THE WORST SUPREME COURT DECISIONS, *EVER*!

(AND RELATED TALES)

THE WORST SUPREME COURT DECISIONS, *EVER*!

(AND RELATED TALES)

C. EVAN STEWART

TWELVE
TABLES
PRESS

To

Patricia M. Stewart
The Love of My Life

and

Gordon G. Chang
My Best Friend

and

Kenneth N. Hart & Stephen J. Friedman
My Legal Mentors

CONTENTS

PREFACE

THE GENESIS OF THIS BOOK comes from a course I have taught for Cornell University since 2006, entitled "Introduction to the American Legal System." The Cornell course is an intense one (three hours a day, five days a week, over a three-week period), designed to give undergraduates an in-depth baptism of what lies ahead in law school. For the enrolled students it is their first exposure to the teaching method known as the Socratic Dialogue—a method not for the faint of heart!

When I was designing the class curriculum in 2005, I thought I should give students exposure to some of the worst Supreme Court decisions—partially because few people study (or are taught) American history, and partially because a number of these decisions are so horrible many law schools and law professors do not like to teach them. My thinking led me from some of the most obvious decisions (*Dred Scott, Plessy, Korematsu*) to other Supreme Court decisions with which few, if any, lawyers or law professors are familiar. After researching these cases, I then began to write and publish articles on them, primarily in the *Federal Bar*

Council Quarterly. For purposes of this book I have adapted those prior articles and (where necessary) updated them.

In our current hyper-charged political environment, the Supreme Court (which Alexander Bickel once called "the least dangerous branch") has come under increased public scrutiny. Not for the first time in the country's history have there been cries to "pack" the Court (i.e., to change its structure to affect an outcome desired by some). I hope as readers go through the various chapters of this book they will see that the Court has made numerous, consequential mistakes over the course of our country's history—mistakes that include and transcend all political views, parties, and factions. That being said, I also hope that readers will gain new insights into how the Court—even with these terrible decisions—has endured as a critically important institution that has contributed to the basic stability of our legal processes.

As an "extra" to the decisions themselves, I have added several chapters on fascinating, little-known vignettes involving the Court and famous Americans. While these chapters are not part of my Cornell class, per se, they have rounded out my knowledge of American history and thus are a sub-text to all that I try to pass on to my students.

THE WORST SUPREME COURT DECISIONS, *EVER*!

(AND RELATED TALES)

CHAPTER I

The *Worst* Supreme Court Decision, *Ever*!

THERE ARE, PERHAPS, MANY CANDIDATES for the *worst* decision by the U.S. Supreme Court, *ever*: *Plessy v. Ferguson*, 163 U.S. 537 (1896), for example, or perhaps *Korematsu v. United States*, 323 U.S. 214 (1944). But there really can only be *one* that ranks at the very bottom: *Dred Scott v. John F.A. Sandford*, 60 U.S. (19 How.) 393 (1856). And it fully deserves that ranking.

Who Was Dred Scott?

Dred Scott was a slave. Born in America, circa 1800, he was owned by several owners. Importantly, in (or about) 1833, Scott was purchased by U.S. Army surgeon John Emerson in Missouri. Transferred to Fort Armstrong in Illinois, Emerson took Scott with him; Emerson also took Scott with him when he was subsequently transferred to Fort Snelling in the northern section of the Louisiana Purchase (now Minnesota). While at Fort Snelling, Scott married another slave also owned by Emerson (this was a legally recognized marriage because it took place in free territory). Scott's wife later gave birth to a daughter in free territory. Ultimately, Emerson moved his family and slaves back to St. Louis, Missouri.

In 1843, Emerson died and his wife inherited Scott and his family. In February 1846, Scott attempted to buy his freedom from Mrs. Emerson, but she refused. Scott, with the encouragement of some White friends in St. Louis, then decided to sue for his freedom, based on his prolonged residence in a free state and a free territory. That began a lengthy legal odyssey that ultimately resulted in the *worst* decision by the U.S. Supreme Court, *ever*.

THE LOWER COURTS

Suing in St. Louis county in April 1846, Scott initially lost because he was unable to prove that he was in fact owned by Emerson and his widow. But a second trial was ordered, a decision that Mrs. Emerson appealed to the Missouri Supreme Court. She lost that appeal, and in 1850 a jury sided with Scott. That outcome was then appealed to the Missouri Supreme Court, which in 1852 rejected prior precedents and overturned the lower court's outcome, ruling that Missouri law governed Scott's status, not the fact that he had resided for a number of years in a free state and a free territory.

With a different set of lawyers, Scott then filed a new suit, this time in federal court. Because Scott's new owner was John F.A. Sandford (Mrs. Emerson's brother—she had transferred legal ownership of Scott and his family over to Sandford), and he was a legal resident of New York, the jurisdictional basis for the federal lawsuit was diversity of citizenship. (Scott claimed Missouri citizenship.) Scott sued Sandford for battery and wrongful imprisonment and sought $9,000 in money damages. The federal district judge, Robert W. Wells, rejected Sandford's pretrial argument that Scott could not be a citizen of Missouri because he was a slave, and allowed the case to go to trial in May 1854. Although Sandford conceded he had "gently laid his hands" on Scott, he nonetheless won the case (based on the prior ruling of the Missouri Supreme Court).

Determined to get his freedom, Scott pressed on, and with two new prominent lawyers (Montgomery Blair and George T. Curtis) leading the charge, he appealed to the U.S. Supreme Court in December 1854. The Court agreed to take the case, first hearing oral argument in February 1856. When the justices met to discuss the case in April 1856, they were deadlocked four to four on the issue of the Court's jurisdiction, with Justice Samuel Nelson (New York) undecided. The Court then agreed to have four days of reargument in December 1856.

POLITICS AFFECTING THE COURT?

Many historians believe that the Court took its time deciding the case in order to push the decision beyond the 1856 presidential election. Once the election had been decided, President-Elect James Buchanan wrote one of the sitting justices (his friend, John Catron, from Tennessee), asking whether the decision was going to be handed down before his inauguration on March 4, 1857 (he hoped it would be, thereby putting to "rest" the slavery issue for the entirety of his presidential term). Buchanan later even went further, pressuring Justice Robert Grier (both men were Pennsylvanians) to join the Southern majority on the Court; the President-Elect wanted the Court's decision not to be perceived as a sectional one. And it was not just the President-Elect. Alexander Stephens, a prominent Georgia congressman (and later the vice president of the Confederacy) wrote to a friend on December 15, 1856: "I have been urging all the influence I could bring to bear upon the Sup. Ct. to get them no longer to postpone the case on the Mo. Restriction [the Compromise of 1820].... I have reason to believe they will [decide] that the restriction was unconstitutional." Then, on January 1, 1857, Stephens penned another letter, stating, "[F]rom what I hear *sub rosa* [the decision] will be

THE DEMOCRATIC PLATFORM.

1856 Cartoon Critical of the Democratic Platform
(Author's Collection)

according to my own opinions upon every point.... The restriction of 1820 will be held to be unconstitutional."

THE SUPREME COURT "FIRST" DECIDES

In 1851, the Supreme Court had decided *Strader v. Graham*, 51 U.S. (10 How.) 82 (1851). In that case, the Court had refused to take an appeal from a decision by the Kentucky Supreme Court, which had ruled that Kentucky slaves taken temporarily to Ohio nonetheless remained slaves under Kentucky law. On February 14, 1857, a majority of the Court actually voted to reaffirm that precedent without elaboration; and Justice Nelson was tasked to write the majority opinion. Justice Benjamin Curtis (Massachusetts) had earlier predicted this outcome to his uncle. And Horace Greeley, editor of the *New York Tribune*, had publicly denounced the Court for its likely "convenient evasion": "The black gowns have come to be artful dodgers." At the same time, Greeley understood the problem of the Court going the other way and embracing slavery; he also warned of "[j]udicial tyranny."

Days later, the majority of justices reversed themselves and decided to go in a different direction. What had changed? It would appear that two dissents coming from Justices Curtis and John McClean (Ohio)—in which they planned to opine that Scott was free under the terms of the Missouri Compromise (a law they were also going to opine *was* constitutional)—shook up the Southern justices. Justice James Wayne (Georgia) asked that the Chief Justice reconsider and issue a broad decision; that petition carried the day. At the same time this was playing out, the Catron-Buchanan-Grier correspondence was going on behind the scenes. (Buchanan's letter to Justice Grier had in fact been encouraged by Justice Catron: "[D]rop Grier a line, saying how necessary it is, and how good the opportunity is to settle the agitation by an affirmative decision of the Supreme Court, one way or the other.")

On March 4, 1857, Buchanan was sworn in as President at the Capitol by Chief Justice Roger Taney (Maryland). In his inaugural address, Buchanan (having been prompted by Justice Catron) told the nation that the vexing question of slavery's status in the territories was "a judicial question which legitimately belongs to the Supreme Court of the United States, before whom it is now and will, it is understood, be speedily and finally settled."

Two days later, *Dred Scott v. John F.A. Sandford* was handed down.

THE SUPREME COURT'S REAL DECISION

Chief Justice Taney delivered the opinion of the Court; it was separately agreed to by six other justices (four Southerners, two Northerners—Grier and Nelson; the latter only concurred based on *Strader v. Graham*). The Chief Justice's first task was to decide whether the Court had jurisdiction: Was Scott a "citizen" of Missouri? As Taney articulated the issue: "It becomes necessary . . . to determine who were citizens of the several States when the Constitution was adopted." In page after page of hard-to-read racism, the Chief Justice listed "evidence" that the Founding Fathers viewed all African-Americans as "being of an inferior order, and altogether unfit to associate with the white race, either in social or political relations, and so far inferior that they had no rights which the white man was bound to respect." According to Taney, African-Americans were certainly not included in the "all men" "created equal" language of the Declaration of Independence, and they also had not been part of the "sovereign people" who were part of the country created by the Constitution. Thus having ascertained that African-Americans were not citizens at the time of the country's founding ("it cannot be believed that the large slaveholding States regarded them as included in the word citizen, or would have consented to a Constitution which might compel them to receive them in that character from another State"), Taney concluded that Dred Scott "was not a citizen of Missouri within the meaning of the Constitution . . . , and not entitled as such to sue in its courts." With no jurisdiction, the Chief Justice could have stopped there, but he had even bigger fish to fry: Stephens's *sub rosa* source(s) were right—Taney was bent on invalidating the Compromise of 1820, an act of Congress that had barred slavery north of 36 degrees, 30 minutes north latitude for the land bought from France in the Louisiana Purchase.

Although the Constitution gave Congress the power to "make all needful rules and regulations" for the territories (Article IV, Section 3), Taney wrote that that power was limited to merely "rules and regulations" and did *not* cover basic, fundamental rights bestowed under the Constitution (e.g., right to bear arms, freedom of the press, etc.). And one of those basic, fundamental rights was the "rights of private property":

> [T]he rights of property are united with the rights of person, and placed on the same ground by the fifth amendment to the Constitution, which provides that no person

shall be deprived of life, liberty, and property, without due process of law. And an act of Congress which deprives a citizen of the United States of his liberty or property, merely because he came himself or brought his property into a particular Territory of the United States, and who had committed no offence against the laws, could hardly be dignified with the name of due process of law.

By those words, the Compromise of 1820 was ruled unconstitutional: all of the territories were now open to slavery and its expansion—without congressional interference; and, *beyond that*, the doctrine of substantive due process had been created—a doctrine that continues to vex legal and political debate over the Court's proper role today. And if that were not enough, Taney then went on to dust up the political doctrine that Stephen Douglas hoped would solve the contentious public debate over the expansion of slavery—popular sovereignty:

And if Congress itself cannot do this—it is beyond the powers conferred on the Federal Government—it will be admitted, we presume, that it could not authorize a Territorial Government to exercise them. It could confer no power on any local Government, established by its authority, to violate the provisions to the Constitution.

The dissents of Justices Curtis and McClean vivisected Taney's historical "evidence," as well as his constitutional limitations on Congress' powers vis-à-vis the territories. Curtis, for example, proved beyond a shadow of doubt that there were many free African-American "citizens" of Massachusetts, New Hampshire, New Jersey, New York, and North Carolina at the time of the Constitution and that they had in fact *voted for its ratification*!

Beyond the obvious point that the Court's invalidation of the Compromise of 1820 was unnecessary (Curtis attacked it as *obiter dicta*), both justices argued that the statutory invalidation was based on sophistry and an explicit repudiation of American history. First of all, "[a]ll needful rules and regulations" obviously meant legislation just like the Compromise of 1820. Furthermore, there were numerous other acts of Congress limiting/banning slavery prior to 1820 that many Founding Fathers *voted for* while in Congress (or signed into law as president), and none had ever expressed any public view that any of those laws were unconstitutional. Furthermore, as posited by Curtis, if this law violated due process, did not the 1807 law banning the importation of slavery from Africa also run afoul of that same property right? And what about the laws in the Northern states that banned slavery? Finally, preventing a slave owner from taking a slave into a territory did not *deprive* the slave owner of that property, it only limited as to where the slave owner could take his "property."

Of course, the dissents garnered only two votes. Nonetheless, the *Dred Scott* opinion ignited a volatile firestorm, and Buchanan's hoped-for peaceful presidential term went the other way in a hurry. It is clear that Taney's decision helped precipitate the Civil War. And, of course, we are still debating the application of substantive due process today (e.g., *Griswold v. Connecticut*, 381 U.S. 479 (1965); *see* Chapter V). The *worst* decision by the Supreme Court, *ever?* It is not even close.

POSTSCRIPTS

The Compromise of 1820, the legislation ruled unconstitutional by the Court in 1857, had already been repealed by Congress when it enacted the Kansas-Nebraska Act of 1854.

After years of wrangling (e.g., the Wilmot Proviso), Congress had tried to legislatively kick the irresolvable political issue of the enforcement of slavery in the territories over to the courts under the terms of the Kansas-Nebraska Act of 1854: "all cases involving title to slaves and 'questions of personal freedom' are referred to the adjudication of local tribunals, with the right of appeal to the Supreme Court of the United States." Ironically, none of the territorial areas that had been the focus of Congress' hand-to-hand combat over the years—Kansas, Nebraska, New Mexico, and Utah—were areas directly at issue in *Dred Scott*.

The political blowback to *Dred Scott* was instantaneous and fierce, and it severely damaged the Court's status as the nonpartisan wing of the federal government. Republicans publicly refused to recognize the legitimacy of the ruling and pledged to "reconstitute" the Court after the election of 1860 to ensure that *Dred Scott* was reversed. Leading Republicans William Henry Seward and Abraham Lincoln deftly turned the decision into a symbol of a slave-power conspiracy that was running/ruining the nation. In 1858, Seward cited the "whisperings" between Taney and Buchanan at the latter's inaugural, followed up by the "salutations" the justices had paid to the president "in the Executive Palace" on March 5, where Buchanan had "received them as graciously as Charles the First did the judges who had, at his insistence, subverted the status of English Liberty." (Taney was so outraged by Seward's attacks that he vowed not to administer the oath of office in 1861 if Seward were to win the presidency.) Lincoln (who Taney did swear in) publicly spoke about the four "conspiring carpenters" who created the *Dred Scott* monstrosity: "Stephen [Douglas], Franklin [Pierce], Roger [Taney], and James [Buchanan]." Lincoln prophesied the conspirators behind *Dred Scott* were planning a sequel: "It is merely for the Supreme Court to decide that no State under the Constitution can exclude it, just as they have already decided that ... neither Congress nor the Territorial Legislature can do it ... [W]e shall lie down pleasantly dreaming that the people of Missouri are on the verge of making their state *free*; and we shall awake to the reality, instead, that the Supreme Court has made Illinois a *slave* State."

Lincoln built on these notions, as well as the dissents in *Dred Scott*, and made them the central tenet of his Cooper Union speech in 1860, a speech that was critical to his getting the Republican presidential nomination (*see* C. Evan Stewart, "Lincoln in the Second Circuit," *Federal Bar Council Quarterly* (Nov. 1, 2011)).

The ruling also led to important fissures in the Democratic Party, which ultimately caused it to split into Northern and Southern wings with different candidates for the presidency in 1860—Stephen Douglas (for the Northern wing) and John Breckenridge (for the Southern wing). After Douglas conceded in his 1858 debates with Lincoln that slavery could in fact be kept out of the territories by the "will and the wishes of the people" of said territories (the Freeport Doctrine), Southern Democrats saw that *Dred Scott* might have given slaveholders an unenforceable property right; as such, a slave code was necessary to govern the territories, to be enforced (as required) by the U.S. Army. Senator Albert Brown (Mississippi): "[If the North] den[ies] to us rights guaranteed by the Constitution ... then, ... the Union is a despotism [and] I am prepared to retire from the concern."

After the decision was handed down, it was revealed that Dred Scott was still in fact owned by Emerson's widow, who was now married to an antislavery congressman from Massachusetts. The congressman's wife quickly transferred ownership of Scott and his family over to the son of Scott's original owner on May 26, 1857. The new owner thereafter manumitted the entire family. Scott, now free, lived one more year.

Of Scott's advocates before the Supreme Court, George Curtis was the brother of Justice Benjamin Curtis, but no one seemed to care. Montgomery Blair was the scion of a powerful Democratic Party family, who had shifted over to the Republican Party because of slavery. He later became a member of Lincoln's cabinet as Postmaster General, resigning in 1864 as part of a deal to ensure that John C. Frémont (the Republican's 1856 standard-bearer) would drop his third-party challenge to Lincoln's reelection.

Ironically, as a young Maryland lawyer in private practice, Taney had taken a different position on slavery when he defended Reverend Jacob Gruber. In 1819, Gruber had been indicted for a sermon he gave in which he attacked slavery and thus was accused of fomenting a social revolution. Arguing to the jury in defense of his client, Taney said that slavery was "a blot on our national character, and every real lover of freedom confidently hopes that it will effectually, though it must be gradually, wiped away." *See* Timothy Huebner, "Roger B. Taney and the Slavery Issue: Looking Beyond—And Before *Dred Scott*," *The Journal of American History* (June 2010). *See also* Michael Schoeppner, "Status Across Borders: Roger Taney, Black British Subjects, and a Diplomatic Antecedent to the *Dred Scott* Decision," *The Journal of American History* (Jan. 2013).

The leading treatise on the *Dred Scott* decision is Don E. Fehrenbacher's *The Dred Scott Case: Its Significance in American Law and Politics* (Oxford University Press 1978). *See also* David Konig, Paul Finkelman & Christopher Bracey, *The Dred Scott Case: Historical and Contemporary Perspectives on Race and Law* (Ohio University Press, 2010); Paul Finkelman, *Dred Scott v. Sandford: A Brief History with Documents* (Bedford Books, 1997). For a fascinating analysis of *Dred Scott*'s impact in Maryland, see M. Jones, "Confronting *Dred Scott*: Seeing Citizenship from Baltimore," in *The Civil War in Maryland Reconsidered* (Louisiana State University Press 2021) (ed. C.W. Mitchell & J.H. Baker). For those who want to have a better understanding of the politics of the Buchanan administration, see *James Buchanan and the Coming of the Civil War* (University Press of Florida, 2014) (ed. John Quist & Michael J. Birkner); *James Buchanan and the Political Crisis of the 1850s* (Susquehanna University Press, 1996) (ed. Michael J. Birkner).

CHAPTER II

THE SECOND WORST SUPREME COURT DECISION

WE HAVE JUST TAKEN A LOOK at the very *worst* decision ever rendered by the Supreme Court. Now, let's take a look at one that is almost as bad: *Plessy v. Ferguson*, 163 U.S. 537 (1896). In *Plessy*, the Court expressly approved of racial segregation!

A PRELUDE TO *PLESSY*

Believing that the Thirteenth and Fourteenth Amendments had not gone far enough to ensure that African-Americans would be given all the rights and privileges accorded White people, Congress passed (and President Ulysses S. Grant signed) the Civil Rights Act of 1875. That law guaranteed African-Americans equal treatment in public accommodations and public transportation, as well as ensured they were not denied the ability to serve on juries. A number of lawsuits thereafter dealt with the constitutionality of the statute. Ultimately, five of them were joined together before the United States Supreme Court, encaptioned as the *Civil Rights Cases*, 109 U.S. 3 (1883) (four were criminal prosecutions against those who barred African-Americans from hotels or theaters; the fifth was a suit by an African-American barred from a railroad car).

By an eight-to-one majority, the Court struck down the first two prongs of the law as unconstitutional. (*See also* Chapter XI.) The Court ruled that the federal government had authority *only* to pass laws prohibiting discriminatory actions by states, *not* those by private citizens (e.g., innkeepers, railroad conductors, theater owners); put another way, excluding African-Americans from privately owned facilities was not unconstitutional. Writing for the majority, Justice Joseph P. Bradley opined that the "state action" doctrine meant that the Fourteenth Amendment only barred states—not individuals—from infringing upon the equal protection and due process of citizens; in his words, if the federal government were allowed to "cover the whole domain of rights appertaining to life, liberty, and property," it would "establish a code of municipal law regulative of all private rights between man and man in society"—and that would be a constitutional bridge too far. As to the Thirteenth Amendment, while it did not have a "state action" limitation, that Amendment was self-executing—it nullified all state laws on slavery, but it went no further; that is, it did not mean that distinctions and/or discriminations based on race or color were inherently unlawful. Not only had free African-Americans experienced discrimination prior to the Civil War, "it would be running the slavery argument into the ground to make it apply to every act of discrimination which a person may see fit to make as to guests he will entertain, or as to the people he will take into his coach or cab or car, or admit to his concert or theater, or deal with in other matters of intercourse or business."

Justice John Marshall Harlan, the only Southerner on the Court and a former slaveholder, issued a stinging dissent to both prongs of the majority's opinion. With respect to the Thirteenth Amendment, he wrote that Congress intended to bar not just the institution of slavery but also "badges of servitude" (interestingly, he cited as authority *Prigg v. Pennsylvania*, 41 U.S. 539 (1842), in which the Court upheld the federal government's—as opposed to the states'—power to enforce the Fugitive Slave Act). As for the Fourteenth Amendment, Harlan wrote that the Civil Rights Act of 1875 was clearly contemplated by that Amendment (the fifth section grants "express power in Congress … to enforce the constitutional provision…."), and the Amendment further created new affirmative rights for *all* U.S. citizens—rights to be free from "discrimination based on race or color, in respect of civil rights." As for the "state action" limitation found by the majority, Harlan was unpersuaded, since nearly every place of the discriminations at issue were public spaces, licensed by the state—hence, "state action" was in fact *not* a legal barrier. As powerful as his words and his logic were, Harlan got only one vote—his own.

Based on the *Civil Rights Cases*, across the South Jim Crow laws began to be enacted; these laws created a "separate but equal" world—separate schools, hospitals, cemeteries, restaurants, bathrooms, water fountains, etc. In 1890, the Louisiana legislature passed Act 111 (the Separate Car Act), mandating that there be "equal but separate accommodations for white and colored races" on railroads. That law set the stage for *Plessy v. Ferguson*.

A Planned Confrontation

In September 1891, a committee of local New Orleans citizens—the Comité des Citoyens ("Committee of Citizens")—wanted to challenge Act 111, and it contacted a Northern lawyer named Albion Tourgée, who had worked for many years after the Civil War to help freed slaves achieve meaningful participation in the American way of life; he agreed to take on the challenge pro bono.

Tourgée wanted to have someone of mixed blood violate the law, so as to test what the classification "colored" actually meant as a matter of law. Homer Plessy, who was born a free man in 1862 and was an "octoroon" (seven-eighths of European descent (his family spoke French) and one-eighth of African descent), agreed to be put up for the test case.

On June 7, 1892, Plessy bought a first-class ticket on the East Louisiana Railroad and boarded a "whites only" railway car in New Orleans, heading on an intrastate journey to Covington, Louisiana. The railroad company, which did not like the law because of the extra expense of separate cars, was a complicit conspirator with the Committee. Indeed, the railroad knew all about Plessy's plans and cooperated with a detective hired by the Committee. After the conductor informed Plessy he would have to vacate the "whites only" car, he refused, the detective swooped in and arrested Plessy. Plessy was then taken off the train at Press and Royal Streets in New Orleans and remanded over to trial.

Between Plessy's arrest and trial, the same judge who was to determine his fate—John H. Ferguson—presided over a similar case. There, Daniel F. Desdunes had been arrested for sitting in a "whites only" car traveling between Louisiana and another state. Ferguson ruled that Act 111 was unconstitutional in its attempt to punish Desdunes because of the federal government's power to regulate interstate commerce. This ruling greatly encouraged the Committee. At Plessy's trial, however, Ferguson ruled that the federal government's power was *not* implicated (and thus the Thirteenth and Fourteenth Amendments had no sway); Plessy had been traveling on an intrastate train and thus, under the *Civil Rights Cases*, the conduct was private conduct that did not trigger constitutional protections. Plessy was convicted and sentenced to pay a $25 fine.

Plessy (and the Committee) immediately sought redress on appeal, but got an unsympathetic hearing at the Louisiana Supreme Court. That court not only rejected the challenge to Ferguson's ruling, it cited Northern states' laws pre–Civil War that expressly sanctioned segregated facilities (e.g., Massachusetts, Pennsylvania). Plessy (and the Committee) then went to the U.S. Supreme Court. On April 13, 1896, the case was argued before the Court;

in addition to Tourgée, Plessy's case was argued by James Walker (a New Orleans attorney) and Samuel Phillips (as U.S. Solicitor General, he had argued—unsuccessfully—for the federal government in the *Civil Rights Cases*).

THE ARGUMENTS OF PLESSY'S ADVOCATES

One broadside against Act 111 was that it violated Plessy's equal protection rights under the Fourteenth Amendment. Albion Tourgée argued that "Justice is pictured as blind and her daughter, the Law ought at least to be color-blind." In furtherance of this "color-blind" point, Tourgée said that racial mixing had rendered the issue of who was "colored" problematic at best—especially given that the laws determining such status differed widely between the states. And in any event, how could such a judgment be placed in the hands of a railroad conductor?

He also argued that belonging to one race versus another was a form of property: "How much would it be worth to a young man entering upon the practice of law to be regarded as a white man rather than a colored one?" Dislodging Plessy from the "whites only" car was depriving him—an "octoroon"—the public recognition/reputation of being a White man, and that deprivation was a taking without due process of law.

Phillips argued that there were constitutional gradations in the states' exercise of their police powers. Given that Washington, D.C., had segregated schools when Congress enacted the Thirteenth and Fourteenth Amendments, he conceded that states could enforce separate but equal schools—education was akin to institutions such as family and marriage (thus, he also conceded that states could constitutionally bar interracial marriages). But the future of such institutions was not implicated by who sat where in railroad cars. Louisiana thus could not exercise its police power in such extenuated, nonessential settings.

Tourgée's most powerful argument was derived from Justice Harlan's dissent in the *Civil Rights Cases*. Congress' Reconstruction Amendments did more than merely end slavery. In particular, the Fourteenth Amendment—"the magna carta of American citizen's rights"—"create[d] a new citizenship of the Untied States embracing new rights, privileges and immunities, derivable in a new manner, controlled by new authority, having a new scope and extent, depending on national authority for its existence and looking to national power for its preservation." Under such *new* rights of citizenship, the treatment of Plessy was clearly a violation of equal protection and due process.

Less than five weeks after oral argument, on May 18, 1896, the Court handed down its decision.

SEPARATE BUT EQUAL

By a seven-to-one vote (one justice did not hear oral argument and did not participate in the decision), the Court held that Louisiana's "equal but separate" statute was constitutional. Six of the seven justices were from Union-aligned states; the seventh was Edmund D. White, a Louisiana citizen who had been active in local white supremacy groups prior to being elevated to the Court. Justice Henry B. Brown (Michigan) wrote the majority opinion.

Brown addressed the Thirteenth Amendment argument first, quickly dismissing it—for the reasons already stated by the Court in the *Civil Rights Cases* (as well as in the *Slaughter-House Cases*, 16 Wall 36 (1873)). In addressing the Fourteenth Amendment, Brown answered yes; he wrote that the Louisiana legislature was "at liberty to act with reference to the established usages, customs, and traditions of the people, and with a view to the promotion of their comfort, and the preservation of the public peace and grand order."

As for Tourgée's property argument, Brown was unfazed—that argument failed on its face since Plessy's "octoroon" status meant he was indisputably "colored" as a matter of Louisiana law. That different states defined "colored" differently stood for nothing, since the issue was exclusively one for each state to decide (and was *not* a federal concern).

Then, in a vein similar to Chief Justice Roger Taney's inability to restrain himself when delivering racist tripe thinly veiled in a legal band-aid, Brown closed his decision by condemning the "underlying fallacy" of Plessy's entire legal complaint: "[T]he assumption that the enforced separation of the two races stamps the colored race with a badge of inferiority. If this be so, it is not reason of anything found in the act, *but solely because the colored race chooses to put that construction upon it.*" (Emphasis added.)

Harlan's Historic Dissent

Justice Harlan started his dissent off in a measured way, delineating (as he had in his *Civil Rights Cases* dissent) that railroads are undeniably "public highways"—public easements, the same as canals or turnpike; and here, the state of Louisiana was regulating "the use of a public highway by citizens of the United States solely upon the basis of race."

Then, again taking from (and building upon) his earlier dissent, Harlan opined that the Thirteenth Amendment not only abolished slavery, it was also enacted to prevent "the imposition of any burdens or disabilities that constitute badges of slavery or servitude." And with the Fourteenth Amendment adding new rights of citizenship to *all* Americans, together the two Amendments "if enforced according to their true intent and meaning, will protect all the civil rights that pertain to freedom and citizenship."

With that warm-up, Harlan became animatedly agitated (rightly so): "In my opinion, the judgment this day rendered will, in time, prove to be quite as pernicious as the decision made by the tribunal in the *Dred Scott* case." The Thirteenth and Fourteenth Amendments had eviscerated Chief Justice Taney's horrible

Portrait of John Marshall Harlan
(Author's Collection)

decision, but the majority ruling in *Plessy* had the effect of turning back the clock. And if Act 111 was to be judged fine and dandy, "why may not the state require the separation in railroad coaches of native and naturalized citizens of the United States, or of the Protestants and Roman Catholics?"

As for the majority's distinction between "political" equality and "social" equality, it was, in Harlan's view, "scarcely worthy of consideration." The purported distinction was merely a cunning device to defeat the "legitimate results" of the Civil War (and the constitutional amendments that followed). *All* citizens were entitled to "equality before the law," irrespective of whether "social equality [could] exist between the white and black races in this country."

The majority's decision was thus out-and-out wrong. Harlan wrote: "Our Constitution is color-blind [lifting Tourgée's words and argument], and neither knows nor tolerates classes among citizens. In respect of civil rights, all citizens are equal before the law."

The majority's decision (and rationale in support) were not only wrong, but they would "certainly arouse race hate" and "perpetrate a fueling of distrust between the races":

> [I]t is difficult to reconcile [the] boast [of freedom] with a state of the law which ... puts the brand of servitude and degradation upon a large class of fellow-citizens, our equals before the law. The thin disguise of "equal" accommodations for passengers in railroad coaches will not mislead any one, nor atone for the wrong this day done.

As in the *Civil Rights Cases*, Harlan got only his vote for his historic dissent.

POSTSCRIPTS

Incredibly, the political response to *Plessy* was relatively benign after it was handed down. On May 19, 1896, for example, the *Union Advertiser* (Rochester, New York) wrote an editorial entitled "State Sovereignty":

> The Supreme Court of the United States yesterday made two important decisions in affirmance of State Sovereignty "within the powers not delegated to the United States by the constitution, nor prohibited by it to the States."
>
> The first declares constitutional the state law of Louisiana involved in what is popularly known as the "Jim Crow" case at the South, which requires railroad companies to provide separate coaches for whites and blacks. Of the nine Justices but one dissented—Harlan.
>
> With the expediency of these the Court had nothing to do. The question was purely one of state power. Of course, in each case, the jurisdiction of the state is over railroads operated within its own territory alone.

In fact, the public's reaction to the *Civil Rights Cases* was far more supercharged (on both sides). Perhaps the difference in reaction is best explained by the differences in time of the two rulings relative to the Civil War, as well as the Northern states' increasing disinterest in the internal affairs of the "Reconstructed" Southern states.

The majority's odious opinion had many awful consequences. One in particular that has never gotten a full airing in American history is the fact that when Woodrow Wilson (Virginia born) became president, he authorized resegregation within the agencies and offices of the federal government. When challenged on this immediate and abrupt reversal of the federal government's prior policy of integration, Wilson personally rebuked the African-American protesters: "Segregation is not a humiliation but a benefit, and ought to be so regarded by you gentlemen." Wilson, of course, also screened at the White House D.W. Griffith's *The Birth of a Nation*, which was based on Wilson's friend Thomas Dixon's book *The Clansman* (extolling the virtues of the Ku Klux Klan). After seeing the movie, Wilson is reported to have said, "It is like writing history with lightning, and my only regret is that it is all so terribly true."

Justice Harlan's famous dissent ("Our Constitution is color-blind") is justly so, and his prediction of the shame that the *Plessy* majority would attach to the Court by its horrible imprimatur of constitutionality upon "separate but equal" laws did come to pass.

In *Brown v. Board of Education*, 347 U.S. 483 (1954), the Court ruled that "in the field of public education the doctrine of 'separate but equal' has no place. Separate educational facilities are inherently unequal." But the Court did not actually expressly overturn *Plessy*, nor did it adopt Harlan's "color-blind" principle; instead, *Brown*'s holding is based on the evidentiary record developed by the National Association for the Advancement of Colored People (and its lead advocate, Thurgood Marshall), which demonstrated that separate schools were *not* in fact equal. That we have struggled to achieve Harlan's "color-blind" Constitution is evidenced by the Court's ongoing difficulties with higher education's admissions policies. *See, e.g., Fisher v. University of Texas*, 570 U.S. ___, 133 S. Ct. 2411 (2013) (*Fisher I*); 579 U.S. ___ (June 23, 2016) (*Fisher II*). The Court recently came close to adopting Harlan's "color-blind" principle in *Students for Fair Admission, Inc. v. President and Fellows of Harvard College*, 600 U.S. 181 (2023), in which the Court held that race-based affirmative action programs in college admissions processes violate the Equal Protection Clause of the Fourteenth Amendment. The Court did not, however, invalidate race-based affirmation action in U.S. military academies (*Id.* at note 4), which the solicitor general urged the Court to allow to continue in the government's amicus brief.

As depicted in the film *Free State of Jones* (IM Global, released June 24, 2016), Newton Knight's great-grandson, Davis Knight (an "octoroon"), was arrested and tried in 1948 in Mississippi for violating that state's antimiscegenation laws—he had married a White woman in 1946. Sentenced to prison for five years, the Mississippi Supreme Court voided his conviction (on evidentiary grounds) in order to avoid a challenge to the laws' constitutionality before the U.S. Supreme Court.

For those who want to read more about *Plessy v. Ferguson*, see Charles A. Lofgren's *The Plessy Case: A Legal Historical Interpretation* (Oxford University Press 1987). *See also* T. Alexander Aleinikoff, "Re-Reading Justice Harlan's Dissent in *Plessy v. Ferguson*: Freedom, Antiracism, and Citizenship," *University of Illinois Law Review* 961 (1962); Brook Thomas, *Plessy v. Ferguson: A Brief History with Documents* (Bedford/St. Martin's 1997).

CHAPTER III

THE THIRD WORST SUPREME COURT DECISION

THE FIRST AND SECOND WORST DECISIONS certainly are very bad. This next one truly ranks with them: *Korematsu v. United States*, 323 U.S. 214 (1944). In *Korematsu*, the Supreme Court held the widespread racial discrimination aimed at one group of American citizens (and one group only)—Americans of Japanese descent—was justified by wartime necessity.

A DATE WHICH WILL LIVE IN INFAMY

At 7:48 a.m. (Hawaiian time) on December 7, 1941, forces from the Imperial Japanese Navy began their attack on the U.S. Pacific Fleet headquartered at Pearl Harbor. All eight U.S. battleships were damaged (four were sunk), 188 planes were destroyed, 2,403 Americans were killed, and 1,178 were wounded. That same day (although it was actually December 8 in Asia), Japan also attacked U.S. bases in the Philippines, Guam, and Wake Island, as well as attacking the British-held colonies of Hong Kong, Singapore, and Malaya.

Also taking place on December 7 was a meeting in Pittsburgh's Soldiers and Sailors Memorial Hall. With a seating capacity of 2,550, the arena was packed with supporters of the America First Committee (AFC), eager to hear Senator Gerald Nye (and others) speak against America getting involved in the armed conflicts raging in Europe and Asia. The AFC had been started on September 4, 1940, by Yale law students (among them, Gerald Ford, Sargent Shriver, Potter Stewart, and Kingman Brewster) and quickly grew into a national movement (800,000 paying members, with supporters such as Walt Disney, John F. Kennedy, Frank Lloyd Wright, E.E. Cummings, and Alice Roosevelt Longworth).

The national spokesman for the group was the famed aviator, Charles Lindbergh. Lindbergh, who had publicly opposed the Roosevelt administration for years (and had also announced to the world how impressed he was with the growing might of Germany's air force), turned up the nature and heat of isolation debate at an AFC rally in Des Moines, Iowa, on September 11, 1941. Blaming the British, the Roosevelt administration, and American Jews for leading America inexorably into the world's conflicts, Lindbergh went on:

> It is not difficult to understand why Jewish people desire the overthrow of Nazi Germany. The persecution they suffered in Germany would be sufficient to make bitter enemies of any race. No person with a sense of the dignity of mankind can condone the persecution the Jewish race suffered in Germany. But no person of honesty and vision can look on their pro-war policy here today without seeing the dangers involved in such a policy, both for us and for them.
>
> Instead of agitating for war the Jewish groups in this country should be opposing it in every possible way, for they will be among the first to feel its consequences. Tolerance is a virtue that depends upon peace and strength. History shows that it cannot survive war and devastation.

A few farsighted Jewish people realize this and stand opposed to intervention. But the majority still do not. Their greatest danger to this county lies in their ownership and influence in our motion pictures, our press, our radio, and our government.

It was in this type of environment that Senator Nye took the stage at 4:45 p.m. and claimed, "Never, never, never again must America let herself be made such a monkey of as she was 25 years go." During his speech, Nye was handed a note that read, "The Japanese Imperial Government and Tokyo today at 4:00 p.m. announced a state of war with the U.S. and Great Britain." He told the crowd about the note, but added, "I can't somehow believe this. I can't come to any conclusions until I know what this is about."

It turned out that Nye had known of the attack on Pearl Harbor before he had gotten up to speak. The next day, the *Pittsburgh Press* denounced the meeting in an editorial: "Never has there been such a disgraceful meeting in all Pittsburgh's history. Those who participated in it should forever hand their heads in shame." More importantly, President Franklin D. Roosevelt addressed Congress that same day and proclaimed that December 7 was "a date which will live in infamy," and asked Congress to declare war against the Empire of Japan. Within 40 minutes, Congress did just that (the Senate: 82 to 0; the House 388 to 1—Jeannette Rankin (R-MT) was the one negative vote; she in fact had also voted against U.S. participation in World War I). Stung by the surprise and enormity of the Japanese attacks, the nation reflexively followed suit, pivoting from isolationism to full support for a vengeful war; not surprisingly, on December 11, the leaders of the AFC disbanded the organization.

PANIC ON THE WEST COAST (AND BEYOND)

In short order, the vengeful American public and their political representatives focused on the approximately 120,000 Japanese Americans who lived among them, almost all of whom were located on the West Coast. One who led the charge was Earl Warren, California's then attorney general (and who later became a liberal icon as Chief Justice of the United States Supreme Court). Warren publicly proclaimed, "I have come to the conclusion that the Japanese situation, as it exists today, may well be the Achilles' heel of the entire civil defense effort. Unless something is done it may bring about a repetition of Pearl Harbor." And the mayor of Los Angeles, Fletcher Bowron, invoked America's greatest president. "There isn't a shadow of a doubt but that Lincoln ... would make short work of rounding up the Japanese and putting them where they could not do harm."

The reported sightings of purported enemy ships and imminent invasions threatening the West Coast exploded. But it was not all frantic fantasy. In late December, three ships were in fact torpedoed off the California coast by a Japanese submarine or submarines. And on February 23, 1942, a Japanese submarine fired some shells at an oil refinery in Galeton, California, causing $500 of damage. The next night brought on "The Battle of Los Angeles," with hundreds of army anti-aircraft rounds fired at the offshore enemy—a U.S. Navy weather balloon (five people died—two of heart attacks, three in car crashes of locals fleeing the City of Angels).

The federal government's team charged with handling this existential threat to the homeland was led by Lieutenant General John DeWitt of the Western Defense Command. DeWitt's basic bottom line was as follows: "A Jap is a Jap! There is no way to determine their loyalty." DeWitt found an ally in Assistant Secretary of War John J. McCloy (*see* C.E. Stewart, "John McCloy in the Second Circuit," *Federal Bar Council Quarterly* (September 2012)), who opined: "We can cover the legal situation ... in spite of the Constitution. Why the Constitution is just a scrap of paper to me." Together, they pressed for an executive order to round up every person on American soil deemed to be of Japanese lineage. McCloy's boss, Secretary of War Henry L. Stimson (*see*

C.E. Stewart, "The Serendipity of History: Henry Stimson and the Saving of Kyoto," *Federal Bar Council Quarterly* (May 2009)), was not comfortable with that approach; Attorney General Francis B. Biddle actually publicly opposed such an action on the ground that it was unconstitutional.

Nonetheless, on February 19, 1942, President Roosevelt signed Executive Order 9066. Roosevelt, however, did not want to publicly embrace this tar baby and issued the order without comment. The order read, in part:

> I hereby further authorize and direct the Secretary of War and the said Military Commanders to take such other steps as he or the appropriate Military Commander may deem advisable to enforce compliance with the restrictions applicable to each Military area herein above authorized to be designated, including the use of Federal troops and other Federal Agencies, with authority to accept assistance of state and local agencies.

Importantly, the order did not mention race or national origin. One reason for that was there was significant sentiment to round up on a wholesale basis German-Americans and Italian-Americans as well. DeWitt, in fact, wanted to intern Joe DiMaggio's parents, who were based in San Francisco and had never applied for American citizenship. (He did not get his wish, but they were barred from using their fishing boat and from visiting the restaurant they owned.)

To the "Camps"

Initially, Japanese-Americans were allowed to "voluntarily" leave the West Coast states—if they relocated east of the Sierra and Cascade mountain ranges. Very few availed themselves of this offer. On March 27, 1942, General DeWitt shut down that option.

Mass departures by bus and train then began in earnest. People were allowed to bring "only what you can carry." A number of "Assembly Centers" were established (mostly in California); these were created to process the deportees on their way to "Relocation Centers"—ultimately, there were 10 such "Centers" (two in California, two in Arizona, two in Arkansas, and one each in Idaho, Utah, Wyoming, and Colorado). These "Centers" were, in fact, concentration camps, surrounded by barbed wired and guarded by armed troops. The government's official line was that the "Centers" had been set up to protect the Japanese-Americans from violence by other Americans; but the people clustered inside the "Centers" noticed that the armed troops, perched on the various guard towers (with search lights), were pointing their machine guns at them, rather than at access routes leading to the "Centers."

FRED KOREMATSU AND MILITARY ORDER NO. 34

Fred Korematsu was an American citizen; his parents had emigrated from Japan. He worked in a shipyard in California, but was fired after Pearl Harbor. He twice tried to enlist, but was rejected. He then procured a forged draft card with the name of Clyde Sarah, claiming Spanish and Hawaiian lineage. Based on his new identity, he was hired at another shipyard in California; and "Clyde" did well there, being promoted to foreman.

During this same period, General DeWitt was busy issuing a whole series of orders, based on the authority delegated to him by Executive Order 9066. On March 27, 1942, for example, he issued Proclamation No. 4, which forbade all persons of Japanese ancestry from leaving Military Area No. 1 "for any purpose." Then, on May 3, DeWitt issued Order No. 34, which excluded all persons of Japanese ancestry from Military Area No. 1. Failure to obey any of the directives issued pursuant to Executive Order 9066 had explicitly been made a crime by a recent act of Congress.

On May 30, Korematsu was arrested on a corner in San Leandro, California. He subsequently was convicted for violating Order No. 34 and the aforementioned congressional statute. A local lawyer, Wayne Collins (at that point a lawyer for the American Civil Liberties Union), urged Korematsu to test the constitutionality of Executive Order 9066. Korematsu agreed, and the case ultimately made its way to the U.S. Supreme Court.

IN THE SUPREME COURT

Writing for a six-justice majority (Chief Justice Stone and Justices Black, Reed, Douglas, Rutledge, and Frankfurter), Justice Hugo Black ruled that Executive Order 9066 and the congressional statute that made a violation thereof a crime were constitutional. Black, who as a young lawyer in Alabama had been a member of the Ku Klux Klan, began his opinion by laying out—for the first time in the Court's history—that "legal restrictions which curtail the civil rights of a single racial group are immediately suspect ... [and are subject] to the most rigid scrutiny."

Notwithstanding such "strict scrutiny," Black believed he was controlled by the Court's prior decision—*Hirabayashi v. United States*, 320 U.S. 81 (1943)—in which the conviction of a Japanese-American for violating a DeWitt curfew order was upheld. Quoting from the earlier decision, Black wrote:

> We cannot reject as unfounded the judgment of military authorities and of Congress that there were disloyal members of that population.... We cannot say that the war-making branch of the Government did not have ground for believing that in a critical hour such persons could not readily be isolated and separately dealt with, and constituted a menace to the national defense and safety, which demanded that prompt and adequate measures be taken to guard against it.

If that were not bad enough, incredibly, Black then wrote that, while it would be a different case if it involved imprisoning a loyal citizen in a concentration camp because of racial prejudice ("our duty [would be] clear"), "we are dealing specifically with nothing but an exclusion order." Of course, that was simply not true; indeed, once Korematsu was arrested he was put into just such a camp (as were nearly 120,000 others). Compounding this strange analysis, Black then wrote that casting "the case into outlines of racial prejudice ... *merely confuses* the issue. Korematsu was not excluded from the Military Area because of hostility to him or his race." (emphasis added).

Black then concluded this train of thought as follows:

> There was evidence of disloyalty on the part of some, the military authorities considered that the need for action was great, and time was short. We cannot—by availing ourselves of the calm perspective of hindsight—now say that at that time these actions were unjustified.

Justice Felix Frankfurter, while he concurred with Justice Black's opinion, felt compelled "to add a few words of [his] own." Opining that the Constitution is "an instrument for dialectic subtleties," Frankfurter could "find nothing in the Constitution which denies to Congress the power to enforce such a valid military order by making its violation an offense triable in the civil courts." And just to sharpen that point, he ended with this thought: When it comes to war, "[t]hat is their [the Executive's and Congress'] business, not ours."

There were three dissents, the first by Justice Owen Roberts. Roberts, as an initial matter, noted that the issue was not "keeping people off the streets at night" (*Hirabayashi*), but rather the conviction of someone who refused to submit to imprisonment in a concentration camp based on his race or national origin. Laying out the history of Executive Order 9066 and DeWitt's various directives pursuant thereto, Roberts laid bare the absurd dilemma

Korematsu faced: "The earlier of [DeWitt's] orders made him a criminal if he left the zone in which he resided; the latter made him a criminal if he did not leave." The only escape from this trap was to voluntarily go to one of the concentration camps. Thus, the internment program itself was indeed at the heart of what was at issue and the whole shebang was clearly unconstitutional.

Justice Frank Murphy was up next, writing that constitutional power had been abused and the internment program fell "into the ugly abyss of racism." Murphy focused on deconstructing the case the government had put forward to justify the "military neces-sity" for excluding "'all persons of Japanese ancestry, both alien and non-alien,' from the Pacific Coast area." That case was based exclu-sively on General DeWitt's *Final Report, Japanese Evacuation from the West Coast*, 1942 (dated June 5, 1943; made public in January 1944). As Murphy made clear, there was "no reliable evidence" cited anywhere in DeWitt's report that the general population of individuals of Japanese descent were disloyal or had done anything wrong. Instead, the report just set forth a litany of racist suppo-sitions, strung one after another ("an accumulation of ... mis-information, half-truths and insinuations"), without any factual basis for support. Murphy then observed that many of these same charges of treason, etc., had been lodged against German-Amer-icans and Italian-Americans, without any wholesale evacuation of those large groups of citizens to concentration camps. He also noted that not one person of Japanese ancestry had been accused or convicted of any activities relating to the attack on Pearl Har-bor. Finally, he demonstrated the Alice-in-Wonderland logic of the DeWitt Report, citing its "amazing statement": "The very fact that *no sabotage* has taken place to date is a disturbing and confirming indication that such *action will be taken*." (emphasis added). He concluded by abhorring the Court's "legalization of racism," which should never have a place "in our democratic way of life."

Justice Robert Jackson then weighed in with a historic dis-sent. Initially, he noted that Korematsu's crime "consists merely of being present in the state whereof he is a citizen, near the place he was born, and where all his life he has lived." The legal dilemma he faced (which could only be solved by agreeing to placement in a concentration camp) was due solely to the birthplace of his parents, notwithstanding that the "fundamental assumption" of our system is that "guilt is personal and not inheritable."

Jackson next turned to the Court's role in passing on DeWitt's various orders. Given the "evidence" in the record, Jackson said he could not judge whether or not the orders were "reasonably expedient military precautions." But to Jackson that was not the issue; the issue was whether or not the orders were constitutional. Making this even more problematic was the DeWitt Report itself, over which there was "sharp controversy as to [its] credibility":

> So the Court, having no real evidence before it, has no choice but to accept General DeWitt's own unsworn, self-serving statement, untested by any cross-examination, that what he did was reasonable. And that it will always be when courts try to look into the reasonableness of military orders.

Jackson's real concern, however, was not with DeWitt's orders, *per se*, because a military commander's order can always be revoked after the military emergency. Rather, his concern was the majority's giving constitutional imprimatur to such orders; for now "the Court for all time has validated the principle of racial discrimination in criminal procedure and of transplanting American citizens." In his dissent's most famous line Jackson then wrote: "The principle then lies about like a *loaded gun* ready for the hand of any authority that can bring forward a plausible claim of an urgent need." (emphasis added).

The U.S. Department of Justice had done its best to time the case before the Supreme Court to ensure that it would have no impact on Roosevelt's campaign for a fourth term. And that effort worked: oral argument took place on October 11 and 12, 1944, and the decision was handed down on December 18, 1944. Not only had Roosevelt been reelected by that time but Korematsu had been released and was working as a welder in Salt Lake City.

The Aftermath of *Korematsu*

For many decades this shameful episode in our nation's history was not widely discussed or acknowledged. But by the 1970s, books began to be written, and President Gerald Ford issued Proclamation 4417 in 1976, which repudiated Executive Order 9066; in doing so he said, among other things: "We now know what we should have known then, not only that evacuation was wrong, but Japanese-Americans were and are loyal Americans." Congress thereafter published a report in 1982; it concluded that "Executive Order 9066 was not justified by military necessity" and that it and DeWitt's various orders were the result of "race prejudice, war hysteria, and a failure of political leadership." Six years later, Congress passed the Civil Liberties Act of 1988. That legislation not only included a formal apology for the evacuations and internments, it also provided payment of $20,000 to each of the approximately 80,000 citizens subject to such treatment who were still living.

More important for Fred Korematsu was that Peter Irons, a professor at the University of Massachusetts at Amherst, and Aiko Yoshinaga-Herzig, a California housewife, independently discovered that Justice Department lawyers had withheld, altered, and/or destroyed evidence while Korematsu's case was winding its way to the Supreme Court. They pooled what they had learned, and a group of Japanese-American lawyers subsequently brought on a *coram nobis* petition to overturn Korematsu's conviction. In the course of that litigation, Korematsu's legal team proved that:

1. the government had withheld intelligence reports from 1942 documenting that Japanese-Americans, as a whole, were loyal;

Desert City, by Roger Shimomura (2020) (acrylic on canvas)
(with permission from the Herbert F. Johnson Museum of Art,
Cornell University)

2. DeWitt's Final Report had been materially altered
    (and it was the altered version that had been submit-
    ted to the Supreme Court as "evidence"); and
3. DeWitt's various suppositions of treasonous acts by
    Japanese-Americans were not only false, they were
    known to be false by government attorneys at the
    time the Court was rendering its decision.

Based on that evidentiary record, Judge Marilyn Hall reversed
Korematsu's conviction, finding that a "manifest injustice" had
been done to all who had been interned. *See Korematsu v. United
States*, 584 F. Supp. 1406, 1416-17 (N.D. Cal. 1984).

Postscripts

Only recently did the Court expressly overrule *Korematsu*, recognizing that it was "gravely wrong the day it was decided." *Trump v. Hawaii*, 585 U.S. ___, 128 S. Ct. 2080 (2018) (slip op. at 38). As the Court has also acknowledged, its decision in *Korematsu* "demonstrates vividly that even the most rigid scrutiny can sometimes fail to detect an illegitimate racial classification" and "[a]ny retreat from the most searching judicial inquiry can only increase the risk of another such error occurring in the future." *Adarand Constructors, Inc. v. Peña*, 515 U.S. 200, 236 (1995).

Ironically, Senator Gerald Nye sponsored the Nye-Lea bill in 1935, which granted citizenship to American veterans of Asian ancestry.

The famed Western photographer Ansel Adams was granted access to the Manzanar camp. His photographs have all been digitalized and are available online at the Library of Congress' website.

By 1943, the federal government had changed its tune, at least insofar as allowing Japanese-Americans to serve in the military. Segregated units were formed, bound for service in Europe; a number of Japanese-Americans also served in the Pacific, most often as translators/interrogators (Major General Charles Willoughby paid tribute to those men as follows: "Never before in history did anyone know so much concerning its enemy.... Those translators saved over a million lives and two years."). The almost entire Japanese-American 442nd Regimental Combat Team, which ferociously fought the Germans in Italy, became the most decorated combat unit (per capita) in American history. Yet when Daniel Inouye (who later represented Hawaii in the U.S. Senate for 50 years) returned from the war (minus his right arm), he went into a San Francisco barbershop in his full-dress uniform (bedecked with medals—he won, *inter alia*, the Medal of Honor), Lieutenant Inouye was told: "You're a Jap and we don't cut Jap hair."

The hysteria that gripped California in the aftermath of Pearl Harbor is captured well in Steven Spielberg's 1979 movie *1941*.

One of the high points of *1941* is the greatest jitterbug dance scene in movie history.

The best, most comprehensive book on the treatment of Japanese-Americans in World War II is Richard Reeves's *Infamy: The Shocking Story of the Japanese-American Internment in World War II* (Picador 2015). An excellent review of the *coram nobis* petition can be found in S.K. Serrano & D. Minami's "*Korematsu v. United States*: A Constant Caution in a Time of Crisis," 10 *Asian American Law Journal* 37 (2003). For a contemporaneous critique of the Supreme Court's handling of *Korematsu*, see E.V. Rostow's "The Japanese American Cases—A Disaster," 54 *Yale Law Journal* 489 (1945).

CHAPTER IV

The Fourth Worst Supreme Court Decision

In *Dred Scott*, the Supreme Court discovered the doctrine of substantive due process—finding in the Fifth Amendment the unwritten constitutional right to protect (and travel with) one's property. Of course, in that case, the property at issue was another human being. The Supreme Court's next expansion of that judicial invention came in the Due Process Clause of the Fourteenth Amendment; this time the Court discovered another unwritten right—the right to economic free will ("freedom of contract"). The case was *Lochner v. New York*, 198 U.S. 45 (1905).

A Man Named Henry Weismann

Without one man—Henry Weismann—there would have been no *Lochner* decision. But he is a figure lost to history. Who was Henry Weismann, and why is he so central to this case?

Henry Weismann was an émigré from Germany, who (after he reached San Francisco) became a force in the Anti-Coolie League of California. His public behavior against Chinese immigration (carrying explosives) resulted in a jail term in 1886.

After six months in the hoosegow, Weismann switched interests; he became a union organizer for bakers. He must have been pretty effective because he was soon recruited to become the editor of the *Bakers' Journal*, which was headquartered in New York City. In that role he developed into a powerful advocate for bakers and against their poor working conditions: "the bakers [have] been robbed daylight, robbed of everything that makes life sweet and desirable, and left to work almost incessantly, day and night." Together with a muckraking journalist, Edward Marshall, Weismann brought a lot of heat and light to the bakers' woeful lot. And that pressure led to petitions to the New York State legislature for action.

In fairly short order, both the Senate and the Assembly unanimously passed a bill, stating, "No employee shall be required or permitted to work in a biscuit, bread or cake bakery or confectionery establishment more than sixty hours in one week, or more than ten hours in one day." (Violating the law was a misdemeanor crime.) On May 2, 1895, New York's governor signed the New York Bakeshop Act into law. On the heels of this legislative success, Weismann one month later was elected International Secretary of the Journeyman Bakers' Union; he was now the union's highest officer, and (like Leonardo DiCaprio) he was "on top of the world."

Two years later, Weismann's world fell in. Found to have his hand in the *Bakers' Journal* cookie jar (skimming off advertisers' money), he was forced to resign his union posts. Thereafter, Weismann opened his own bakery (and then another). Becoming an owner caused his sympathies to morph. He experienced "an intellectual revolution, [seeing] where the law had succeeded in having passed was unjust to the employers"; soon he was working with other bakery owners to eviscerate the Bakeshop Act.

Besides switching from labor's side, Weismann started to study the law, enrolling in 1901 in the first class (14 men) of the fledgling Brooklyn Law School. Weismann graduated in 1903 at the top of his graduating class (he also had been elected president of the school).[1]

A MAN NAMED JOSEPH LOCHNER

Joseph Lochner, an immigrant from Bavaria, owned a small bakery (Lochner's Home Bakery) in Utica, New York. One of his bakers was Arron Schmitter, and Schmitter worked more than 60 hours in one week in April of 1901. Shortly thereafter, Lochner was arrested and criminally charged with violating the Bakeshop Act—for the second time (in 1899, he had been fined $25 for violating the statute). The matter was referred to an Oneida County grand jury, which returned an indictment on October 22, 1901.

On February 12, 1902, the case went to trial; Lochner was represented by William S. Mackie. For some reason, Mackie presented no defense, and Lochner was found guilty; he was subsequently sentenced to pay $50 or spend 50 days in jail.

Mackie appealed the Appellate Division, Fourth Department in Rochester. His argument was that "laws which impair or trammel the right of one to use his facilities in lawful ways, to earn his livelihood in any lawful calling, to pursue any lawful trade or vocation, are infringements upon fundamental rights of liberty which are under constitutional protection." The Fourth Department (by a three-to-two vote) was not persuaded—the court ruled that the law was not a prohibition, but merely a regulation and, as such, a valid exercise of the state's police power. *See* 79 N.Y.S. 396 (4th Dep't 1902).

---

[1] I am grateful that Weismann's granddaughter, Ann Weismann Gehring, who contacted me prior to publication to correct an error that I had adopted from Professor Paul Kens's book (*see* page 47)—to wit, Kens's assertion that Weismann was not an accredited lawyer licensed in New York State (pp. 114-15). Ms. Gehring provided me more than sufficient proof that Weismann was in fact a member of the bar.

Mackie made the same argument to the New York State Court of Appeals in 1904. And while he again found some sympathetic judges, he did not find enough, losing in that court by a four-to-three vote. *See* 69 N.E. 373 (N.Y. 1904). (The majority opinion was written by Chief Judge Alton B. Parker, who later that year ran unsuccessfully for president against Theodore Roosevelt.)

ON TO THE U.S. SUPREME COURT

That ended William Mackie's formal involvement in representing Lochner. But obviously the case did not end at this point. So, who stepped in as Lochner's legal representation? None other than Henry Weismann! After fumbling around procedurally on how to get to the U.S. Supreme Court, Weismann brought on board a fellow Brooklynite Frank Harvey Field. Field, with Weismann listed as "of counsel," put together sufficient certiorari papers ("writ of error") to pass muster, and Justice Rufus W. Peckham granted the petition. Briefing proceeded (Weismann was now listed as co-counsel), and Lochner's lawyers took dead aim at the due process right at stake: "the treasured freedom of the individual ... should [not] be swept away under the guise of the police power of the state." Mindful of *Holden v. Hardy*, 169 U.S. 366 (1898), however, where the Court had upheld a Utah law establishing an eight-hour workday for miners in order to protect their health, they argued that the Bakeshop Act could hardly be deemed a health-related statute since the "average bakery ... is well ventilated, comfortable both summer and winter, and always sweet smelling."

The case was argued on February 23, 1905 (with Weismann *pro hac vice* participating in oral argument). Two months later, on April 17, 1905, the Supreme Court handed down its decision.

FREEDOM OF CONTRACT

Technically speaking, the five-to-four decision overturning New York's Bakeshop Act was not the first Supreme Court decision to find that freedom of contract was a substantive constitutional right found in the Fourteenth Amendment. Seven years earlier, Justice Peckham, writing for a unanimous Court, discovered such a right when a Louisiana statute concerning the sale of marine insurance was struck down: *Allgeyer v. Lou Liana*, 165 U.S. 578 (1897). (And its original antecedent came from Justice Stephen J. Field's dissent in the *Slaughter-House Cases*, 83 U.S. 36 (1873), where he wrote of the Fourteenth Amendment empowering "the liberty of citizens to acquire property and pursue happiness.")

In *Allgeyer*, Justice Peckham did not define the parameters of this new right (or the limits of a state's police power to infringe on this new right), leaving the law's development to "each case as it arises." And as noted above, in the year after *Allgeyer*, the Court expressly declined to rule in *Holden* that the right to contract "freely" could be invoked successfully to allow Utah miners to "freely" decide to work underground more than eight hours a day.

Justice Peckham, who had been in the minority in *Holden*, was now writing for the majority in *Lochner*, and he undertook to put some meat on the constitutional bone he had discovered seven years earlier. First off, Justice Peckham addressed head-on the *Holden* precedent, which, on its face, seemed a pretty big obstacle. But according to him, no problemo, and for two reasons: (1) the Utah law only dealt with "peculiar conditions"—that is, the very dangerous situation of working in underground mines (and the Utah legislature had specifically limited the law to those "peculiar conditions"), and (2) the Utah law provided for cases of emergency, where the law would not apply. Neither situation "covers the case now before [the Court]": "there can be no fair doubt that the trade of a baker, in and of itself, is not an unhealthy one"; furthermore, the Bakeshop Act had no emergency clause. New York's law was thus not "within any fair meaning of the term, a health law, but [was] an illegal interference with the rights of individuals ... to make contracts." And, as such, it was a clear violation of the federal Constitution.

While aware of what Justice John Marshall Harlan had written for the Court just two years earlier in *Atkin v. Kansas*, 191 U.S.
207 (1903) (acts of a legislature should be upheld "unless they
are plainly and palpably, beyond all question, in violation of the
fundamental law of the Constitution."), Justice Peckham simply
proclaimed that "[t]his is not a question of substituting the judgement of the [C]ourt for that of the legislature." It was instead a
question of whether the legislature could interfere "with the liberty
of person or the right of the free contract." And according to the
majority's view, New York's legislators had "no reasonable ground"
for doing so.

Justice Peckham then moved on to the slippery slope. If laws
restricting the freedoms of bakers were to be upheld, whose freedoms would be next? Why, lawyers' freedoms, of course. Repeatedly invoking lawyers, Peckham worried that someone might want
to try to restrict the working hours of lawyers (especially young
lawyers), those "condemned to labor day after day in buildings
where the sun never shines"; we would never want to forbid such
professionals also from "fatiguing their brains and bodies by prolonged hours of [work]"!

There were two dissenting opinions, both famous. The first
was by Justice Harlan, in which Justices Edward Douglas White
and William R. Day joined. Some have speculated that Harlan's
opinion at one point had been the majority opinion; if so, some-
where along the line he lost Justices Henry Billings Brown and
Joseph McKenna, both of whom had been in the *Atkin* majority.
Undeterred, he reiterated the basic tenet of a restrained judiciary
in our democracy:

> If there be doubt as to the validity of the statute, that
> doubt must therefore be resolved in favor of its validity,
> and the courts must keep their hands off, leaving the leg-
> islature to meet the responsibility for unwise legislation. If
> the end which the legislature seeks to accomplish be one
> to which its power extends, and if the means employed

to that end, although not the wisest or best, are yet not plainly and palpably unauthorized by law, then the court cannot interfere.

Justice Harlan then took up the notion of whether a baker's lot was a "happy one," free from a dangerous work environment. First, he cited to a leading treatise in which it was written "[t]he labor of the bakers is among the hardest and most laborious imaginable." Next, in a review that would have caused Justice Antonin Scalia apoplexy, Justice Harlan compared working men's hours in the United States to those of various European nations. Finally, he circled back to the fact that the majority's ruling could not be squared with *Atkin* and the "plainly and palpably" standard enunciated by a six-justice majority just two years before.

The Yankee from Olympus, Justice Oliver Wendell Holmes, also dissented, issuing a brief opinion under just his name. Not mincing words, he quickly (and famously) got to the point: "This case is decided upon an economic theory which a large part of the country does not entertain. The Fourteenth Amendment does not enact Mr. Herbert Spencer's Social Statics." (Spencer was an English "Social Darwinist" in fact, he has been credited with inventing the phrase "survival of the fittest.") Then, with a tip of his hat to James Madison's Federalist No. 10, Justice Holmes wrote that the Constitution "is not intended to embody a particular economic theory.... [Rather,] [i]t is made for people of fundamentally differing views, and the accident of our finding certain opinions natural and familiar or novel and even shocking ought not to conclude our judgment upon the question whether statutes embodying them conflict with the Constitution of the United States."

THE AFTERMATH OF *LOCHNER*

Historian William E. Leuchtenberg has written that *Lochner* is "the high-water mark of usurpation by the courts of legislative authority." The majority decision has been widely criticized by legal and constitutional scholars and political scientists as being, at bottom, anti-democratic: unelected justices, by judicial fiat, using substantive due process to overturn laws enacted by elected officials. *Lochner* also ushered in an era of judicial activism—on the politically "conservative" side.

For the next three decades, the Supreme Court generally hewed to the *Lochner* brand of "laissez-faire constitutionalism." Thus, for example, in *Adkins v. Children's Hospital*, 261 U.S. 525 (1923), the Court struck down a statute that created a minimum wage for women and children working in the District of Columbia. (Following *Lochner*, Justice George Sutherland also justified the majority's ruling under a feminist flag: "we cannot accept the doctrine that women of mature age, *sui juris*, require or may be subjected to restrictions upon their liberty of contract which could not lawfully be imposed in the case of men under similar circumstances.") And when President Franklin Roosevelt pushed through Congress his "New Deal" legislation, the Court simply nullified one after another. *See, e.g., A.L.A. Schecter Poultry Corp. v. United States*, 295 U.S. 495 (1935) (striking down the National Industrial Recovery Act). Only in the face of President Roosevelt's "court-packing scheme"—when a "switch in time save[d] nine"— did the Court do an immediate about-face in *West Coast Hotel v. Parrish*, 300 U.S. 379 (1937) (upholding Washington State's minimum wage law; reversing *Morehead v. New York ex rel. Tipaldo*, 298 U.S. 587 (1936), which a year earlier had struck down New York's minimum wage law (following *Lochner* and *Adkins*)). *See* Chapter XIV.

This judicial about-face saved the Court, averted a separation of powers crisis, and ended the invocation of substantive due process by judicial "conservatives" to achieve certain policy ends (and block "progressive" legislation). But would those on the other end of the spectrum feel so constrained once they came into the majority and wanted to achieve their policy goals? We will see in Chapter V.

FURTHER READINGS

For those who wish to do a deeper dive on *Lochner*, recommended is Paul Kens's *Lochner v. New York: Economic Regulation on Trial* (Kansas 1998). *See also* Charles W. McCurdy's "The Roots of 'Liberty of Contract' Reconsidered: Major Premises in the Law of Employment, 1867-1937," *Yearbook of the Supreme Court Historical Society* (1984); Bernard H. Siegan's "*Rehabilitating Lochner*," 22 *San Diego Law Review* 453 (1985); David E. Bernstein's "*Lochner v. New York*: A Centennial Retrospective," 83 *Washington Univ. Law Review* 1469 (2005).

CHAPTER V

How an Uncommonly Silly Law Led to a Host of Consequential Supreme Court Decisions

In 1879, Connecticut passed a law barring the use of "any drug, medicinal article or instrument for the purpose of preventing conception"; the penalty was "not less than fifty dollars" or between 60 days and one year in prison. And the state legislature also made it a crime to aid or abet such activity.

Connecticut's law was challenged repeatedly in the years thereafter, even reaching the U.S. Supreme Court several times, but without effect. In 1965, the Court decided to address the law head-on, a law one justice derided as "uncommonly silly." Yet the outcome of that case, *Griswold v. Connecticut*, 381 U.S. 479 (1965), was far from silly. For the first time the nation's highest court declared that the Constitution implied a fundamental right to privacy, thereby setting in motion the direct doctrinal basis for some of the most consequential social policy rulings of our time: *Roe v. Wade*, 410 U.S. 113 (1973) (abortion), *Lawrence v. Texas*, 539 U.S. 558 (2003) (right of same-sex sex), and *Obergefell v. Hodges*, 576 U.S. 644 (2015) (same-sex marriage). All of those decisions, whether acknowledged or not, involved the Court's application of substantive due process.

"BAD" SUBSTANTIVE DUE PROCESS

The Supreme Court's track record on substantive due process is far from stellar. It made many terrible decisions before it began experimenting with substantive due process in what many people consider a "good" way in the 1960s. As we know (*see* Chapter I), the *worst* decision, in my judgment, was the invention of substantive due process in *Dred Scott v. John F.A. Sandford*, 60 U.S. (19 How.) 393 (1856), where the Fifth Amendment was held to protect the right to travel with one's "property" (i.e., one's slave). The Court thereafter expanded on that "original sin," via the Fourteenth Amendment, into protecting the right of economic "free will" in *Lochner v. New York*, 198 U.S. 45 (1905), which struck down a New York law that sought to regulate the number hours a baker could work per week (*see* Chapter IV). The Court rejected New York's "arbitrary" and "unreasonable" interference with an individual's "freedom of contract"; *Lochner* was subsequently used to promote "laissez-faire constitutionalism" throughout the first part of the twentieth century, as one by one the Court struck down virtually all of President Roosevelt's "New Deal" legislation. It likely would have continued on that path were it not for FDR's threat to pack the Court in 1937. In response to that constitutional crisis, the Court did an abrupt 180-degree turn. *See* Chapter XIV.

Many lawyers and political scientists have been very critical of the foregoing substantive due process decisions by the Court; and a good number of those critics have not liked unelected justices weighing in on obviously political matters, as well as the policy ends promoted by those decisions (e.g., racism, striking down "progressive" legislation, etc.). But what if substantive due process were to be used going the other political way?

"GOOD" SUBSTANTIVE DUE PROCESS

The first time the Court started experimenting with substantive due process in a "good" way came in the 1960s, and involved the "uncommonly silly" Connecticut law that had been challenged over the years—but always unsuccessfully. In 1961, the Supreme Court seemed to put an end to all repeal efforts in *Poe v. Ullman*, 367 U.S. 497 (1961), when it dismissed a lawsuit directed against the Connecticut law for failure to state a case or controversy. In his dissent, however, Justice John Marshall Harlan II (Justice Harlan's grandson) suggested a legal path forward through a broad reading of liberty rights under the Fourteenth Amendment:

> [T]he full scope of the liberty guaranteed by the Due Process Clause cannot be found in or limited by the precise terms of the specific guarantees elsewhere provided in the Constitution. This "liberty" is not a series of isolated points pricked out in terms of the taking of property; the freedom of speech, press, and religion; the right to keep and bear arms; the freedom from unreasonable searches and seizures; and so on. It is a rational continuum which, broadly speaking, includes a freedom from all substantial arbitrary impositions and purposeless restraints, ... and which also recognizes, what a reasonable and sensitive judgment must, that certain interests require particularly careful scrutiny of the state needs asserted to justify their abridgment.

That language would become transformative for much of the Supreme Court's Fourteenth Amendment jurisprudence over the next six decades.

A TEST CASE IS BORN

In addition to Harlan's doctrinal approach, Justice William Brennan's concurrence in *Poe*—that a "true controversy" did not exist because no one had been arrested in violation of Connecticut law—provided the law's opponents with a plan. Planned Parenthood decided first to open a clinic in Connecticut and thereafter to "get Estelle Griswold [the Executive Director of Planned Parent-hood's Connecticut operation] arrested." On November 1, 1961, the facility opened in New Haven. Several days later, New Haven police detectives began assembling prearranged evidence that demonstrated that Griswold and Leo Buxton, a professor at Yale Medical School and the medical director at the clinic, were giving birth control devices, as well as advice related thereto, to a number of local, married women. On November 10, arrest warrants were issued for both Griswold and Buxton for violating the aiding and abetting provision. The test case had begun.

At the trial stage, the defendants were found guilty and each fined $100. The intermediate appellate court affirmed the verdict (the court declined to pass judgment on the "wisdom or unwis-dom" of the law unless it was "plainly violative of some constitu-tional mandate"). On April 28, 1964, the Connecticut Supreme Court affirmed the lower courts, noting that "every attack now made on the statute ... has been made and rejected" by each and every court, over many years. Next up: the U.S. Supreme Court.

ON TO THE SUPREMES

Griswold and Buxton's lawyers invoked 28 U.S.C. § 1257 (where a statute is "repugnant to the Constitution") in their peti-tion to the U.S. Supreme Court, invoking Amendments One, Four, Nine, and Fourteen as the affected Constitutional provi-sions. In December of 1964, a unanimous Court agreed to grant certiorari, and briefing took place at the beginning of the next year.

On March 29, 1965, the Court began to hear oral argu-ment, and it was tough sledding for both sets of advocates; each was constantly interrupted by questions, unable to get to many of the points they had intended to raise. At one point, Justice Hugo Black suggested to appellants' counsel that his side was advocating the same kind of (discredited) substantive due process doctrine endorsed by *Lochner* and its progeny; that led to some very heated back and forth. Notwithstanding, appellants' counsel did try to focus on that which had been advanced in the briefs—what Harlan had been getting at in *Poe*: an emerging constitutional right of privacy, grounded in the First, Third, Fourth, Fifth, and Ninth Amendments. Justice Harlan piped in at that point and asked whether appellants' counsel was planning to say anything more on the First Amendment issue. His reply: "Well, I'm not getting far on any of my arguments...." After laughter throughout the courtroom subsided, he concluded: "I can't guarantee that I'll get back to the First Amendment, no." The argument then moved on to the fact that the Connecticut law did not "conform to current community standards."

Counsel for the state of Connecticut was equally hammered, especially on the fact that Connecticut was the only state that prohibited the use of contraception. The Court adjourned midway through his presentation, and took up argument the following day. The focus the next day was on whether the statute was a proper use of Connecticut's police power and whether the seldom-enforced law was really a "dead letter."

In his rebuttal, appellants' counsel tried to focus on broad public policy issues. But then a series of questions from the Court on the unbriefed subject of abortion took center stage. At one point, Justice Byron White observed: "I take it abortion involves killing a life in being, doesn't it? Isn't that a rather different problem from conception?" Appellants' counsel agreed, but was unable to stop Justice Black from probing farther on this hot-potato issue and its possible application to the case before the Court.

Finally, at 10:45 a.m. on March 30, oral argument concluded. And as with most cases argued before the Court, no one could predict how the nine justices would resolve the weighty matters briefed and orally vetted.

The Court Decides

On June 7, 1965, Justice William Douglas (who had not asked a single question at oral argument) delivered the opinion of the Court. Justice Arthur Goldberg wrote a concurring opinion, which was joined by Chief Justice Earl Warren and Justice Brennan. Justice Harlan wrote a separate opinion, concurring in the result, as did Justice White. Justices Black and Potter Stewart each wrote dissenting opinions.

Justice Douglas noted at the outset that there was not a problem of standing (which had defeated a prior challenge to the statutes) because Estelle Griswold and Leo Buxton had been found guilty of the aiding and abetting provision. That was the easy part.

Moving on to the merits, Douglas, in striking down Connecticut's law, recognized that the result might sound a lot like *Lochner* and its substantive due process progeny. Not so: "We do not sit as a super-legislature to determine the wisdom, need, and propriety of laws that touch economic problems, business affairs, or social conditions." Instead, the Court was *only* substituting its wisdom for the Connecticut legislature because the legislators had passed a law that "operates directly on an intimate relation of husband and wife and their physician's role in one aspect of that relation."

In justifying the Court voiding the law, Douglas first invoked Harlan's dissent in *Poe*; but then he went a step farther, finding that various provisions of the Bill of Rights (the First, Third, Fourth, Fifth, and Ninth Amendments) have privacy guarantees that "have *penumbras*, formed by *emanations* from those guarantees that help give them life and substance" (emphasis added). Douglas then cited a number of prior Supreme Court "penumbra-like" cases that "bear witness that the right of privacy which presses for recognition here is a legitimate one."

Obviously concerned about how wide a door he might be opening by recognizing a constitutional "right of privacy" for the first time in the country's history, Douglas indicated that this new right would be a *very* limited one:

We deal with a right of privacy older than the Bill of Rights—older than our political parties, older than our school system. Marriage is a coming together for better or for worse, hopefully enduring, and intimate to the degree of being sacred. It is an association that promotes a way of life, not causes; a harmony in living, not political faiths; a bilateral loyalty, not commercial or social projects. Yet it is an association for as noble a purpose as any involved in our prior decisions.

Justice Goldberg's concurrence agreed with the newly discovered constitutional "right of marital privacy" (even though it "is not mentioned explicitly in the Constitution"). His justification, however, was not based on "penumbras" or "emanations." With the help of his imaginative law clerk, Stephen Breyer, Goldberg emphasized the importance of the Ninth Amendment ("The enumeration in the Constitution, of certain rights, shall not be construed to deny or disparage others retained by the people."). Why emphasize the Ninth Amendment? Because "this Court has had little occasion to interpret" that constitutional provision, so perhaps the jurisprudential vacuum could be used to say that the "forgotten" amendment actually "lends strong support" to this new right of marital privacy. The sole authority for this dubious assertion, however, was a "cf." citation to an opinion of the Court interpreting the Hatch Act![1] As for how to determine "which [other] rights are fundamental" enough to receive constitutional protection, Goldberg provided a facile solution: "look to the 'traditions and [collective] conscience of our people.'"

Perhaps recognizing the foregoing was not on the most solid ground (and anticipating caustic attacks from Black and the usually mild-mannered Stewart), Goldberg spent the rest of his concurrence agreeing and reagreeing with Harlan's dissent in *Poe*.

---

[1] The Hatch Act ("An Act to Prevent Pernicious Political Activities") is a 1939 statute (most recently amended in 2012) barring civil service employees in the executive branch of the federal government—except the president and vice president—from engaging in various forms of electoral activity.

Justice Harlan concurred with the result, but rejected the imaginative way the majority got there. Rather than trying to avoid the *Lochner* stigma—by invoking "penumbras" and "emanations," let's call a spade a spade—obviously, this is substantive due process; but now it is being used (as he wrote in *Poe*) not in a bad *Lochner* way, but instead to vindicate one of the "basic values implicit in the concept of ordered liberty." As for those who would worry about opening a Pandora's box with this approach, don't worry: "Judicial self-restraint" will ensure that the Court does not go crazy in the future. And such self-restraint will be achieved through (1) respecting history, (2) recognizing the aforementioned "basic values," and (3) appreciating federalism and the separation of powers.[2]

Justice White, also concurred in the result, but took on an even more direct approach than did Harlan. In essence, he wrote that Connecticut's law was so stupid, it violated due process. In an opinion littered with "cf." citations,[3] White questioned how a ban on contraception affecting married people could somehow prevent illicit sexual relations. Because of the broad impact of the statute on compelling societal interests (i.e., children), Connecticut was bound to justify the law; and because the state could not, the law must be voided.

---

[2] Ironically, Harlan's grandfather, John Marshall Harlan, had espoused exactly the opposite approach in his *Lochner* dissent. Underscoring that a basic tenet of our democracy is restrained judiciary, he wrote: "If there be doubt as to the validity of the statute, that doubt must therefore be resolved in favor of its validity, and the courts must keep their hands off, leaving the legislature to meet the responsibility of unwise legislation. If the end which the legislature seeks to accomplish be one to which its power extends, and if the means employed to the end, although not the wisest or best, are yet not plainly and palpably unauthorized by law, then the court cannot interfere."

[3] A "cf." citation is a convention that lawyers and judges use when there is no authority even closely related to the proposition being advanced (and they want the reader to be aware of that fact).

Justice Black's dissent, while less famous than Stewart's, presented a telling critique of the opinions of his judicial brethren who voided Connecticut's law. While initially agreeing that the Connecticut law was dumb, he wrote that that did not rise to a constitutional violation. As for a constitutional right of privacy, obviously it exists nowhere in the Founders' document (nor are there any "emanations" therein); indeed, the first time the concept emerged was in an 1890 article in the *Harvard Law Review*![4] With respect to the embrace of substantive due process, Black wrote that he thought the Court had rid itself of that noxious doctrine when the Court did its pivot in the 1930s and stopped voiding FDR's New Deal legislation. In any event, "[s]uch an appraisal of the wisdom of legislation is an attribute of the power to make laws, not of the power to interpret them ... [the former is] a power which was specifically denied to federal courts by the convention that framed the Constitution." As to White's burden point, Black countered that White got it exactly wrong: laws are *presumed* to be constitutional. Regarding Goldberg's proposed standard of the "traditions and [collective] conscience of our people," where and/or how does the Court determine them?: "Our Court certainly has no machinery with which to take a Gallup Poll." Finally, as to the notion that the Court must "keep the Constitution in tune with the times," that is precisely what led to all the mischief in *Lochner* and its progeny; if people want to update the Constitution, the Founders provided a precise mechanism to do that (a mechanism that does not involve the Court). On this last point, Black ended by quoting the late Judge Learned Hand's disparaging of judges using substantive due process to favor their "personal preferences": "For myself it would be most irksome to be ruled by a bevy of Platonic Guardians, even if I knew how to choose them, which I assuredly do not."

---

[4] Samuel D. Warren II & Louis Brandeis, "The Right to Privacy," 4 Harvard L. Rev. 193 (1890). In this article, the right of privacy was envisioned as giving rise to a cause of action in tort law.

Justice Stewart began his dissent with his famous observation: "this is an uncommonly silly law. As a practical matter, the law is obviously unenforceable, except in the oblique context of the present case." He then warmed to the task at hand, chastising the majority for being afraid to label what they were really doing: reviving substantive due process—at least Harlan and White had the courage to call it what it was. As for Douglas's "emanations" and "penumbras" of marital privacy, they are nowhere to be found in any of the enumerated Amendments. And as for Goldberg's hyping of the Ninth Amendment, that is "to turn somersaults with history": "the idea that a federal court could ever use the Ninth Amendment to annul a law passed by the elected representatives of the people of the state of Connecticut would have caused James Madison no little wonder." Stewart then addressed the comment made at oral argument about nonconformity with "current community standards": "it is not the function of this Court to decide cases on the basis of community standards." If people do not like a law, the correct way to proceed is "to persuade their elected representatives to repeal it. That is the constitutional way to take [a] law off the books."

Pre- and Post-Blowback

Well before the various opinions were made public, it was evident to some Court insiders that what was to come would have great significance. Most importantly, two memoranda written by Chief Justice Warren's clerk, John Hart Ely, foresaw much of what lay ahead. The first was dated February 26, 1965, before oral argument, and it was distributed beyond Warren to a number of other justices. In his memorandum, Ely warned that "some of [the arguments] urged by appellants have dangerous implications": "Just as I think the Court should vigorously enforce each clause in the Constitution, I do not think the Court should enforce clauses which are not there. No matter how strong a dislike for a piece of legislation may be, it is dangerous precedent to read into the Constitution guarantees which are not there. Despite Justice Brandeis's lifelong crusade for a right of privacy, ... the Constitution says nothing about such a right." And as for Justice Harlan's approach in his *Poe* dissent, that would constitute "in my opinion, the most dangerous sort of 'activism.'" Ely concluded his February memorandum by advising Warren that to reverse the lower courts on a right to privacy ground "would, in my opinion, have very dangerous implications."

Later on, when Justice Douglas was circulating drafts of his opinion, a number of other Supreme Court clerks were taken aback by the weakness of the analysis, with a few openly mocking his "penumbras" and "emanations." More ominous was Ely's second memorandum to Warren, written after Douglas's nearly finalized opinion: "This opinion incorporates an approach to the Constitution so dangerous that you should not join it."

It appears that the only person in the Supreme Court's building who actually liked what Douglas had come up with was Justice Tom Clark. On April 28, he penned a note to Douglas: "Bill, Yes I like all of it—it emancipates femininity and protects masculinity—TC."

After the ruling, the immediate reaction by the media was fairly predictable. The liberal press (e.g., *New York Times, Washington Post, Life, New Republic*) hailed the Court's action to protect "the people" from troglodyte state legislators. The mainstream press (e.g., *Richmond Times-Dispatch*), however, thought the dissents were right: "The fact that members of the court simply *don't like* a law is no basis for throwing it out." (emphasis in original); and a number of publications (e.g., *Waterloo Daily Courier*) lampooned and/or lambasted Douglas's "penumbras" and "emanations."

Perhaps more important were the first wave of law review articles. The annual Supreme Court edition published by the *Harvard Law Review* in 1965 opined that the two approaches endorsed by Justices Douglas and Harlan "differ more in tone than in results to which they lead." What the *Review*'s editors found more curious was Justice Goldberg's hyping of the Ninth Amendment, which had never been the basis for a single decision by the Court since its adoption in 1791. Later in 1965 came an entire issue of the *Michigan Law Review* devoted to *Griswold*; while most of the legal academics praised the result—a constitutional right to privacy— many questioned the means to get there. Professor Paul Klapper, for example, found Douglas's opinion "curious," "puzzling," "confusing," "uncertain," and "ambiguous." Professor Robert Dixon wrote: "The actual result of *Griswold* may be applauded, but was it necessary to play charades with the Constitution?" And a consensus among the various academics seemed to form around the notion that—notwithstanding the various approaches of Douglas, Goldberg, Harlan, and White—they all were, at bottom, "treading a worn and familiar path." And that path subsequently became known as "liberal *Lochner*ism."

WHAT IS THE FUTURE OF *GRISWOLD*?

At first blush, after the Court's decision in *Dobbs v. Jacskon Women's Health Organization*, 597 U.S. ___, 142 S. Ct. 2228 (2022) (overturning both *Roe v. Wade* and *Planned Parenthood v. Casey*, 505 U.S. 833 (1992)), one might conclude that the Court would, *seriatim*, reverse *Griswold* and its other progeny (e.g., *Lawrence v. Texas*). Yet the tenor and text of Justice Samuel Alito's majority opinion in *Dobbs* clearly suggests otherwise. Indeed, the *only* justice calling for a complete rejection of the doctrine of substantive due process is Justice Clarence Thomas. And (perhaps ironically) the one clear effect of the *Dobbs* decision has been to transfer the abortion issue back into the political branches of government—and into electoral politics itself—an effect that has had a decidedly pro-abortion orientation. So, perhaps until there is another seismic shift in the balance of power on the Court, *Griswold* and its (non–*Roe v. Wade*) progeny appear safe; at the same time, it also seems probable that the current Court will not be finding new substantive due process rights in the Constitution any time soon.[5]

Postscripts

For those who wish to know more about *Griswold,* the first stop should be John Johnson's *Griswold v. Connecticut: Birth Control and the Constitutional Right of Privacy* (University Press of Kansas 2005). The 1965 *Michigan Law Review* referenced above is in Volume 64. A more recent scholarly law review take on *Griswold* is Ryan William's "The Path to *Griswold,*" 89 *Notre Dame Law Review* 2155 (2014). And Jill Lepore has weighed in on *Griswold* (and related subjects) in two *New Yorker* articles: "To Have and To Hold" (May 25, 2015) and "The History Test" (March 27, 2017).

Justice Potter Stewart's "uncommonly silly law" phrase was later cited with approval by Justice Clarence Thomas in his dissent in *Lawrence v. Texas.*

Justice Arthur Goldberg's Ninth Amendment opinion in *Griswold* would be his last as a Supreme Court Justice. At President Lyndon Johnson's importuning, he left the Court to replace Adlai Stevenson as the U.S. Ambassador to the United Nations. His seat on the Court was filled by Abe Fortas; and Goldberg's clerk ultimately became Justice Stephen Breyer.

John Hart Ely became one of America's leading legal scholars (ranked as the fourth most-cited legal authority—after Richard Posner, Ronald Dworkin, and Oliver Wendell Holmes), and served as Dean of the Stanford Law School. His 1980 book, *Democracy and Distrust: A Theory of Judicial Review* (Harvard University Press,

---

[5] This may explain why the nomination process involving Justices Amy Coney Barrett and Ketanji Brown Jackson was far less heated than the process that Justices Neil Gorsuch and Brett Kavanaugh had to go through; in other words, the ideological balance of the Court was much more settled during the former, as opposed to the latter.

1980), is considered one of the most important and influential books about Constitutional law ever written. In 1973, after the Court had decided *Roe v. Wade*, Ely published an article in the *Yale Law Journal* (Volume 82). In it he posited that the two rights discovered by the *Griswold* and *Roe* Courts were made from the same "whole cloth" as *Lochner*. He went on to write that "although *Lochner* and *Roe* are twins to be sure, they are not identical. While I would hesitate to argue that one is more defensible than the other in terms of judicial style, there are differences in that regard that suggest *Roe* may turn out to be the more dangerous precedent." Ely supported the availability of abortions as a matter of public policy, but *Roe* (he wrote) "is not constitutional law and gives almost no sense of an obligation to try to be."

CHAPTER VI

THE SUPREME COURT'S WORST DECISION ON CAMPAIGN FINANCES!

JESSE UNRUH WAS A LEGENDARY FIGURE in California (and national) politics for virtually his entire adult life. And one of his most famous statements was: "money is the mothers' milk of politics."[1] He, of course, was right. That is, until this basic truism ran into the United States Supreme Court, when the Court truly split the baby: sometimes money *is*, and sometimes money *is not*. Huh?!

WATERGATE AND THE ROOT OF ALL EVIL: MONEY

For the movie *All the President's Men*, William Goldman (the screenwriter) attributed the phrase "follow the money" to Deep Throat (aka Mark Felt), in his advice to Bob Woodward on how to disentangle the web of intrigue that was broadly labeled

---

[1] Mark Hanna, William McKinley's presidential campaign manager in 1896 (and later senator from Ohio), expressed this sentiment slightly differently: "There are two things that are important in politics. The first is money, and I can't remember what the second one is." W. Safire, *Safire's Political Dictionary*. p. 237 (Oxford University Press 2008).

"Watergate." And in reaction to Watergate, Congress in 1974 passed a number of amendments to the Federal Election Campaign Act of 1971 in an effort not just to "follow the money," but to limit severely its impact on federal elections. The key provisions of the 1974 amendments were (1) to limit to $1,000 what individuals or groups could contribute to federal office candidates, and (2) to limit independent expenditures by an individual or a group advocating any one federal office candidate. (Other provisions (e.g., public disclosure of the names of contributors of more than $100, creation of the Federal Election Commission, etc.) were also part of the new regime; and while those (and other provisions) were also challenged to the Supreme Court, in my judgment they were not so highly controversial, consequential, or impactful, and thus will not be the focus of this chapter.)

BUCKLEY V. VALEO

To challenge the constitutionality of the 1974 amendments, an odd coalition of discordant political and legal forces (e.g., James Buckley (Conservative Senator, New York), Eugene McCarthy (former Democratic Senator, Minnesota), the New York Civil Liberties Union, the American Conservative Union, etc.) came together and sued the Secretary of the U.S. Senate (Francis Valeo) and the Clerk of the U.S. House of Representatives, both in their official capacities and as the ex-officio members of the Federal Election Commission (also named as defendants were the Commission, the U.S. Attorney General, and the U.S. Comptroller General). Through a complicated process, the lawsuit went quickly to the D.C. Circuit Court of Appeals. And with one minor exception, the Court of Appeals upheld the 1974 amendments, finding "a clear and compelling interest" in preserving the integrity of the electoral process. *Buckley v. Valeo*, 519 F.2d 817, 841 (D.C. Cir. 1975). With that judicial determination, the plaintiffs moved on to U.S. Supreme Court.

Lead counsel for the challengers was Ralph K. Winter, a Yale law professor (and later a distinguished judge for the Second Circuit); assisting him (among others) was a young ACLU lawyer, Joel M. Gora, who has gone on to a distinguished academic career at the Brooklyn Law School. The challengers argued that "the law was the greatest frontal assault on the First Amendment protection of political speech and association since the Alien and Sedition Acts. It would stifle the voices of outsiders, political underdogs, and dissidents, and thereby ... entrench the incumbents in Congress[,] who had written the law precisely to barricade themselves in power." Arrayed against them, defending the federal statute, was a cavalcade of legal heavyweights, including Archibald Cox, Lloyd Cutler, and Solicitor General Robert Bork.

The case was argued before the Court on November 10, 1975. On January 20, 1976, in a 143-page *per curiam* opinion, with five separate concurring and dissenting opinions by different justices, the Court rendered its decision(s).[2] The *per curiam* opinion soared with First Amendment rhetoric:

> The First Amendment denies government the power to determine that spending to promote one's political views is wasteful, excessive, or unwise. In the free society ordained by our Constitution it is not the government but the people individually as citizens and candidates and collectively as associations and political committees who must retain control over the quantity and range of debate on public issues in a political campaign.

---

[2] The *per curiam* nature of the opinion is itself a tad confusing/misleading. Justice John Paul Stevens recused himself from the case and the only thing the other eight justices seem to have agreed on was that there was a proper "case or controversy" before the Court. Three justices (Brennan, Powell, and Stewart) did in fact sign on to the whole enchilada. As we will see, the other five justices could only agree with certain disparate parts of the Court's *per curiam* opinion.

But then the *per curiam* Court, in applying this soaring rhetoric, drew a line of enormous consequence—delineating a constitutional difference between a campaign *contribution* and a campaign *expenditure*. Thus, some federal limits on campaign *contributions* were fine and dandy, while federal limits on campaign *expenditures* were unconstitutional.

The Court determined that any and all restrictions placed on what could be spent in federal political campaigns (i.e., *expenditures*) clearly violated First Amendment rights; such moneys constituted protected speech, irrespective of amount(s). At the same time, however, the $1,000 limitation imposed on individual *contributions* was consistent with the First Amendment because of Congress' express concern with avoiding the fact (or appearance) of corruption. (The limits on contributions were further defended on the ground that they would "act as a brake on the skyrocketing cost of political campaigns.") And yet this did not apply to wealthy individuals underwriting their own campaigns; since the wealthy could not "corrupt" themselves, any limitations on what they could spend on their own individual races violated their (the wealthy's) First Amendment rights.

On its face, the Court's constitutional distinction between *contributions* and *expenditures*—one is not speech, the other is— made (and makes) no sense; neither did the constitutional carve-out for the wealthiest Americans who want to hold high political office. And it did not take any period of great reflection to figure these (and other) problems out; many of the justices noted a number of them in their own separate opinions.

Chief Justice Warren Burger's concurrence and dissent went right after the most obvious flaw. Agreeing with the *per curiam* opinion's determination that campaign *expenditures* were protected political expressions that could not be restricted consistent with the First Amendment, Burger contended that "contributions and expenditures are two sides of the same First Amendment coin." He went on, belittling the "word games" employed to distinguish between the two—saying that such games "will not wash." Burger went on to predict that the contributions rulings would "foreclose some candidacies" and "also alter the nature of some electoral contests drastically." He also noted that the Court's approved finance regime would give "a clear advantage" to candidates with personal fortunes over less affluent opponents, constrained by the fund-raising limits of $1,000; other losers in this system would include minority parties and little-known, first-time candidates.

Justice Byron White, in his concurrence and dissent, agreed with Burger's poo-pooing of the delineation between *contributions* and *expenditures*. But then he arrived at exactly the opposite conclusion. According to White, neither *contributions* nor *expenditures* constituted speech—rather, caps on spending of any kind are "neutral" vis-à-vis political speech. While it made no sense to cap *contributions* and not *expenditures*, White would have deferred to those with political expertise (i.e., Congress and the president) to determine what should be done "to counter the corrosive effects of money in federal election campaigns." White also disagreed with the *per curiam* opinion's carve-out for wealthy candidates' spending as much as they would like on themselves: "Congress was entitled to determine that personal wealth ought to play a less important role ... than it has in the past. Nothing in the First Amendment stands in the way of that determination."

Justice Thurgood Marshall's opinion was directed at the *per curiam* opinion's carve-out for wealthy candidates, pointing out that the political landscape going forward would definitely favor millionaires. Justice Harry Blackmun's opinion dissented from the determination that the $1,000 limit on contributions was constitutional. Justice William Rehnquist's opinion was directed at the *per curiam* opinion's ruling on public financing of campaigns, believing it would serve to entrench the two-party system and unconstitutionally penalize minority parties.

THE AFTERMATH OF *BUCKLEY*

While some hailed the *per curiam* ruling for "declaring for the first time that campaign funding limits violated First Amendment rights," others with political experience knew better. Indeed, as former Senator (and later District of Columbia Circuit Judge) Buckley would later write on the fortieth anniversary of the *Buckley* ruling:

> In the wake of the *Buckley* decision, we are left with a package of federal election laws and regulations that have distorted virtually every aspect of the election-process. The 1974 amendments to the Federal Election Campaign Act were supposed to deemphasize the role of money in federal election campaigns. Instead, the limit on individual contributions has made the search for money a candidate's central preoccupation.
>
> * * *
>
> [And for those] reformers [who] complain about the power of political action committees—the notorious PACs ... their proliferation and growth are a direct consequence of the restrictions placed on individual giving.

And as Buckley further noted, the still-current delineation between *contributions* and *expenditures* "makes politics the playground of the super-rich who can finance their own campaigns." Indeed (and not surprisingly), since 2012, a majority of the members of Congress and Senate are millionaires many times over.

As noted by Justice White, the Court—then (and now) made up of folks who have never run for political office—does not have first-hand expertise or experience with money's role in politics. And in subsequent decisions, the Court often displayed similar proclivities when it came to assessing the role of money in politics.[3]

---

[3] *See, e.g., Austin v. Michigan Chamber of Commerce,* 494 U.S. 652 (1990) (holding that the Michigan Campaign Finance Act, which barred corporations from making expenditures in political campaigns, did not violate the First and Fourteenth Amendments); *McConnell v. FEC,* 540 U.S. 93 (2003) (holding that

But in more recent years, perhaps influenced by Justice Antonin Scalia's dissents in *Austin* and *McConnell* (that campaign restrictions at issue in those cases were intended to, and had the effect of, stifling critics of elected officials), the Court has moved in the direction of attempting to correct the crazy-quilt campaign finance system it created by its 1976 ruling in *Buckley*. The first such case was *Citizens United v. FEC*, 558 U.S. 310 (2010). Because so much heat (and very little light) has been directed at *Citizens United*, perhaps a brief recap is in order. At issue in that case was whether a nonprofit corporation could produce and distribute a movie entitled *Hillary: The Movie*; the movie was critical of Hillary Rodham Clinton who was (at that time) the front-runner for the Democratic Party's presidential nomination in 2008. (In 2004, Michael Moore had done a similar movie critical of President George W. Bush entitled *Fahrenheit 9/11*.) The District Court for the District of Columbia ruled that the Bipartisan Campaign Reform Act (upheld in *McConnell*) barred corporations (and unions) from making independent expenditures in political campaigns (with criminal penalties for noncompliance). At oral argument before the Supreme Court, Justice Samuel Alito asked the government's lawyer defending the law (Deputy Solicitor General Malcolm Stewart) whether it could also be used to bar a publishing company from distributing a book critical of Senator Clinton. Stewart answered, "yes"; at reargument six months later, Elena Kagan (then Solicitor General, now a Supreme Court Justice) essentially affirmed Stewart's candid response—that position may have been the straw that broke the camel's back.

On January 21, 2010, Justice Anthony Kennedy issued the Court's (five-to-four) opinion, ruling that the Bipartisan Campaign Reform Act's provision violated the First Amendment: "If the First Amendment has any force, it prohibits Congress from

---

the Bipartisan Campaign Reforms Act's restrictions on "soft money" contributions did not violate the First Amendment).

Hillary Clinton Punching Bag, from the 2016 Campaign
(Author's Collection)

fining or jailing citizens, or associations of citizens [including corporations or unions], for simply engaging in political speech." By
this ruling, the Court's prior decision in *Austin* was overturned,
and *McConnell* was partially overruled as well. (Professor Gora, in
writing about *Citizens United*, has taken to task Clinton for her
"chutzpah" in the 2016 election, in which she "repeatedly promised—to great applause each time—not to nominate anyone to
the Supreme Court who was not prepared to overrule [*Citizens
United*]." Gora not only thought such a litmus test improper, but
noted "the irony of a leading presidential candidate attacking a
decision that permitted a group of citizens to question her fitness
for office." *See* J. Gora, "Money, Speech, and Chutzpah," *Litigation*
48, 52 (Summer 2017).

More recently, the Court had the opportunity to review some
of the 1974 amendments to the Federal Election Campaign Act.

In *McCutcheon v. FEC*, 572 U.S. 185 (2014), the Court (by a five-to-four vote) struck down the limit on contributions an individual can make over a two-year period to national party and federal candidate campaign committees. In Chief Justice John Roberts's plurality decision: "The government may no more restrict how many candidates or causes a donor may support than it may tell a newspaper how many candidates it may endorse." Justice Clarence Thomas concurred separately (thus providing the fifth vote), but argued that *all* limits on contributions are unconstitutional (i.e., *McCutcheon* left intact the limits on how much individuals can give to an individual political candidate (which now maxes out at $2,700 per election)).

Buckley—what the *Wall Street Journal* has called the Court's "original First Amendment sin"—thus still stands, albeit significantly weakened in breadth and devoid of much (if not all) sense. And notwithstanding the *Buckley* Court's prediction, discussed above, money keeps flooding exponentially into our political campaigns at ever faster rates. So, let me give the last word to the principal litigant in *Buckley*, Senator/Judge Buckley, who wrote: "The answer ... is not to place further restrictions on the freedom of speech, as so many continue to argue.... [Rather,] [o]ur current law addresses the problem [of corruption] by requiring a timely disclosure of all contributions over a specific amount. That enables opponents to publicize any gift that might arise to an adverse influence, and the public can then judge whether the contribution in fact is apt to corrupt the recipient."

POSTSCRIPTS

For those wanting to delve deeper into the legacy of *Buckley v. Valeo*, see Volume 25, Issue 1 of Brooklyn Law School's *Journal of Law and Policy* (December 2, 2016).

Floyd Abrams, who successfully argued *Citizens United v. FEC* in the Supreme Court, published a wonderful book: *The Soul of the First Amendment* (Yale University Press 2017). As Abrams makes abundantly clear, the purpose of the First Amendment is to protect Americans from governmental attempts (to quote Justice Robert Jackson) to seize "guardianship of the public mind." Abrams has been castigated by the political left for aligning himself with the political right in that case. But Abrams does not view the constitutional principle (and Amendment) at issue in political terms. As he has written: "What threatens democracy is any law, such as that at issue in *Citizens United*, that makes criminal the showing on television of a documentary—like movie denouncing a candidate for the presidency of the nation simply because the organization that prepared it had received some corporate grants. The film at issue in *Citizens United—Hillary: The Movie*—was, in my view, grotesquely unfair to then-Senator Clinton. But that sort of political speech is precisely what the First Amendment most obviously protects."

CHAPTER VII

YET ANOTHER TERRIBLE DECISION BY THE SUPREME COURT: THIS TIME ENDORSING *EUGENICS*!

OLIVER WENDELL HOLMES WROTE and said many famous things during his long and illustrious judicial career. One of my personal favorites is: "The life of the law has not been logic, it has been experience." As I tell my law students, that gem can be trotted out whenever one is in a jam for something to say; its elasticity (and opaque meaning) will usually suffice to end whatever tough spot in which one finds herself.

Unfortunately, when Holmes penned his most infamous opinion in *Buck v. Bell*, 274 U.S. 200 (1927), neither "logic" nor "experience" carried the day.

EUGENICS

Although eugenics got its start in England in the 1880s, it quickly took hold in America. Proponents believed there were "genetically inferior" groups threatening the well-being and future of the country. By the 1920s, eugenics was being taught at 376 leading colleges and universities—Earnest Hooton, Chairman of Harvard's Anthropology Department, opined that well-educated

Americans were throwing away their "biological birthright for a mess of morons." Supporters of the eugenics movement included John D. Rockefeller Jr., Alexander Graham Bell, W.E.B. Du Bois, Theodore Roosevelt, and Margaret Sanger.

In 1896, Connecticut became the first state to enact a law prohibiting marriage to anyone who was "epileptic, imbecile or feeble-minded." In 1907, Indiana became the first state to pass sterilization legislation for "defective" people.

Legislative efforts that followed in various states fed upon public enthusiasm for ensuring that America would continue to be a nation of and for "high grade" people. By the 1920s, Congress was holding hearings at which the biological and genetics differences between various national groups was openly vetted. Eugenics "expert" Harry H. Laughlin (a Princeton Ph.D. in biology and head of the Eugenics Record Office), who testified in support of the Immigration Act of 1924 (which barred immigration to Southern and Eastern Europeans—"inferior stock," while allowing immigration for Northern Europeans—"old stock"), was strident in his advocacy that the "lowest one-tenth" of Americans (15 million people) should be sterilized.

Also in 1924, based in large part on a "model" eugenics law devised by Laughlin (in consultation with legal experts), Virginia adopted a statute that authorized the compulsory sterilization of "mental defectives." Aubrey E. Strode—a prominent Virginia lawyer—was the principal drafter of the legislation; and he would also be its defender/advocate in the lower courts and before the U.S. Supreme Court. Dr. Albert S. Priddy, the superintendent of Virginia State Colony for Epileptics and Feebleminded, did not want to proceed under the new law (for which he had lobbied the state legislature) until the courts had blessed it. Accordingly, it was decided there should be a test case. And Carrie Buck was chosen to be the "testee."

Who Was Carrie Buck?

Carrie Buck had been at the Colony for only two months in 1924, but in many ways she was the perfect candidate for Priddy's purposes. For one thing, her mother had been in the Colony for several years, having been declared a "moron" and being someone who exhibited "a lack of moral sense and responsibility" (she had had two additional children out of wedlock, was "without means of support," and may have resorted to prostitution to help support herself and her children). Carrie had been taken away from her mother at an early age and had been living with a local family since she was four. For a time, Carrie's life with a new family seemed for the better: she attended school, had friends, and in her free time went fishing and hiking. After the sixth grade, however (her last teacher's comments were "very good—deportment and lessons"), her foster parents pulled her out of school and relegated her to domestic chores, both at home and for hire. When she was 17, Carrie was raped by her foster mother's nephew and became pregnant. Faced with this most unfortunate situation, Carrie's foster parents made the decision not only to get her out of their home but also to institutionalize her.

Petitioning the Virginia Commission of Feeblemindedness, Carrie's foster parents falsely represented that she was both feeble-minded and epileptic. And at the time of Commission's hearing, Carrie was seven months pregnant. This latter fact—an unmarried and pregnant minor, who was also purportedly feebleminded—was a defining third strike, because it reinforced many public fears driving the eugenics movement: immoral young woman carrying venereal diseases, and giving "birth to children who are as defective as themselves." (Dr. Walker E. Fernald). The Commission dutifully found Carrie to be "feebleminded or epileptic"—without setting forth any criteria or evidence of either; and after Carrie gave birth to a daughter (Vivian), she was delivered to the Colony and Dr. Priddy's care, where she was promptly designated a "Middle grade Moron."

A Test Case

Dr. Priddy's decision to pick Carrie for his test case was easy: he already had the determination by the Commission; he had the Colony's own "medical" assessment of her; he had her mother's track record at the Colony; Carrie was an unwed, teenage mother (stoking the aforementioned fears); and she was young—once sterilized, Carrie could be released back into society (free from years of taxpayer care, but not able to engage in immoral activity leading to more feebleminded children). Following the procedures set forth in the new law, Priddy initiated legal proceedings to sterilize Carrie, and hired Aubrey Strode as his counsel. A local court then appointed a lawyer (Robert G. Shelton) as Carrie's guardian to protect her interests; his compensation: $5 a day (with a cap of $15).

Next came a hearing of the Colony's Special Board of Directors to obtain permission to proceed. At the hearing, Priddy was the principal witness, and much of his testimony was false; the worst part was his statement that Carrie's two-month-old daughter, Vivian, was also feebleminded—something he could not possibly have known. Unfortunately, Shelton's cross-examination was pathetic and Priddy was actually able to bolster his case for sterilization. At the end of the hearing, Carrie was asked one question: "Do you care to say anything about having this operation performed on you?" Not surprisingly, no one had ever explained to her what "this operation" was. Her answer was "No, Sir, I have not, it is up to my people." There was no follow-up, not even who she believed to be her "people" (or why she thought they were looking out for her). Not surprisingly, the Special Board in short order granted Priddy's petition.

Virginia's statute allowed Carrie a right to appeal to a court; Priddy wanted a test case, and Shelton willingly agreed to appeal the matter. Shelton then hired another lawyer, Irving P. Whitehead, to handle the appeal. Unfortunately for Carrie, Whitehead—an enthusiastic proponent of eugenics—had close ties to Strode, the Colony, and Priddy (and Priddy agreed to pay Whitehead's legal fees).

Six weeks after the Special Board's decision, a local Virginia court held a trial on Carrie's appeal. It was a disaster. Strode presented six fact witnesses, virtually all of whom gave testimony based on supposition, hearsay, or opinion(s). Whitehead stood silent to such objectionable garbage, and his cross-examination of each only made things worse. Then came three "experts" whose testimony would most certainly never even get to serious *Daubert* scrutiny.[1] Their expertise on Carrie, her mother, and her daughter makes for shocking reading; it is uninformed and untethered to any actual medical or scientific work. Nevertheless, it all came in without objection, and (again) Whitehead's cross-examination of these experts only made matters worse. Although there are a multitude of examples of egregious "expert" testimony, the worst (in my view) came from Arthur Estabrook, who worked for Harry Laughlin. Estabrook not only misrepresented that he had given Carrie an accredited medical test to determine her mental capacity, he also gave the *only* testimony about Vivian's mental capacity, and that testimony (about an eight-month-old baby) was on its face absurd and went unchallenged by Whitehead on cross-examination. [This testimony would constitute the *sole* "evidence" with respect to *three* generations of mental impairment in Carrie's family.]

At the conclusion of the "expert" testimony, Strode rested his case. Whitehead, who was the one challenging the sterilization order, called no witnesses, fact or expert. The entire trial took one day. The complete evidentiary record for any appeal going forward had thus been established.

Three months later, the court duly issued its decision, upholding the Colony Special Board's order and finding that the statute was constitutional. The court, however, stayed its ruling to allow Shelton to appeal further. Shelton, as ever, followed the playbook and authorized an appeal to the Virginia Supreme Court of Appeals. A new party had to be added to the caption, however, because Priddy had died. His successor at the Colony, Dr. John

---

[1] In *Daubert v. Merrell-Dow Pharm., Inc.*, 509 U.S. 579 (1993), the Supreme Court established standards for the admissibility of experts' opinion.

Bell, readily agreed to be substituted as the name opposite Carrie Buck. And Bell was no reluctant participant. Not only was it Bell who first "examined" Carrie when she arrived at the Colony, in a presentation he made to the Medical Society of Virginia, Bell had ominously predicted "a world peopled by a race of degenerates and defectives, a world gone topsy-turvy, and sunk into the slough of despond."

APPEAL OF THE TEST CASE

Notwithstanding the appalling evidentiary record below, Carrie Buck's legal chances on appeal did not look so bad. Between 1913 and 1921, there had been eight challenges to state sterilization laws (Indiana, Iowa, Michigan, Nevada, New Jersey, New York, Oregon, Washington), and all eight had been successful. The state statutes were voided on various constitutional grounds: cruel and unusual punishment, due process, and equal protection. Would Virginia's statute suffer a similar fate?

Irving Whitehead raised the enumerated constitutional grounds that had worked to void the other states' statutes. But he did so in a half-hearted way: his brief to Virginia's highest court was five pages long, and it focused primarily on the weakest point: due process—that the statute did not provide enough procedural protections before sterilization could be effected. Bizarrely (and without any seeming irony), he contended that due process was especially violated because his client had insufficient means or opportunity to refute the testimony presented against her, especially that of the expert witnesses.

Aubrey Strode (who as drafter of Virginia's statute had been fully aware of the other states' determinations of the flaws in their laws) put together a formidable, 45-page response. First and foremost was the overwhelming evidence that went in unchallenged and uncontradicted at trial. Invoking the state's police power to protect its citizens, Strode then cited *Jacobson v. Massachusetts*, 197

U.S. 11 (1905), in which the U.S. Supreme Court upheld Massachusetts' mandatory vaccination laws. (Harry Laughlin's treatise on eugenics sterilization had also prominently cited *Jacobson*.) As for the constitutional issues, Strode quickly dealt with cruel and unusual punishment (Carrie was not being "punished" for any crime) and due process (the Virginia statute was replete with all the procedural niceties for which the other states' laws had been found lacking). As far as equal protection, Strode knew this was the weak link (and had known it when he drafted the statute) because the law applied only to those in state hospitals, not to the population generally. That bifurcation had already doomed the laws of New Jersey, New York, and Michigan. In addressing this point, Strode did some rope-a-dope, arguing that there were not in fact two classes of Virginians, because at some point *anyone* in Virginia could be committed to a state hospital and be a candidate for sterilization!

On November 12, 1925, Virginia's Supreme Court of Appeals unanimously affirmed the trial court in all respects; and it adopted Strode's arguments and legal authority *in toto*. One month later, Strode and Whitehead met with the Colony's Special Board, jointly telling that group that the case "was in admirable shape" to go up to the U.S. Supreme Court. Thereafter, Shelton again followed his marching orders and authorized the case to be reviewed by the nation's highest court. What kind of justice would Carrie Buck receive from the Yankee from Olympus and his colleagues?

Justice Holmes and the Supremes

Unfortunately, the make-up of the Court was not a good one for Carrie Buck. Chief Justice William Howard Taft had chaired the Life Extension Institute, a health organization with ties to Harry Laughlin's Eugenics Record Office. Holmes's father, a prominent doctor, had coined the phrase "Boston Brahmin," and of that elite bloodline, he was deemed the "greatest Brahmin." His son had written in 1923 that he wanted laws to "keep certain strains out of our blood." Many of the other justices were racists, bigots, or anti-Semites.

Oral argument was held on April 22, 1927, and the decision was handed down less than two weeks later, on May 2, 1927. Clearly, the justices did not spend a great deal of time agonizing over the merits of the case. When Taft assigned the majority opinion to Holmes, he sent along the following advice:

> Some of the brethren are troubled about the case, especially [Justice Pierce] Butler. May I suggest that you [explicate] the care Virginia has taken in guarding against undue or hasty action, the proven absence of danger to the patient, and other circumstances tending to lessen the shock that many feel over such a remedy? The strength of the facts in three generations of course is the strongest argument for the necessity for such state action and its reasonableness.

Holmes quickly completed his opinion and sent it to be printed on April 25, 1927. It would be his worst.

Holmes hastily prepared opinion was short (less than three pages), not artfully done, and reflected his own prejudices on the subject at hand. Based on Strode's recitation of the evidence adduced below, Holmes started off by declaring as a fact that Carrie, her mother, and her daughter were all feebleminded; and he also accepted the trial experts' representations that "insanity, imbecility, etc." were transmitted by heredity. He then turned to the "very careful provisions" of the Virginia statute, detailing all the procedural steps put in the law by Strode, and concluding that "[t]here can be no doubt that ... the rights of the patient [were] most carefully considered, and ... every step in this case was taken in scrupulous compliance with the statute." He thus declared that Carrie had certainly received due process.

Holmes next turned to the dangers the Virginia statute was designed to address: it was there "to prevent our being swamped with incompetence." Taking *Jacobson* straight from Strode's brief, he wrote that "[t]he principle that sustains compulsory vaccination is broad enough to cover cutting the Fallopian tubes." Then came the infamous words: "Three generations of imbeciles are enough."

In his last paragraph, Holmes briefly addressed the equal protection issue. Obviously convinced by Strode's argument, Holmes rejected this as no big deal, deeming it "the usual last resort of constitutional arguments to point out shortcomings of this sort." He reasoned that once hospitals sterilized inmates and returned them to the world, the hospitals would be "open ... to others, [and] the equality aimed at will be more nearly reached."

Eight justices signed on to Holmes's decision (including Louis Brandeis and Harlan Fiske Stone). The lone dissent was Justice Pierce Butler, the Court's only Catholic. Butler's dissent, however, came without an opinion.

The Aftermath of *Buck v. Bell*

Media reaction to the Holmes opinion was generally favorable. The first female presidential candidate (Victoria Woodhull Martin) hailed the decision (the "first principle of the breeder's art is to weed out the inferior animals"). Cornell Law Professor Robert E. Cushman lauded Holmes and called the statute "reasonable social protection." Not everyone was pleased, however. A group of Catholic lawyers sought rehearing of the matter in the Supreme Court; their petition was denied. And Dr. Bell received a postcard from New York, with this message: "May God protect Miss Carrie Buck from [feebleminded justice] injustice." (The "feebleminded justice" had been crossed out.)

On October 19, 1927, Carrie was operated on by Dr. Bell. She recovered well and was released on "furlough" by the Colony on November 12, 1927. After Christmas, she came back to the

Colony. At that point, Dr. Bell picked up on Albert Priddy's sworn representations that Carrie was wanted back at the home of her foster parents (who had custody of Vivian); he contacted them, but they replied they did not want Carrie under their roof and asked that she be kept at the Colony (permanently). Ultimately, Carrie was placed with a different family in far-away Bland, Virginia, where she did well and corresponded with Bell on an ongoing basis; the basic goal of her correspondence was to be formally discharged, which was ultimately granted on January 1, 1929.

In 1932, Carrie married a 63-year-old widower, with whom she had been "going" for three years. Seven weeks after the wedding, Vivian—who was eight and who Carrie had seen only a few times—died of a stomach infection (following a bout with the measles). Before she died, Vivian had made the honor roll at school. (Years later, Harvard biologist Stephen Jay Gould examined Vivian's school records and concluded that she was a "quite average student and perfectly normal.")

After her husband died in the 1940s, Carrie moved to Front Royal, Virginia. On her own, she took on several jobs, including taking care of elderly people. In 1965, Carrie married again. In 1980, the director of the Colony (now renamed the Lynchburg Training Center) convinced Carrie to return to the facility. She came mainly to see her mother's grave site; when confronted with the building where Dr. Bell had sterilized her, Carrie could not bring herself to revisit the operating room.

After that trip, Carrie was interviewed by a local paper. For the first time, it was publicly revealed that her pregnancy had resulted from being raped by her foster parent's nephew. And Carrie also revealed that—far from being a willing participant to sterilization (as repeatedly testified to by Dr. Priddy)—she was never told (by anyone) that the operation would cause her to become sterile.

Carrie died in 1983. She was buried near the graves of her daughter and her foster parents.

Postscripts

Was Carrie Buck feebleminded? Contemporary evidence strongly suggests not. Not only did she do well at school—through the sixth grade—but those who interacted with her (outside of those who wanted to institutionalize and sterilize her) all seem of the view that she was not mentally impaired. Most telling is the voluminous cache of her articulate letters to Dr. Bell after the operation—which survive; they belie that she was feebleminded, as well as the label Dr. Bell affixed to her in 1924: a "Middle grade Moron." At the end of her life, Carrie was an avid newspaper reader and a devotee of crossword puzzles. Stephen Gould, who met her at that time, concluded that "she was neither mentally ill nor retarded."

The starting places for those who want to know more about this sad and grotesque story are Adam Cohen's *Imbeciles: The Supreme Court, American Eugenics, and the Sterilization of Carrie Buck* (Penguin 2016) and Paul Lombardo's *Three Generations, No Imbeciles: Eugenics, the Supreme Court, and* Buck v. Bell (Johns Hopkins University Press 2008).

After his testimony, Arthur Estabrook's career took a nosedive. First, he got caught trying to double bill for his trial expenses. And Estabrook (who had called Carrie a "moral degenerate") was also unmasked as a sexual predator of college interns who worked for him. As a result, he was dismissed from the Eugenics Record Office.

Harry Laughlin's career trajectory was a bit different. Other states now enacted the model law he had drafted, as did European countries. In 1933, the Nazi regime adopted its Law for the Prevention of Hereditarily Diseased Offspring (ultimately at least 375,000 sterilization orders were issued under that law). In 1936, Laughlin—an admirer of the Nazi's racial policies—was awarded an honorary doctorate by the University of Heidelberg.

At the Nuremberg trials, Otto Hoffman, who led the SS Race and Settlement Main Office, defended his role in sterilizing hundreds of thousands by citing America's sterilization laws and Oliver Wendell Holmes's opinion in *Buck v. Bell*. This *Buck v. Bell* defense was explicitly referenced in the movie *Judgment at Nuremberg* (United Artists 1961).

Irving Whitehead's atrocious/conflicted representation of Carrie Buck's interests was never publicly revealed during his lifetime, and, as such, it went unpunished.

Incredibly, *Buck v. Bell* is still good law. It has never been overturned by the Supreme Court. *See Skinner v. Oklahoma*, 316 U.S. 525 (1942). Indeed, it was cited by Justice Harry Blackmun in *Roe v. Wade*, 410 U.S. 113, 154 (1973). For recent citations to this odious opinion, see *Vaughan v. Ruoff*, 253 F.3d 1124, 1129 (8th Cir. 2001).

Under the various state sterilization laws, it is estimated that approximately 70,000 Americans were sterilized in the twentieth century, the great majority of whom were woman.

CHAPTER VIII

THE SUPREME COURT WRESTLES WITH THE GOLD CLAUSE

THE GREATEST ECONOMIC DISASTER in our country's history was undoubtedly the Great Depression. It also destroyed Herbert Hoover's presidency, and made Franklin Roosevelt's election in 1932 to replace him a certainty. It is interesting that Roosevelt's campaign rhetoric on how to dig out of the crisis was vague and sometimes contradictory (for example, one of his central tenets for economic revival was to balance the federal budget).

Desperately trying to win reelection, Hoover directly attacked Roosevelt, warning the country that, if elected, his opponent would follow William Jennings Bryan's 1896 opiate and "issue greenback currency." Hoover further warned that that would inevitably lead to the country going off the gold standard, which would create "one of the most tragic disasters to ... the independence of man."

Roosevelt, recognizing the danger of this attack, replied that Hoover was conducting a "campaign of fear," that he (Roosevelt) was not a "devolutionist," and that he (Roosevelt) believed in "sound money." This reply was carefully chosen to obfuscate the fact that Roosevelt (and his "Brain trust") really did not have a set of definitive plans. What was more candid and revealing was what

Roosevelt voiced publicly as his overriding, governing principle: "The country needs and, unless I mistake its temper, the country demands bold, persistent experimentation. It is common sense to take a method and try it. If it fails, admit it frankly and try another. But above all, try something."

Once he became president on March 4, 1933, Roosevelt lived up to his promise of experimentation. One result of that was immensely consequential litigation up to the Supreme Court that is little remembered today.

FIRST WE MUST DEVALUE THE CURRENCY

One of President Roosevelt's first priorities was to get monetary relief for the country's farmers—to raise (somehow) the price of farm commodities. Although there were many ways to perhaps achieve that goal over the mid to long term, the only way to do that quickly was to (1) give up the gold standard, and (2) devalue the dollar.

This first step came with Executive Order No. 6102 on April 5, 1933, in which the president decreed that all gold held by private citizens had to be sold to the Federal Reserve. This was followed by Executive Order 6111 on April 20, which prohibited (indefinitely) all exports of gold from the United States. By these two actions, the United States effectively went off the gold standard. (Roosevelt's Budget Director, Lewis Douglas, said privately that this was "the end of Western Civilization.")

At the same time, legislation was moving through Congress to give the president the authority to end deflation by, *inter alia*, doing exactly what Hoover had warned of: issuing greenback currency and monetizing silver (at a 16-to-1 ratio to gold—one of Bryan's campaign slogans in 1896). And while these steps would likely help to jump-start farm commodity prices by devaluing the dollar, there was one last leg of the monetary stool that also had to be fixed, and that was the gold clause.

Deep-Sixing the Gold Clause

In virtually all private contracts, as well as in government-issued securities (and World War I debt incurred by foreign countries), there was a provision known as the gold clause. This meant that the contracting parties agreed to all debts being paid in gold or gold equivalents. If these clauses remained in place, devaluation of the currency would make matters exponentially worse: the dollar would be worth much less, but all debts would have to be repaid at the official price of gold: $20.67 per ounce (set by the Gold Standard Act of 1900). In other words, farmers (and others) would have even less money (in terms of value) to make good on their fixed contractual obligations; the bankruptcies prior to Roosevelt's election would be a trivial number if this state of play was allowed to exist. Roosevelt's advisors (principally George F. Warren, a professor of agricultural economics at Cornell) were aware of this danger, but believed there was an easy answer: if Congress could devalue the dollar, it could also void the gold clause in contracts.

On May 7, 1933, Roosevelt gave his second "fireside chat" to the nation over the radio. Still within the famous, first 100 days of his administration, the President recounted all that had already been done to tackle the Great Depression. He also addressed the country's currency and, in particular, the fact that the government and public had approximately $120 billion in debt that was subject to the gold clause. Roosevelt explained that this was much ado about nothing, since "all the gold in the United States amounted to only between three and four billions and that all of the gold of the world amounted to only eleven billion." Thus, according to the President, few could really be repaid in gold; instead, virtually all debtors would repay in paper currency, and every creditor would therefore have no recourse but to accept that paper.

Like much of his campaign rhetoric, Roosevelt was dissembling in his "fireside chat." The gold clause did not actually require a physical delivery of gold; rather, it required that the debt be repaid

DIOGENES . . . THE GREEK CYNIC PHILOSOPHER
Born about 412 years before Christ . . . Walked the streets of Athens with a Lantern, looking for an Honest Man

UNCLE SAM MEETS DIOGENES and asks him for advice . . . DIOGENES gives him his Lantern.

UNCLE SAM takes the Lantern, goes to the Capitol, finds FRANKLIN D. ROOSEVELT and gives him his Lantern.

Franklin Roosevelt Cartoon upon Assuming the Presidency in 1933
(Author's Collection)

in gold *or* in currency valued at the price of gold (*see* the *Legal Tender Cases* decided by the Supreme Court after the Civil War; e.g., *Knox v. Lee*, 79 U.S. 457 (1871); *Juilliard v. Greenman*, 110 U.S. 421 (1884)). Thus, the problem still remained—notwithstanding the President's facile dismissal—and it had to be addressed pronto.

On May 26, the administration—contemplating the issuance of new government securities in June *without* the gold clause—asked Congress to void (permanently) the gold clause for all future *and past* contracts. There was immediate (and strong) push back. Carter Douglas, Democratic Senator from Virginia (and someone who had been a key ally in repelling Hoover's economic attacks on Roosevelt during the 1932 campaign), publicly denounced "the proposal to repudiate all outstanding gold contracts [as] unconstitutional and the courts will so hold if there is any integrity left in the courts with respect to the sanctity of contracts." He subsequently attempted to exempt government securities and debts owed to the United States arising out of World War I, but that failed to carry the day in the Senate. Notwithstanding predictions that foreign governments owing America many billions in World War I obligations would default on their debts if the legislation became law, the House of Representatives overwhelmingly approved the measure on May 29; the Senate quickly followed suit on June 3. Two days later, Roosevelt signed the legislation. Where people stood on this law depended on, among other things, their political party, not to mention their status as creditor versus debtor. Although the executive and legislative branches had spoken and acted, the issue had be resolved by the courts and, ultimately, by the Supreme Court.

WAS THE LAW CONSTITUTIONAL?

In short order, there were a variety of legal challenges to the retroactive voiding of the gold clause; four of them ultimately were consolidated together before the Supreme Court—and they became known as the "Gold Clause Cases": *Norman v. Baltimore and Ohio Railroad* (New York State), *United States v. Bankers' Trust Co.* (8th Cir.), *Perry v. United States* (Court of Claims), and *Nortz v. United States* (Court of Claims). The key issues teed up by these cases were as follows:

1. Was the party relying on the gold clause entitled to receive in legal tender what was owed at the equivalence of the legal price of gold?
2. Was the party relying on the gold clause entitled to money damages as a result of Congress' abrogation of the gold clause?

In the government's briefs, the principal argument was that Congress' action was based on a national "necessity"; as articulated by Assistant Solicitor General Angus MacLean: "[I]f the gold clauses were maintained [at the same time the other steps were taken to devalue the currency] ..., this meant bankruptcy on a national scale." (It had been estimated that it would take $1.69 to make good on a gold clause's $1.00 value.) Thus, Congress *had* to act and the Supreme Court was *obligated* to uphold that action "in order to save the country."

The government also argued (in addition to Roosevelt's specious contention that this was all no big deal because there was not enough actual gold to make good on $120 billion in contractual obligations) that the plaintiff had suffered no actual (and actionable) damages; because of wide-scale deflation, the same amount of paper currency actually had far more purchasing power in 1934-35 than it had prior to October of 1929. As precedent for its various positions, the government cited to the *Legal Tender Cases*, where the Court, *inter alia*, had written: "Whatever power there is over the currency is vested in Congress."

Oral argument on the consolidated "Gold Clause Cases" took place on January 8, 9, and 10 of 1935. The general consensus was that the government had not done well before a skeptical Court, and there were apocalyptic predictions of what would happen if the Court struck down the legislation. Not surprisingly, financial markets reacted negatively, as did commodity prices. Foreign nations, owing huge sums to the United States in World War I obligations, publicly fretted about what to do. According to a report in the *New York Times*, unnamed members of the Senate were studying increasing the number of Supreme Court Justices to get to whatever number of votes were needed to sustain such a law (shades of Roosevelt's court-packing scheme of 1937! *See* Chapter XIV). Subsequently, the New York Stock Exchange (fearing the worst) publicly announced that it would (if necessary) suspend trading upon the Supreme Court's decision. Also fearing the worst, Roosevelt's administration began thinking up a "Plan B"—among the contingencies contemplated in the face of an adverse decision were:

1. the declaration of a national emergency by the president for 90 days (or longer, up to a year)—staying payment of any debts greater than the nominal dollar amount of the obligation,
2. new legislation voiding any counterparty's rights to sue the government based on the gold clause,
3. new legislation changing the jurisdiction of the Court of Claims (so no gold clause claims could be brought therein), and
4. an unprecedented attack by the president on the Supreme Court over the airwaves.

While Roosevelt and his advisors pondered these and other scenarios, they, the nation, and the world waited for the Supreme Court to render a decision.

The Supreme Court Decides

On February 18, 1935, Chief Justice Charles Evans Hughes announced the Court's decisions in open Court. In the two cases involving private debt (*Norman* and *Bankers' Trust*), by a five-to-four vote the Court ruled that Congress' nullification of the gold clauses was constitutional—that Congress had been granted power over such matters by the Constitution. ("We are not concerned here with the wisdom of [Congress' enactment]. We are concerned with power, not with policy.")

But with respect to the two cases involving public debt (that is, government bonds: *Perry* and *Nortz*), by an eight-to-one vote the Court ruled that Congress' nullification of the gold clauses was unconstitutional—that Congress, having been granted the power to authorize such debt, had "not been vested with authority to alter or destroy those obligations." Notwithstanding, by a five-to-four vote the Court went on to rule that the public debt holders (for example, *Perry*) had not suffered "any loss whatsoever"—that to permit "payment to the plaintiff ... would appear not a recoupment of loss ..., but an unjust enrichment."

In other words, the law was unconstitutional as applied to government bonds (only), but there would be no actionable remedy in money damages.

On behalf of the "Four Horsemen" (Justices Pierce Butler, George Sutherland, and Willis Van Devanter), Justice James Clark McReynolds issued a vociferous dissenting opinion (although they obviously concurred with the first holding in *Perry* and *Nortz*): "Just men regard repudiation and spoliation of citizens by their sovereign with abhorrence; but we are asked to affirm that the Constitution granted power to accomplish both." According to McReynolds, the Founding Fathers never "intended that the expected government should have the authority to annihilate its own obligations and destroy the very rights which they were endeavoring to protect." Noting that the "gold clause promise" had existed for more than 100 years in U.S. contracts, both private and governmental, what Congress had done was contrary both to the sanctity of contracts (private and public) and the country's most solemn obligations: "[I]t destroys directly" and thus violates the Fifth Amendment, there being "no provision for compensation"—that is, "[o]bligations cannot be legally avoided by prohibiting the creditor from recovering the thing promised." Then, invoking Alexander Hamilton (regarding the government's moral and constitutional obligations to honor matters of contract), as well as the fact the sanctity of contracts had built America into the greatest nation in the world, McReynolds questioned who would do business in the future with such a government. He ended the opinion as follows: "Loss of reputation for honorable dealing will bring us unending humiliation; the impending legal and moral chaos is appalling." (When he read his opinion in open Court on February 18, McReynolds started off by saying: "The Constitution as many of us understood it, the instrument that has meant so much to us, is gone." He ended with these words: "Shame and humiliation are upon us now. Moral and financial chaos may be confidently expected.")

The subject of little focus at the time was Justice Harlan Stone's separate opinion on the public debt cases (*Perry* and *Nortz*). It was Stone's view that, once Chief Justice Hughes had opined that the debt holders had no damages, the Court should *not* have then gone on and ruled (unnecessarily, in his opinion) that the law—as it applied to public obligations—was unconstitutional (having determined the opposite for private obligations). By that extra step, the Court had "imposed restrictions upon the future exercise of the [Congress'] power to regulate the currency." Even so, in Justice Stone's mind the formality of said "restrictions" perhaps did *not* in fact kick in because the Hughes opinion on the constitutionality of canceling the gold clause vis-à-vis public debt had gotten only four votes (he dissented on that ruling, and Justice McReynolds's opinion had a different rationale vis-à-vis Congress' statute); Stone privately wrote that the "Court has not declared, decided, or adjudged that the Government is bound by the Gold Clause."

The media's immediate reaction to what the Court decided was, to say the least, "confused." The Associated Press announced that the government had "lost." The *Atlanta Constitution's* headline read: "'New Deal' Upheld in High Court." Closer to what actually happened was headlined by the *Wall Street Journal*: "Moral Defeat, Practical Victory, for Government." Similarly, the *Times of London* opined that "[y]esterday's judgement ... leaves the Administration free to act as if what is declared unconstitutional were in fact constitutional." And as Walter Lippmann wrote a week later, the decision constituted "a victory but not ... a vindication of the government.... The abrogation destroys a vested right. It repudiates a contract.... And unless one is prepared to agree that legitimate rights can never be extinguished, the gold clauses cannot be dealt with on the theory that contracts are absolute."

Irrespective of the media's confusion, Roosevelt and his advisors were relieved and "very jolly." While they could not foresee the New Deal's setbacks in the Court that would lead to the court-packing scheme in 1937, for now they had radically devalued the currency and gotten the Court to uphold Congress' retroactive invalidation of the nation's contracts. As for the financial markets—which had been braced for bad news—they reacted positively; not so much for the Court's validation of the nation acting like a banana republic (i.e., repudiating its legal obligations), but rather for the certainty that seemed the clear result of the Court's decisions.

Although Milton Friedman and Anna Jacobson Schwartz would later write that the Supreme Court's rulings retarded the country's emergence from the Great Depression (*A Monetary History of the United States, 1867-1960* (Princeton University Press 1963)), the U.S. government in fact had no difficulty going back to the financial markets and issuing new debt in short order. Thus, unlike when third-world countries have defaulted on their debts and investors punished them severely, our nation radically changed the rules of the game at halftime and seemingly paid no price for it (indeed, benefited from it). Could this work a second time?

POSTSCRIPTS

Like, I presume, most lawyers, I was never taught about the "Gold Clause Cases" when I was in law school. Rather, I just learned about them at a fascinating symposium at the Council on Foreign Relations, which featured a presentation by Sebastian Edwards, an economics professor at UCLA. His book, *American Default* (Princeton University Press 2018), is a must read for anyone seeking more information on this little remembered but fascinating part of our nation's legal and economic history.

The devaluation of our currency and abrogation of the gold clause did not seem to have a beneficial impact on foreign countries' willingness to repay their World War I obligations to America. Of the 17 countries that borrowed over $10 billion from the

United States (a huge sum in 1914-18 dollars), only Finland paid its debts in full.

Dean Acheson was Undersecretary of the Treasury in early 1933, and because of the illness of the Secretary he was pretty much running the department on a day-to-day basis. He (like so many establishment figures) considered Roosevelt's plan to go off the gold standard and to devalue the currency, etc., to be improper and illegal. As such (and depending on which version of history you believe), he was either asked to resign or resigned of his own volition. In any event, in doing so Acheson wrote a short letter to Roosevelt, thanking the President for allowing him to serve in such "stirring times." Thereafter, Acheson—despite his views—never expressed them publicly. Roosevelt never forgot Acheson's "appropriate" behavior, and when another subordinate tendered a very different type of resignation, the President told his press secretary: "Return it to him and tell him to ask Acheson how a gentleman resigns." Acheson's actions also had the effect of allowing him back into the government during World War II to a high-level post in the U.S. Department of State (and later, under President Harry S. Truman, he became the Secretary of State).

The last word on the Gold Clause Cases is given to the legendary Harvard Law Professor Henry M. Hart Jr., who wrote a seminal piece in the May 1935 issue of the *Harvard Law Review* ("The Gold Clause in United States Bonds"). In Hart's view: "Few more baffling pronouncements, it is fair to say, have ever been issued from the United States Supreme Court.... Seldom has a legal controversy been touched with ramifications so various and extensive. So much the more astonishing, therefore, is the Delphic character of the Court's utterance in the most difficult of the cases before it.... [With respect to the public debt plaintiffs,] [a]lmost the only thing which is possible to say with assurance is that the plaintiff[s] ... did not recover."

CHAPTER IX

BUSH V. GORE

MORE THAN 20 YEARS AGO the country almost went through a constitutional crisis of epic proportions. For 37 days after the presidential election of 2000, no one knew which candidate had won the nation's highest office. Then, on December 12, 2000, the United States Supreme Court decided *Bush v. Gore*, 531 U.S. 8 (2012).

SETTING THE STAGE

The day after the national election (November 8), 37 electoral votes were still undecided (Florida, Oregon, and New Mexico). The biggest prize was Florida with 25 electors at stake. On that day, the Florida Division of Elections reported that George W. Bush led Al Gore by 1,784 votes. The next day, a machine recount required under Florida's Election Code reduced Bush's lead to 327 votes (ultimately, Bush's lead was determined to be 537 votes). Also on November 9, the Florida Secretary of State (Katherine Harris) declined to waive the statutory November 14 deadline for hand recounting, and Gore petitioned for hand recounts in four

Florida counties in which he hoped to find the necessary votes to defeat Bush (Volusia, Palm Beach, Broward, and Miami-Dade).

Seven Decisions

The foregoing triggered seven judicial decisions that predated the Supreme Court's December 12 ruling. And that December 12 ruling cannot be understood without an analysis of those earlier seven decisions:

1. Florida Circuit Judge Terry Lewis's decision upholding the Florida Secretary of State's refusal to extend the deadline for hand recounting beyond November 14 (November 17, 2000),
2. the Florida Supreme Court's reversal of Judge Lewis (November 21, 2000),
3. the U.S. Supreme Court's vacation of the Florida Supreme Court's decision (December 4, 2000),
4. Florida Circuit Judge N. Sanders Sauls's decision dismissing the contest proceeding brought on by Gore (December 4, 2000),
5. the Florida Supreme Court's reversal of Judge Sauls (December 8, 2000),
6. the U.S. Supreme Court's stay of the Florida Supreme Court's December 8 decision (December 9, 2000), and
7. the Florida Supreme Court's decision "clarifying" its November 21 decision (December 11, 2000).

Under Florida law, vote totals had to be submitted to the Secretary of State by November 14 (seven days after the election). Within that seven-day period, a "protest" could be interposed, with a hand recount ordered; if a recount was undertaken but not completed within that period, the Secretary of State "may ... ignore" the incomplete results. Once the Secretary of State certified the election winner, a "contest" could be interposed by means of litigation.

By November 14, only one Florida county in which Gore interposed a protest had completed a recount. Counting an additional 98 Gore votes, the Secretary of State certified Bush the winner of Florida's electoral votes by a 930 vote margin. With respect to the incomplete recounts, the Secretary of State refused to waive the deadline, absent evidence of fraud or some other calamity (for example, an act of God) interrupting the recount. Although Judge Lewis upheld the Secretary of State's discretion and decision, the Florida Supreme Court did not, extending the "protest" period to November 26.

This latter action was wrong on the law, and had profound consequences. As a practical matter, it meant that the inevitable "contest" period could not begin until after November 26, which rendered the amount of time for that process to an almost certain to be too short a period; the political, as well as legal, fallout from the resulting compressed "contest" period had much to do with the crisis(es) that ensued (both actual and perceived). Legally, the decision was at odds with the Florida statute because it essentially rewrote "error in the vote tabulation" (the only statutory grounds for a hand recount—an error of that sort had clearly *not* occurred) to mean "error by the voter," with the latter constituting the basis for extending the certification deadline. The Florida Supreme Court explicitly acknowledged its ex post facto handiwork—criticizing "sacred, unyielding adherence to statutory scripture," and "hyper-technical reliance upon statutory provisions," and citing to "the will of the people [as expressed in the Florida constitution] ... [as the] fundamental principle ... guid[ing] our decision today."

On December 4, the U.S. Supreme Court *unanimously* vacated and remanded that decision back to the Florida Supreme Court. Although perhaps it was too oblique (or restrained, or unable to agree on a unifying reason), the U.S. Supreme Court's decision signaled to the Florida Supreme Court that its reliance on the *Florida* constitution could not be a vehicle to negate or limit the power granted exclusively to the Florida legislature by Article II of the U.S. Constitution (each state shall pick presidential electors "in such manner as the Legislature thereof shall direct"). The U.S. Supreme Court, besides seeking clarification of the Florida Supreme Court's interpretation of Florida's election law, also sought that court's view of whether the Florida legislature had wanted to come within the "safe harbor" provisions set forth in the U.S. Code (a deadline—December 12—by which a state's presidential electors, if certified by that date, could not be challenged when Congress met in January to count the electoral votes). This latter inquiry was a stickier wicket than most observers understood at the time. Beyond the timing issue, a precondition of the safe harbor is the application of the state law existing as of the date of the election (that is, November 7, not November 21 or November 26). If the Florida Supreme Court persisted in its view(s) in rewriting the legislature's election law, the safe harbor could be forfeited; if, on the other hand, the legislature wanted the safe harbor, then the Florida Supreme Court's November 21 decision could well be at odds with state law *and* Article II of the U.S. Constitution.

On the same day as the U.S. Supreme Court's decision, Judge Sauls handed down his decision rejecting Gore's "contest" action, which had been brought against Palm Beach and Miami-Dade Counties. After a two-day trial, the judge ruled that the two canvassing boards had not abused their discretion—Palm Beach in its recount methodology, and Miami-Dade in deciding not to complete a recount that it had started. There was no evidence of voter fraud or similar kinds of shenanigans put before Judge Sauls; rather, the trial focused on the questions of voter error(s), the nature thereof, and the methodologies by which recounts to ascertain voter intent could be/would be/should be employed.

Four days later, the Florida Supreme Court (by a four-to-three vote) reversed Judge Sauls. In a remarkable decision, the Florida Supreme Court (1) stripped the county canvassing boards of their discretion in the "contest" period (having already done so previously to the Secretary of State in the "protest" period), (2) ordered recounted votes that Gore had gained in Palm Beach and Miami-Dade Counties to be added to the totals, and (3) ordered a hand recount of all remaining "undervotes" throughout the entire state (but *not* any "overvotes"). ["Undervotes" are where the voter seems to have decided *not* to make a specific choice and thus not detected by voting machines such as, punch card ballots with no *holes* (or holes only slightly indented). "Overvotes" are where a voter selected more than the maximum number of available options.]

The Florida Supreme Court's December 8 decision offered no standard for how the hand recounts were to be determined, notwithstanding that the trial before Judge Sauls indisputably demonstrated that the various counties employed wildly different standards (with attendant disparate results). This was but one critical flaw in the court's decision. Another was to focus only on undervotes, to the exclusion of overvotes. A third was its mandate that the process be completed and certified as of December 12 (to preserve the safe harbor); there was simply no way the approximately 60,000 undervotes could have been recounted (with the certain legal challenges to follow) by that date. The Chief Justice of the Florida Supreme Court pointed out those (and other) flaws in his vociferous dissent. He went on to predict (presciently) that the inevitable review his court's decision would receive would not be a pleasant one.

The next day (December 9) the U.S. Supreme Court (by a five-to-four vote) stayed the recount ordered by the Florida Supreme Court. The ground for issuing the stay was "irreparable harm" to the petitioning party (Bush). Some/many have argued that only "political" harm would have accrued to Bush if the stay had not been granted; certainly harm of that type might well have been suffered by him, as well as possible harm of that nature to the U.S. Supreme Court itself (if it had waited until after a standardless recount of only the undervotes, and then reversed the Florida Supreme Court). But other "real" harm also loomed for Bush if

Bush and Gore Cigars from the 2000 Election
(Author's Collection)

the "contest" period were to be deemed completed and the afore-mentioned recount (with all of its flaws) had pushed Gore's totals across the finish line. I believe another reason underlay the U.S. Supreme Court's quick action: the Florida Supreme Court had acted on December 8 without any reference, or response, to the U.S. Supreme Court's earlier ruling. Such institutional insubordination, directly manifested in such a charged atmosphere (as we will see) appears to have prompted the Court's desire to weigh in at that point.

On December 11, the Florida Supreme Court (the same day oral argument in the U.S. Supreme Court took place) finally responded to the U.S. Supreme Court's decision of December 4. The Florida court's "clarifying" opinion set forth: (1) it had engaged only in everyday statutory construction it its November 21 decision, (2) it had not changed the Florida statute after the election, (3) it had not based its decision on the Florida constitution, and (4) in its view, the Florida legislature wanted to take advantage of the safe harbor. Those first three assertions (as we have seen) were dubious, at best; and the final assertion meant that the Florida Supreme Court believed everything was required to be wrapped up the next day—an obvious impossibility (thanks in large part to its earlier extension of the "protest" period).

THE U.S. SUPREME COURT DECIDES

On December 12 (16 hours after oral argument), the Supreme Court handed down its decision in *Bush v. Gore.* Seven of the nine justices (William Rehnquist, Sandra Day O'Connor, Antonin Scalia, Anthony Kennedy, Clarence Thomas, Stephen Breyer, and David Souter) believed that the Florida Supreme Court's December 8 decision was unconstitutional because of the recount procedure ordered. And because they believed time had run out (it being December 12), five justices (Rehnquist, O'Connor, Scalia, Kennedy, and Thomas) basically shut down any further recounts. By those two determinations, Bush's lead in certified votes was allowed to stand; he was subsequently awarded Florida's 25 electoral votes, and thereafter was sworn in as president on January 21, 2001.

The constitutional ground on which seven justices agreed was that the standardless recount (on the basis of the widely disparate interpretation in play on the ground in Florida) constituted a violation of equal protection. I believe that this was not a persuasive constitutional argument. Throughout our history (before and after 2000), localities—which control the electoral process—have used (and will continue to use) different methods for voting and for the counting of votes. Undoubtedly recognizing that equal protection could open a litigation Pandora's box of future challenges to close elections, the Court's *per curiam* opinion stated that its equal protection analysis was "limited to the present circumstances, for the problem of equal protection in the election process generally presents many complexities."

According to Evan Thomas's biography of Justice O'Connor,[1] she was the author of this limiting phrase (p. 332). O'Connor also appears to have played an important role in cobbling together the

---

[1] Evan Thomas, *First* (Penguin 2019).

diverse coalition of seven justices who signed on to the equal protection analysis (principally authored by Justice Kennedy).[2] Also
according to Evan Thomas, Justice Scalia held his nose and voted
for equal protection, but later said that argument was "as we say in
Brooklyn, a piece of shit."[3]

Evan Thomas's biography also revealed that many of the justices were not pleased by the Florida Supreme Court's institutional
insubordination. For example, he wrote that O'Connor (who, by
all accounts, was one of the most collegial and least confronta-
tional of all the justices) "did not disguise her annoyance at the
Florida Supreme Court.... [T]he judges on the Florida high court
had essentially ignored the gentle nudge from the justices in Washington to come up with a fair method of counting votes and a
rationale for doing so. Now time was running out."[4]

I believe the Article II concerns identified in Chief Justice
Rehnquist's concurrence would have been a far better ground upon
which to base the Court's decision. Clearly, the Florida Supreme
Court (despite what it said on December 11) had in fact voided
the legislature's law—after the election—and put in place its own
view of what the law should have been (acting in the name of "the
will of the people"). But in the 16-hour, rushed process imposed
on the Court, the Chief Justice could only get two other justices
(Scalia and Thomas) to sign on to that view.

The remedy ordered by the five justices has usually taken the
biggest hit from critics. Ironically, in my view, this has always been
the least objectionable part of what the Court did. First, the Florida Supreme Court had indicated that December 12 was the drop-
dead day for the safe harbor; and December 12, of course, was the
date of the U.S. Supreme Court's decision.

---

[2] *Id.*

[3] *Id.*

[4] *Id.* at 330.

Second, even if December 18 was viewed (by some) as an alternative date (the date on which the Electoral College met and voted for president), there was no way a recount (based on a single standard—acceptable to both candidates, or ordered by a court—after the issue had been litigated), with subsequent litigation challenges, etc., could have been completed by December 18.

Third, if the issue went unresolved by December 18 and/or competing slates of electors had been submitted to Congress, the country would have been faced with the very likely result of the speaker of the house (Dennis Hastert) or the president pro tempore of the Senate (Strom Thurmond) becoming acting president of the United States (or, if those two declined the honor, Secretary of the Treasury Lawrence Summers), while Congress decided the winner—a complicated (to say the least) process, for which the 1876-77 precedent provides little historically helpful guidance.

The two justices who found an equal protection violation dissented on the remedy (Breyer and Souter), did so in large measure because they saw nothing magical about December 12 and believed that it was possible to meet the December 18 date. As set forth above, however, and even putting aside Florida's view of the safe harbor, it just seems a virtual impossibility that an accepted, orderly recount process (with subsequent challenges thereto) could in fact have been completed in six days.

The two justices who did not agree with either part of the Court's decisions (Ruth Bader Ginsburg and John Paul Stevens) wrote dissenting opinions that were especially bitter and cast aspersions particularly upon the good faith of the remedy resolution determined by the five justices. One quotation from Stevens's dissent should suffice on this score: "[The decision] by the majority of this Court can only lead credence to the most cynical appraisal of the work of judges throughout the land.... Although we may never know with complete certainty the identity of the winner in this year's Presidential election, the identity of the loser is perfectly clear. It is the Nation's confidence in the judge as an impartial guardian of the rule of law."

In his memoir *The Making of a Justice*,[5] Justice Stevens spent most of his time on *Bush v. Gore* with a critique of the Court's equal protection analysis; he also attacked "the Majority's second guessing the Florida Supreme Court's interpretation of its own state's law," quoted the above-cited language from his dissent, and closed with he "remain[s] of the view that the Court has not fully recovered from the damage it inflicted on itself in *Bush v. Gore*."[6]

CONCLUSION

I believe the Court's decision saved the country from an immense political and constitutional crisis. That it did so under a less-than-perfect constitutional rationale is also clear to me. But given the gross liberties that the Florida Supreme Court took in rewriting (after the election) its own state's election law, if that court's decisions had been left standing Vice President Gore would likely have become President Gore; and that kind of banana republic precedent would have been far worse than the one set by *Bush v. Gore*.

Seventy-five years ago, Justice Robert Jackson wrote: "I do not think we can run away from the case just because Eisler has." *Eisler v. United States*, 338 U.S. 189, 196 (1949); and I am thankful that the Supreme Court did not "run away" from the case that was presented to it.

POSTSCRIPTS

Not surprisingly, a lot of ink has been spilled on (and over) *Bush v. Gore*. Alan Dershowitz published *How the High Court Hijacked Election 2000* (Oxford University Press 2001); in it, he

---

[5] John Paul Stevens, *The Making of a Justice: Reflections on My First 94 Years* (Little Brown 2019).

[6] *Id.* at 374.

wrote that the ruling "may be ranked as the single most corrupt decision in Supreme Court history." Vincent Bugliosi, a former Los Angeles deputy district attorney, published *The Betrayal of America: How the Supreme Court Undermined the Constitution and Chose Our President* (Thunder's Mouth Press 2001); in it, he wrote that the justices in the majority were "criminals in the very *truest* sense of the word" (and as to public comments by Chief Justice Rehnquist and Justice Thomas that politics played no part in the outcome, Bugliosi wrote: "Well, at least we know they can lie as well as they can steal.").

On the other hand, Judge Richard Posner wrote *Breaking the Deadlock: The 2000 Election, the Constitution, and the Courts* (Princeton University Press 2001); in it, he criticized the equal protection analysis, argued that Article II was the better basis for reversing the Florida Supreme Court, and contended that the U.S. Supreme Court acted (on balance) appropriately (rendering "a rather good" decision) and averted a national crisis (if the matter had ended up before Congress). Obviously, I come down on Judge Posner's side of things.

Regardless of how one views the various opinions handed down on December 12, 2000, most (if not all) should agree that they do not reflect the justices' best work. But given the median age of the Court at the time and the fact that the justices had to pull (essentially) all-nighters to get their opinions written and finalized (within the 16-hour window), is that surprising?

I will give the last word to the late Justice Scalia. Noting that post-election analyses have confirmed that George W. Bush actually did win Florida (in large part because of confusion caused by Florida's butterfly ballot—which was *not* a litigated issue in the various decisions discussed above), Scalia's final comment to critics was: "I say nonsense. Get over it. It's so old by now."

CHAPTER X

PLESSY BY ANY OTHER NAME? THE SUPREME COURT AND THE INSULAR CASES

As with the Gold Clause Cases (*see* Chapter VIII), let us now examine another set of linked, troubling decisions—again, not taught to law students: the *Insular Cases* (e.g., *Huus v. N.Y. & P.R.S. Co.*, 182 U.S. 392 (1901); *Downes v. Bidwell*, 182 U.S. 244 (1901); *Armstrong v. United States*, 182 U.S. 243 (1901); *Dooley v. United States*, 182 U.S. 222 (1901); *Goetze v. Unites States*, 182 U.S. 221 (1901); *De Lima v. Bidwell*, 182 U.S. 1 (1901)). By these cases, the Supreme Court defined the applicability and reach of the Constitution to territories acquired by the United States from Spain after the Spanish-American War of 1898.

The U.S. Ambassador to Great Britain (and soon-to-be Secretary of State) John Hay remarked that the conflict with Spain had been "a splendid little war." When it ended (per the Treaty of Paris), the United States had acquired the Philippines, Guam, and Puerto Rico; Cuba became "independent"; and Spain received $20 million. But with the United States now an international empire came the question: What constitutional rights did the people in these new U.S. territories have?

HISTORICAL BACKGROUND

In the odious *Dred Scott* decision (*see* Chapter I), the Court—extraneous to its rulings—had written:

> There is certainly no power given by the Constitution to the Federal Government to establish or maintain colonies bordering on the United States or at a distance, to be ruled and governed at its own pleasure; nor to enlarge its territorial limits in any way, except by admission of new States.... [N]o power is given to acquire a territory to be held and governed [in a] permanently [colonial] character.

60 U.S. (19 How.) 393, 446 (1856).

Notwithstanding, as American commerce became increasing focused on Asia, we acquired the Guano Islands (1856), as well as Alaska (1867) and Midway (1867). This expansion of the country's reach only whetted the appetite of many (e.g., Theodore Roosevelt) to go further and establish an empire akin to what many European nations had done. And the collapsing empire of the Spanish in the Caribbean and in the Philippines seemed a promising choice.

With extensive native rebellions in both Cuba and the Philippines, President William McKinley had stationed the *U.S.S. Maine* off Cuba to pressure the Spanish to end their acts of uncivilized "extermination." After the *Maine* exploded on February 15, 1898, Roosevelt—then the Assistant Secretary of the Navy—ordered Commodore George Dewey to take the Pacific fleet to Manila Bay. That order was allowed to stand and a reluctant president soon asked for a declaration of war; Congress approved, so long as Cuba would not be taken on as a U.S. possession (the Teller Amendment). Dewey defeated the Spanish in the Battle of Manila Bay in six hours. Thereafter, an army of U.S. troops (including now Colonel Roosevelt) was dispatched to Cuba and Puerto Rico. Within less than four months, the "splendid little war" was over. Not content to stop there, we also acquired Hawaii (1898), and then half of Samoa (1899) as well as Wake Island (1899).

With respect to the Spanish territories acquired as a result of the spoils of war, those tropical areas were densely populated places that (unlike the American West) did not offer potential farming opportunities for recent European immigrants to move to from crowded northeastern cities. Suddenly, the United States was a global behemoth, but with new and large groups of people thousands of miles away from the mainland who had no racial, ethnic, or cultural ties to the American citizenry. How would these acquired territories be governed, and (more pertinent to this chapter) what rights would these eight million people have?

SETTING THE STAGE

Although the U.S. government had exercised authority over various North American territories since the country's founding (in very different ways), to many Americans these far-off tropical territories posed a whole new set of issues. And these issues were formally teed up by Congress' passing of the Foraker Act in 1900. That controversial legislation[1] established the civil government for Puerto Rico. The taxation component of that legislation as to goods flowing to and from Puerto Rico (a tariff was imposed on all such trade) would set the spark for the constitutional brouhaha. Specifically, did the Uniformity Clause of the Constitution (Article I, Section 8, cl. 1)—"all Duties, Imports and Excises ... [shall] be uniform throughout the United States")—apply to the taxation of commerce between the United States and Puerto Rico. That is, was Puerto Rico part of or excluded from the "United States"?

---

[1] The Senate's committee report stated that Congress should withhold "the operation of the Constitution and the laws of the United States" from "people of [a] wholly different character, illiterate, and unacquainted with our institutions, and incapable of exercising the rights and privileges guaranteed by the Constitution to the States of the Union."

THE *INSULAR CASES*

The Supreme Court heard oral arguments on the first cluster of *Insular Cases* between early December 1900 and mid-January 1901. Importantly, it was essentially the same Court that had established the "separate but equal" principle in *Plessy v. Ferguson* (*see* Chapter II). Having already found that African-American citizens could legally be deemed constitutionally inferior, how would the Court treat the inhabitants of these new, far-off colonies?

There was heavy lobbying on the Court's members (e.g., Philippine Governor William Howard Taft on Justice John Marshall Harlan); and the economic interests of key American industrial groups (e.g., the Sugar Trust) were also weighing heavily on the Court's deliberations. Most public predictions on the decisions were (1) the Court would rule that "the Constitution does not follow the flag 'ex proprio vigore'" [of its own force], and (2) the Court's members, based on the oral arguments, would likely be quite divided in their views. The cases were decided as a group on May 27, 1901, and the most important was *Downes v. Bidwell*, in which the constitutionality of the Foraker Act was front and center. (*New York World*: "No case [has] every attracted wider attention.").

DOWNES v. BIDWELL

With five votes, the Court upheld the constitutionality of the Foraker Act, but those five justices differed in their approaches. In the Court's lead opinion, for which there was only one vote, Justice Henry Billings Brown (author of *Plessy v. Ferguson*) took the view that the "United States" was made up only of its actual states; Congress was thus free to impose taxes on Puerto Rico or any other territory (this narrow construction adopted the U.S. government's arguments). Although he distinguished *Dred Scott* and other Supreme Court cases, Brown (warning of "savages" and "alien races") also wrote: "It is obvious that in the annexation of outlying and distant possessions grave questions will arise from

differences of face, habits, laws and customs of the people ...
which may require action on the part of Congress that would be
quite unnecessary in the annexation of contiguous territory inhab-
ited only by people of the same race, or by scattered bodies of
native Indians."

Justice Edward D. White, in a concurrence joined by Justices
George J. Shiras and Joseph McKenna, took a different tack. Adopting an approach advanced by Harvard Professor Abbott Lawrence
Lowell, White endorsed the "incorporation" doctrine—a territory
acquired with the intention of incorporating it into the United
States would be treated differently from a territory not acquired for
that purpose. By White's calculation, because the Treaty of Paris
contained "no conditions for incorporation, ... [and] expressly
provides to the contrary," until Congress declared that the territory
"should enter into and form a part of the American Family" Puerto
Rico, while "not a foreign country ... was foreign to the United
States in a domestic sense": "the island had not been incorporated
into the United States, but was merely appurtenant thereto as a
possession." White's opinion shared the racial bias of Brown's,
worrying that the country had acquired territories consisting of
"people with an uncivilized race ... absolutely unfit to receive" the
rights of U.S. citizenship. (Justice Horace Gray, while concurring
with White's opinion, also wrote a separate opinion endorsing the
prerogatives of Congress and the president to deal with territories
and tariffs.)

Chief Justice Melville Weston Fuller issued a dissent on behalf
of Justices Harlan (the lone dissenter in *Plessy*), David Josiah Brewer,
and Rufus Wheeler Peckham. Fuller wrote that the Constitution
clearly stated that the "United States" included all of its territories, regardless of whether statehood existed. He also directly took
on White's new doctrine: "Great stress is thrown upon the word
'incorporation,' as if possessed of some occult meaning.... That
theory assumes the Constitution created a government empowered to acquire countries throughout the world, to be governed by

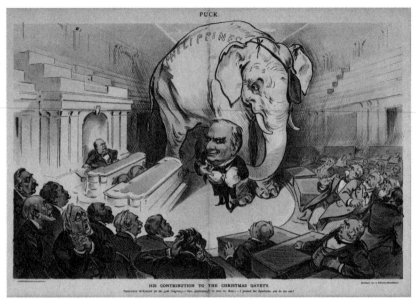

Cartoon Depicting McKinley's Acquisition of Philippines
(author's collection)

different rules than those obtaining in the original states and territories." Giving Congress such "unrestrictive power" was in contra-
vention of constitutional provisions "too plain and unambiguous
to permit its meaning to be thus influenced."

Harlan also wrote a separate dissent, emphasizing that the
Constitution "speaks ... to all peoples, whether of States or territories, who are subject to the authority of the United States." He
went on to criticize the incorporation doctrine as something alien
to our republican form of government, it being something more
likely to be utilized by "[m]onarchical or despotic governments,
unrestrained by written constitutions." And he concluded: "The
idea that this country may acquire territories anywhere upon the
earth, by conquest or treaty, and hold them as mere colonies or
provinces—the people inhabiting them to enjoy only those rights
Congress chooses to accord them ... is wholly inconsistent with
the spirit and genius as well the words of the Constitution."

Incredibly (or perhaps not so much), the press coverage of the rulings was a mess, with some newspapers declaring "The Constitution Follows the Flag," and others pronouncing "The Constitution Does Not Follow the Flag." Some wrote that it was a victory for the government, and some the opposite. At the end of the day, two things were clear: those in favor of the new American empire were happy, while those opposed to American "imperialism" were not.

THE *INSULAR CASES* GO ON

The *Insular Cases* decided on May 27, 1901, related to various tariff issues, and those decisions all reflected divergent judicial approaches to the newly acquired territories.

What was also clear in these (almost all) five-to-four decisions was that Justice Henry Billings Brown was the swing vote; he sided with the *Downes* minority to form the majority in *De Lima*;[2] he would do so again later that year in *Fourteen Diamond Rings v. United States*.[3] And Brown flipped yet again in *Dooley v. United States*.[4] With this messy jurisprudence, what did the future hold, especially with a shifting group of justices?

Many Supreme Court decisions that followed expanded the jurisprudential legacy of the cluster of *Insular Cases* beyond tariff issues; but at least four stand out. The first was *Hawaii v. Mankichi*, 190 U.S. 197 (1903).

---

[2] Duties levied after the Treaty of Paris, but before the Foraker Act, were impermissible because Puerto Rico was not a "foreign country" as defined by the congressional statute at issue.

[3] 183 U.S. 176 (1901). Rings brought back from the Philippines by a soldier could not be subject to import duties. Brown's concurrence was based on the fact that the tax in question was only reflected in a Senate resolution.

[4] 183 U.S. 151 (1901). Taxes on imports into Puerto Rico did not violate the Constitution's ban on taxing state exports: Article I, Section 9. Another five-to-four split.

The criminal defendant in *Mankichi* had been found guilty by a petit jury (by a nine-to-three vote) of murder. He appealed on the grounds that the Fifth, Sixth, and Fourteenth Amendments had been violated because he had not been indicted by a grand jury nor convicted unanimously. Justice Brown, on behalf of Justices Oliver Wendell Holmes Jr. and William R. Day, continued to reject the incorporation doctrine; instead he believed that only some of the Constitution's protections extended to the people in Hawaii: "the two rights alleged to be violated in this case are not fundamental in their nature, but concern merely a method of procedure." Justice White concurred (joined by Justice McKenna), rejecting the defendant's claims on the ground that Hawaii had not been incorporated into the United States at the time of the trial and conviction and thus *Mankichi* could not invoke constitutional rights.

The following year came *Dorr v. United States*, 195 U.S. 138 (1904). There, the issue was whether the Fifth Amendment guarantees of a jury trial and an indictment process were available in the Philippines. For the majority, Justice Day ruled that the incorporation doctrine resolved the question without further ado. He then added: "if the United States shall acquire territory peopled by savages, ... if this doctrine is sound [defendant's argument], it must establish there the trial by jury. To state such a proposition demonstrates the improbability of carrying it into practice."

Next came *Rassmussen v. United States*, 197 U.S. 516 (1905). In that case, a convicted criminal in Alaska was ruled to be entitled to constitutional protections because the treaty with Russia (unlike the Treaty of Paris) expressly manifested a "contrary intention to admit the inhabitants of the ceded territory ... to the enjoyment of all the rights, advantages, and immunities of citizens of the United States." The real jurisprudential importance of *Rasmussen* was that the Brown versus White conflict over how not to give the territories constitutional protections came to an end. White's incorporation doctrine had now won a seven-vote majority; thereafter (and to this day) that doctrine would be the law of the land.

Finally, even after U.S. citizenship had been granted to the residents of Puerto Rico by the Jones Act of 1917, that did not mean they were (or are) entitled to full constitutional protections. In *Balzac v. People of Puerto Rico*, 258 U.S. 298 (1922), Chief Justice William Howard Taft, for a unanimous Court, wrote that Puerto Ricans did not have a constitutional right to a jury trial under the incorporation doctrine (which had "become the settled law of the court"). While Puerto Ricans were entitled to "fundamental rights," without express congressional action, the Fifth and Sixth Amendments were not deemed to be "fundamental" due process rights for people in certain territories. ("Alaska was a very different case from that of Puerto Rico. It was an enormous territory, very sparsely settled, and offering opportunity for immigration and settlement by American Citizens.")

SO WHERE ARE WE TODAY?

Alaska and Hawaii are, of course, now U.S. states. After World War II, the Philippines became an independent nation. That leaves Puerto Rico, Guam, the Virgin Islands, the Northern Marianas, and American Samoa. The people in those U.S. territories—while they can serve in the U.S. military—cannot vote, are not represented in Congress, do not have full constitutional rights, and have federal laws disparately applied to them. Although Supreme Court justices have (on occasion) mused on whether to reconsider the incorporation doctrine and its impact on the "unincorporated Territories," the basic line of cases discussed here (e.g., *Downes*; *Balzac*) are (as stated above) still good law. *See, e.g., Financial Oversight and Management Board for Puerto Rico v. Aurelius Investment, LLC.*, No. 18-1324, 590 U.S. ___ (June 1, 2020); *Boumediene v. Bush*, 553 U.S. 723, 757-59 (2008); *Harris v. Rorsario*, 446 U.S. 651 (1980); *Tuava v. United States*, 951 F. Supp. 2d 88 (D.D.C. 2017), *aff'd*, 788 F. 3d 300 (D.C. Cir. 2015); *Davis v. Commonwealth Electric Comm'n*, 844 F. 3d 1087 (9th Cir. 2016). *See also* Sam Erman, *Almost Citizens: Puerto Rico, the U.S. Constitution, and Empire* (Cambridge 2019) ("the rare and shocking spectacle of cases as racist as [the *Insular Cases*] remaining largely untouched by time").

POSTSCRIPTS

Leading the charge to have the *Insular Cases* jurisprudentially rejected and full constitutional status granted to the U.S. territories was (until his death) Juan R. Torruella, a judge on the U.S. Court of Appeals for the First Circuit and chief judge from 1994 to 2001. *See* "The *Insular Cases*: The Establishment of a Regime of Political Apartheid," 29 U. Pa. J. Int'l L. 283 (2007). For those wanting to understand the *Insular Cases* in a greater historical context, I recommend Bartholomew H. Sparrow's *The* Insular Cases *and the Emergence of American Empire* (University Press of Kansas 2006). And for those wanting the best and most comprehensive explanation of America's global expansion during this era, I recommend Walter LaFeber's *The American Search for Opportunity, 1865-1913* (Cambridge University Press 1993).

It is important to note that the Court's distinction between "fundamental" and other (less "fundamental") constitutional rights came at a time when the Court had not yet found the protections found in the Bill of Rights to be "incorporated" to the states via the Fourteenth Amendment. *See* Christina Duffy Burnett, "United States: American Expansion and Territorial Deannexation," 72 U. Chi. L. Rev. 797 (2005).

The decisions were called the *Insular Cases* because the territories were islands under the jurisdiction of and administered by the War Department's Bureau of Insular Affairs.

CHAPTER XI

THE SUPREME COURT GETS IT WRONG (AGAIN): THE *CIVIL RIGHTS CASES*

B Y 1875, THE FEDERAL GOVERNMENT'S EFFORTS to compel the Southern states that fought the Civil War to grant former slaves even a modicum of "life, liberty, and the pursuit of happiness" were coming to a disastrous conclusion. Mainly because of Southern Whites' intransigence (and widespread acts of terrorism against African-Americans who sought to live as free men, vote, etc.), and partly because of weariness on the part of the Northern population, the Reconstruction Era was on its last legs. In a final legislative gasp at doing something, Congressman Benjamin Butler (aka "Beast Butler"—his nickname stemming from his oversight of New Orleans during the Civil War) introduced the Civil Rights Act of 1875.

THE ORIGINS AND PASSAGE OF THE CIVIL RIGHTS ACT

Butler's legislative proposal had its direct antecedent in the civil rights legislation first offered by Massachusetts Senator Charles Sumner in 1870. Initially designed to "protect all citizens in their civil and legal rights" across every conceivable aspect of civilian life, Sumner's bill went nowhere. In successive congressional sessions, the reintroduced legislation got watered down—ultimately eliminating all references to schools, churches, cemeteries, etc.—leaving protection only for places of "public accommodation." Notwithstanding, the legislation remained bottled up in Congress; and Sumner died in March of 1874.

The congressional election of 1874 was a historic disaster for the Republican Party—in some part because it was a referendum on Sumner's proposed bill. Returning to a lame-duck session of Congress in December 1974 were 100 Republican congressmen (including Butler) who had been defeated at the polls—the entire House at that time had only 273 members. Apparently with many legislators now not fearing their constituents' wrath, the public accommodation law moved toward passage, also in large part thanks to parliamentary maneuvering in the House by Speaker James G. Blaine and Congressman (and future President) James A. Garfield.

The bill passed the House on February 4, 1875 (by a 162-100 vote) and the Senate on February 27 (by a 38-to-26 vote). President Ulysses S. Grant signed the legislation into law on March 1. The new law, on the one hand, represented (in the words of historian Eric Foner) "an unprecedented exercise of national authority, and breached traditional federalist principles more fully than any previous Reconstruction legislation." At the same time, however, it also was an example of the Republican Party's loss of appetite for governmental interference in and control of the day-to-day oversight of Southern affairs: enforcement of the law would primarily be in the hands of former slaves seeking redress in federal court.

Public Accommodation and the Supreme Court

As historian John Hope Franklin has written, the Civil Rights Act of 1875 did not amount to much in practice. Public opinion (in both sections of the country) was opposed to the law, and there were not that many court cases brought. Nonetheless, by the early 1880s, five separate cases did make their way up to the U.S. Supreme Court. Challenging hotels, theaters, and railroads for discriminatory treatment, the five cases (*United States v. Stanley*, *United States v. Ryan*, *United States v. Nichols*, *United States v. Singleton*, and *Robinson v. Memphis & Charleston Railroad*) consolidated together as the *Civil Rights Cases*, 109 U.S. 3 (1883).

Writing for the Court's majority was Justice Joseph P. Bradley. This was significant because, although he dissented from the *Slaughter-House Cases*, 83 U.S. (16 Wall.) 36 (1873) (the Privileges and Immunities Clause of the Fourteenth Amendment was held to protect only federal citizenship rights, not those relating to state citizenship), Bradley had firsthand judicial experience with the Colfax massacre of 1873 (what historian Eric Foner has described as "the bloodiest single act of carnage in all of Reconstruction"—60 African-Americans were killed at a political rally in Louisiana by a white mob). Presiding at a second trial of the accused conspirators as a federal circuit judge for the Fifth Circuit, Bradley dismissed the convictions, ruling (among other things) that the charges violated the state action doctrine and failed to prove a racial motive for the slaughter. On appeal to the Supreme Court as *United States v. Cruikshank*, 92 U.S. 542 (1876), the Court affirmed Bradley's dismissal, holding that the Enforcement Act of 1870 (the congressional statute utilized to prosecute) applied (via the Fourteenth Amendment) only to state action and not to acts of private individuals (the Court also ruled that the First and Second Amendments did not apply to the acts of state governments or individuals). This decision opened the door in the South to heightened terrorism that suppressed Black voting, forced Republicans from office, and ultimately put in place solid Democratic state legislatures. (*See* Bennette Kramer's "The Origins of Jim Crow," *Federal Bar Council News* (November 2020).)

At the outset of the *Civil Rights* opinion, Justice Bradley declared that "[i]t is obvious that the primary and important question in all the cases is the constitutionality of the law, for if the law is unconstitutional, none of the prosecutions can stand." After an extensive discussion, he ruled that the Civil Rights Act of 1875 was indeed "unconstitutional and void." In Butler's view (on behalf of himself and seven other justices), the Thirteenth Amendment "simply abolished slavery"; and the Fourteenth Amendment only "prohibited the States" from depriving citizens of due process or equal protection. Nothing gave Congress the authority to govern the conduct (discriminatory or otherwise) of individuals: "Can the act of a mere individual, the owner of an inn, ... refusing an accommodation, be justly regarded as imposing a badge of slavery or servitude upon the applicant, or only as inflicting an ordinary civil injury, properly cognizable by the laws of the State and presumably subject to redress by these laws until the contrary appears? ... [W]e are forced to the conclusion that such an act of refusal has nothing to do with slavery or involuntary servitude.... It would be running the slavery argument into the ground to make it apply to every act of discrimination which a person may see fit to make as to guests he will entertain ... or deal with in other matters of intercourse or business." Former slaves, Bradley reasoned, had achieved the "rank of mere citizens"; they were not entitled "to be the special favorite of the laws." And since "[m]ere discriminations on account of race or color were not regarded as badges of slavery [by free African-Americans before the Civil War]," there was no reason to view them as "badges" now.

Just as the foregoing language prefigures/foreshadows the Court's even more odious ruling in *Plessy v. Ferguson,* 163 U.S. 537 (1896) (*see* Chapter II), as in *Plessy* the single dissent came from Justice John Marshall Harlan, the only Southerner on the Court and a former slaveholder (Bradley was from New Jersey).

Harlan began his dissent by observing "that the substance and spirit of the recent amendments of the Constitution have been sacrificed by a subtle and ingenious verbal criticism." In his view, the Court had "departed from the familiar rule requiring, in the interpretation of constitutional provisions, that full effect be given to the intent with which they were adopted."

According to Harlan, the Thirteenth and Fourteenth Amendments gave Congress the authority to enact laws to protect people from deprivations "on account of their race, of any civil rights enjoyed by other freemen." With respect to the state action argument, Harlan demonstrated that, by the Court's own jurisprudence, railroads, theaters, and inns operated under the color of state law. With the Court ignoring those decisions and rejecting the usual "broad and liberal connection" given to constitutional provisions, that left "the civil rights under discussion [of African-Americans] practically at the mercy of corporations and individuals wielding power under public authority." Harlan concluded presciently: "Today it is the colored race which is denied, by corporations and individuals wielding public authority, rights fundamental in their freedom and citizenship. At some future time it may be some other race that will fall under the ban."

POSTSCRIPTS

The *Civil Rights Cases* fed the fire started by *Cruikshank* and soon the Southern states had codified a system of economic and social discrimination that the Supreme Court officially blessed in *Plessy*. Amazingly, the Court's *Civil Rights* ruling has never been overturned, and its analysis on the reach of the Fourteenth Amendment was reaffirmed in *United States v. Morrison*, 529 U.S. 598 (2000). While the Civil Rights Act of 1964 banned discrimination in public accommodations, it was found to be constitutional because the law was based on the Commerce Clause. *See Heart of Atlanta Motel v. United States*, 379 U.S. 241 (1964).

The starting point for anyone wanting to know more about the Reconstruction Era is Eric Foner's magisterial work: *Reconstruction: America's Unfinished Revolution (1863-1877)* (Harper & Row 1988). John Hope Franklin's article on the Civil Rights Act is

"The Enforcement of the Civil Rights Act of 1875," *Prologue Magazine* (Winter 1974). For the best biography on "Beast Butler," see Elizabeth Leonard's *Benjamin Franklin Butler: A Noisy, Fearless Life* (Chapel Hill 2022).

Besides his role in effectively nullifying the Fourteenth Amendment (at least in the nineteenth and early twentieth centuries) (the Ku Klux Klan and the Knights of the White Camelia publicly thanked Justice Bradley for his jurisprudential work), Joseph P. Bradley is best known to history as the deciding vote in the 1876 Electoral Commission that voted (eight to seven) to rule that Rutherford B. Hayes had won the disputed presidential election over Samuel J. Tilden.

CHAPTER XII

THE SUPREME COURT TACKLES (AND FUMBLES) THE SHERMAN ANTITRUST ACT

After the Civil War (and its aftermath, the Reconstruction of the Union, which remains one of the least understood periods in American history (*see* Eric Foner's *Reconstruction: America's Unfinished Revolution, 1863-1877* (Harper 1988)), America entered the Gilded Age. One of that period's most notable aspects was the rise of industrial trusts, whereby entire product lines (e.g., sugar, steel, oil, etc.) were controlled by national conglomerates that enforced vertical integration of their products (i.e., control over raw materials, production, and distribution).

Because the states seemed unable (or unwilling) to deal with the consequences of the trusts, pressure grew on the national government to do something. Ultimately, in 1890, Congress passed the Sherman Antitrust Act, sponsored by the powerful senator from Ohio, John Sherman. With virtually no debate in either house, the bill passed the House of Representatives 242 to 0, and the Senate 51 to 1. The language of the statute was both sweeping and undefined: "Every contract, combination in the form of trust or otherwise, or conspiracy, in restraint of trade or commerce among the several States, or with foreign nations, is declared to be illegal." Although signed into law by President Benjamin Harrison, his administration did nothing to enforce it. Enforcement fell to his successor (who was also his predecessor) President Grover Cleveland.

More specifically, it fell to Cleveland's Attorney General, Richard Olney, who had previously been a Boston-based railroad attorney. Olney was not a fan of the new law, and publicly opined (as attorney general) that the statute's scope was limited. Nonetheless, he did file an action against the American Sugar Refining Company, challenging the 1892 acquisition of E.C. Knight Company and three other Philadelphia sugar manufacturers (which gave American Sugar 98 percent of the country's sugar refining capacity); the goal of the suit was to reduce American Sugar's market share to approximately 65 percent.

The U.S. Court of Appeals for the Third Circuit dismissed the action, in large part because the government had done a poor job of providing definitive record evidence of monopoly pricing. In its petition to the Supreme Court, the government relied more on what was ineluctably obvious: the trust refined virtually all of the sugar in the country and thus it controlled the price of sugar sold in every state. With the Court agreeing to take the case on certiorari, it would for the first time interpret what Congress had in mind in barring "every contract . . . in restraint of trade."

Arguing the case for American Sugar was John G. Johnson, a lawyer best known for representing J.P. Morgan. Johnson conceded the obvious—that the trust was a monopoly. His argument was that its monopoly was only in the manufacture of sugar; as to the pricing of the product in interstate commerce, the trust exercised no monopoly power because the hidden hand of the market set sugar price(s). (The market was not influenced by sugar produced offshore because of the tariff barriers effected by the McKinley Tariff of 1890.)

Chief Justice Melville Fuller, on behalf of seven of his colleagues, bought into the architectural dichotomy constructed by

Johnson, writing that the question before the Court was whether "the act of Congress of July 2, 1890 ... [could] suppress a monopoly in the manufacture of a good, as well as its distribution?" In an opinion that principally focused on protecting the "police power" prerogative of the states against encroachment by the federal government (*United States v. E.C. Knight Co.*, 156 U.S. 1 (1895)), Fuller determined that:

> Congress did not attempt ... to limit and restrict the rights of corporations created by the States or the citizens of the States in acquisition, control, or disposition of property.... [W]hat the law struck out was combinations, contracts, and conspiracies to monopolize trade and commerce among the several States or with foreign nations.

Because the only activity was the acquisition of sugar refineries in Pennsylvania, there was no connection to commerce between the states or with foreign countries (the "object was manifestly private gain in the manufacture of the commodity, but not through control of interstate or foreign commerce"). In truly tortured logic, Fuller went on to concede that "the products of these refineries were sold and distributed among the several States, and that all the companies were engaged in trade or commerce with the several States and with foreign nations; but that was no more than to say that trade and commerce served manufacture to fulfil its function." Thus, while there was a monopoly in the manufacturing of sugar, it did not follow that that meant there was an attempt ("whether executory or consummated") to monopolize commerce—"even though, in order to dispose of the product, the instrumentality of commerce was necessarily invoked."

Justice John Marshall Harlan (already famous for his dissents; *see* Chapters II, IV, X, and XI) filed the sole dissent. Harlan began his dissent by emphasizing that American Sugar's corporate charter set forth that it was organized "for the purpose of buying, manufacturing, refining, and selling sugar in different parts of the

Puck Cartoon Depicting the Antitrust Snake Threatening Columbia
(Author's Collection)

country," and that the stated purpose of the 1892 acquisitions was
to obtain "more perfect control over the business of refining and
selling sugar in the country." He then gave a realistic assessment of
what, in fact, constituted commerce among the states (as opposed
to Fuller's tortured construct) and opined that the majority's decision unduly limited Congress' authority to address an important
societal/economic issue.[1]   Harlan next reviewed a lengthy set of
state court decisions that had found precisely such corporate com-
binations to be illegal restraints of trade.

---

[1] "[T]he general government is not placed by the Constitution in such
a condition of helplessness that it must fold its arms and remain inactive while
capital combines, under the name of a corporation, to destroy competition, not
in one State only, but throughout the entire country, in the buying and selling
of articles—especially the necessities of life—that go into commerce among the
States." This latter point was a consistent theme in Harlan's jurisprudence.

Noting that, while the Court had not declared the Sherman Antitrust Act to be unconstitutional, Harlan observed that the majority opinion "defeats the main object for which it was passed." He then turned to the evidentiary record:

It is said there are no proofs in the record which indicated an intention upon the part of the American Sugar Refining Company and its associates to put a restraint upon trade or commerce. Was it necessary that formal proof be made that the persons engaged in this combination admitted in words, that they intended to restrain trade or commerce? Did anyone expect to find in written agreements ... a distinct expression of a purpose to restrain trade of commerce? ... Why, it is conceded that the object of the business is making and selling refined sugar throughout the entire country ... And now it is proved—indeed, is conceded—that the object has been accomplished to the extent that the American Sugar Refining Company now controls ninety-eight per cent of all the sugar refining business in the country, and therefore controls the price of that article everywhere. Now, the mere existence of a combination having such an object and possessing such extraordinary power is itself, under settled principles of law—there being no adjudged case to the contrary in this country—a direct restraint of trade in the article for the control of the sales of which in this country that combination was organized. And that restraint is felt in all the States, for the reason, known to all, that the article in question goes, was intended to go, and must always go, into commerce among the several States, and into the homes of people in every condition of life.

Notwithstanding the logic and common sense of the foregoing, Harlan's voice was a lonely one.

Public protests followed the *Knight* decision (particularly in agricultural communities).

But this defeat caused the Cleveland administration to throw in the towel on the Sherman Antitrust Act; Attorney General Olney declared: "The government has been defeated on the trust question. I always supposed it would be and have taken the responsibility of not prosecuting under a law to be no good."

A decade later, Harlan's lonely dissent became the law in *Swift and Company v. United States*, 196 U.S. 375 (1905). In *Swift*, Justice Oliver Wendell Holmes, writing for a unanimous Court (that included Fuller and Harlan), upheld the Roosevelt administration's attack on the "Beef Trust." Key to that ruling was the Court's adoption of a "stream of commerce" concept that allowed Congress to regulate the Chicago-based slaughterhouse industry under the Commerce Clause. (Rather than expressly overruling *Knight*, Holmes merely waived it aside: *Swift* simply was "not like" *Knight*.)

POSTSCRIPTS

The Supreme Court had signaled a new, emboldened view of the Sherman Antitrust Act in 1904 in *Northern Securities Co. v. United States*, 193 U.S. 197 (1904). In a five-to-four decision, the Court struck down a merger effected by Northern Securities to dominate the railroad industry. Justice Harlan wrote the plurality opinion. Justice Holmes's dissent included the memorable phrase: "Great cases like hard cases make bad law." Robert Bork, in his seminal *The Antitrust Paradox* (Free Press 1978), was critical of both Harlan's "ineptitude in doctrinal disputation," as well as Holmes's "famous, though very uneven dissent, [which has] misled generations of lawyers into thinking the case a precedent for the illegality of all horizontal elimination of rivalry."

For readers wanting a comprehensive biography of Justice Harlan, see Peter S. Canellos, *The Great Dissenter: The Story of John Marshall Harlan, America's Judicial Hero* (Simon & Schuster 2021).

CHAPTER XIII

The Pentagon Papers: The First Amendment Case That Wasn't

WHAT A DIFFERENCE A FEW DAYS CAN MAKE. On Saturday, June 12, 1971, President Richard M. Nixon was about as happy in his personal life as he had ever been. That day, as 59 million Americans watched on television, his daughter, Tricia Nixon, was married in a wonderful ceremony in the White House Rose Garden. Thereafter, a giddy president danced at the wedding reception with numerous women, including (for the first time in public) his wife.

The following day, the *New York Times* began publishing what would soon be called the Pentagon Papers—a highly classified study (commissioned years earlier by Robert McNamara, John F. Kennedy, and Lyndon Johnson's Secretary of Defense) of how the United States became embroiled in the Vietnam War. Although labeled "top secret," the Pentagon Papers were essentially historical in nature.

As Nixon initially viewed the *Times*' first installment, the Papers were "really tough on Kennedy, McNamara, and Johnson," with virtually nothing to do with his administration. That night Nixon's Chief of Staff, H.R. "Bob" Haldeman, opined that "[t]he key now is for us to keep out of it and let the people that are affected cut each other up on it."

MONDAY, JUNE 14, 1971

By Monday morning, things started to change. Henry Kissinger, Nixon's National Security Adviser, perhaps overly concerned that future installments of the Papers would divulge some of his back-channel handiwork during the prior Democratic administrations, called the president and directly challenged his manhood. Telling Nixon that the *Times'* publication "shows you are a weakling, Mr. President," and that "these leaks are slowly and systematically destroying us," Kissinger whipped the president (in Haldeman's words) into "a frenzy."

While Nixon and Kissinger were raising each other's blood pressure, a group of distinguished lawyers and journalists was having lunch at the University Club in New York City. They had assembled to hear a presentation by Yale Law Professor Alexander Bickel on a draft he had prepared for an *amicus curiae* brief in *Branzburg v. Hayes*, 408 U.S. 665 (1972).

Bickel had been recruited for the project—testing whether reporters had First Amendment rights not to reveal sources before a grand jury—by a former student, Floyd Abrams. When Abrams first contacted Bickel, Bickel warned Abrams that he was "no First Amendment voluptuary." Voluptuary or not, Bickel gave the assembled group what Abrams called a "dazzling" and "golden" presentation.

After Bickel concluded, the group (which included James Goodale, the *Times'* general counsel) started to talk about the publication of the Pentagon Papers. Both Bickel and Abrams gave them a fair amount of gratuitous advice—mainly that the government would not try to bring a prior restraint proceeding, but that if it did (according to Bickel), "[t]hat's one you can't lose."

On the evening of June 14, Attorney General John Mitchell sent a telegram to the *Times*; in it, he cited Section 793 of the Espionage Act, and directed the paper not to publish another word from the "top secret" Pentagon Papers.

The *Times* responded to Mitchell that it would "respectfully" not follow his directive. That decision was arrived at relatively easily inside the newspaper-in-large mainly because there had already been a fractious internal debate prior to the first publication, a debate that had only been resolved by the *Times*' publisher, Arthur Sulzberger.

But there was another problem immediately facing the paper: Who would represent them in the impending legal battle with the federal government? Lord, Day & Lord, the venerable New York firm that had represented the *Times* for over 60 years, refused to handle the assignment.

Herbert Brownell, Lord Day's senior partner and former attorney general under President Dwight D. Eisenhower, had previously advised the *Times* that publishing the Pentagon Papers would be unpatriotic (and un-*Times*-like), would violate the Espionage Act, and might land Sulzberger in jail. Brownell (who had already received a call from Mitchell on the 14th, in which Mitchell urged him not to represent the *Times*) that night told Goodale his firm could not take on the matter, citing as his reason the executive order establishing the national security classification system that he had drafted as attorney general.

A little after 1:00 a.m. that same night, Goodale picked up the telephone and woke up Abrams at home. Succinctly explaining the pickle in which the newspaper found itself, Goodale asked Abrams if he and Bickel—in light of their earlier expressed, breezy confidence—would represent the *Times*.

Abrams would later recount that the call from Goodale was "like a dream." He excitedly agreed to take on the matter (subject to checking with the powers that be at his firm, Cahill Gordon & Reindel, in the morning); Abrams then told Goodale that he and

Bickel would go to the office immediately and get started. Abrams thereupon scooped up Bickel in a taxi, and the *Times'* new lawyers headed straight to the law firm's library.

Bickel's "Vision"

Bickel and Abrams first tackled Section 793 of the Espionage Act. After reviewing the statute, both men were puzzled: Section 793 was a criminal statute, but the proceeding contemplated in Mitchell's telegram was injunctive and noncriminal; also, Congress had not contemplated or set forth in the statute a basis for the prior restraint of any kind of publication (top secret documents or anything else).

And, although Abrams believed that the main line of attack should be on pure First Amendment grounds (i.e., prior restraints on the press were "all but unthinkable"), Bickel immediately seized upon the Espionage Act's inapplicability and envisioned a compelling separation of powers argument. As Abrams would later write:

> While [Bickel] viewed as useful existing First Amendment law making prior restraints extremely difficult to obtain, he regarded it as insufficient in itself to persuade the courts to rule in our favor. We needed more, he thought, and congressional refusal to enact legislation explicitly criminalizing behavior like the *Times'* or, at the least, permitting it to be enjoined was central to his vision of the case.

Later that morning, Bickel and Abrams met with the key decision makers at the *Times*. At that meeting, Bickel's approach was premised entirely upon what Justice William Brennan always said was the most important quality needed by a Supreme Court justice: the ability to count to five.

In other words, Justices Black, Brennan, Douglas, and Marshall were all safe bets to side with the *Times*. To pick up a fifth vote, however, it would be necessary to *not* argue for an absolute

First Amendment protection; instead, the *Times* should concede that there might indeed be some circumstances justifying prior restraints (the Supreme Court had already articulated one in *Near v. Minnesota*, 283 U.S. 697 (1931)—Chief Justice Charles Evans Hughes had written: "No one would question but that [during war] a government might prevent the publication of the sailing dates of transports or of the number and location of troops.") and emphasize instead that Congress had never given the president the authority to pursue the remedy sought.

Even before Bickel finished his presentation, the *Times* was contacted by the U.S. Attorney's Office for the Southern District of New York about the government's application for a temporary restraining order, which was about to be heard before Nixon appointee, Murray Gurfein.

Beginning at noon, the parties had a brief oral argument in open court. Judge Gurfein then called the principals into his chambers.

Prefacing his remarks with "we are all patriotic Americans," Gurfein asked Bickel if his client would (de facto) acquiesce to the temporary restraining order, at least for a few days so he could review the documents about which the government claimed that public dissemination would prove ruinous to national security.

Bickel, after conferring with his client (and Goodale calling the *Times*), replied in the negative. Thereupon, Gurfein entered an order granting the temporary restraining order, and set an evidentiary hearing for three days later (June 18).

The Litigation Context

It may be hard to remember or imagine what all the hubbub was about, but the stakes seemed enormous at the time and peoples' emotions ran to extremes.

One of Abrams's law partners, who was added to the litigation team for the evidentiary hearing, was asked by the president

Nixon and Mao Playing Ping Pong
(Author's Collection)

of his largest client: "Since when does your firm represent traitors?" Without missing a beat, the Cahill lawyer responded: "What the fuck do you know about the First Amendment?!"

Back at the *Times*, there was rumbling about whether to obey Judge Gurfein's order. Abrams advised that to defy the order "would be self-destructive" and poison the litigation well for the newspaper all the way up to the Supreme Court. Bickel added that "the reason we are here is to vindicate the law." Sulzberger followed his lawyers' advice and quelled any dissent.

Meanwhile, within the walls of the White House, the angst levels were rising higher. Nixon, spewing forth anti-Semitic diatribes about the leadership of the *Times*, on-again/off-again flirted with having Mitchell institute parallel criminal proceedings.

At the same time, the president not only began to lecture his staff on comparisons to the *Hiss* case (which had propelled Nixon to national fame), he also began to see opportunities to damage JFK's legacy (implicating him in the 1963 assassination of South Vietnam's President Diem) and to blackmail LBJ (over his deceptions to the American public vis-à-vis various wartime decisions). Nixon even pondered aloud the possibility of him arguing the government's case before the U.S. Supreme Court.

FRIDAY, JUNE 18

The evidentiary hearing before Judge Gurfein went poorly for the government. The witnesses proffered to speak about threats to national security were long on rhetoric and short on specifics. Repeatedly, the judge asked for concrete examples, but none were offered up. Incredibly, one high-ranking Defense Department official testified that he had called his Pentagon colleagues at lunch, but even at that late date had been unable "to come up with a list of, a lengthy list, of specifics."

As a result, when Gurfein handed down a decision the next day, he ruled that the government had not met its burden in "convinc[ing] this Court that the publication of these historical documents would seriously breach the National security." Judge Gurfein also latched onto Bickel's argument, agreeing that the Espionage Act had nothing to do with preventing the publication of anything.

The *Times* was not out of the woods yet, however. The Department of Justice quickly got a stay from Judge Irving Kaufman of the Second Circuit, pending review by that court of Judge Gurfein's decision. Oral argument on the appeal was set for three days after Kaufman entered the stay.

TUESDAY, JUNE 22

In its brief to the Second Circuit, the *Times* continued to follow Bickel's strategic approach; in fact, only three pages of the 48-page brief focused on the First Amendment. By Abrams's own admission, the brief "made little difference," however, because oral argument "was a disaster." Before Bickel could even get to the substance of his argument, Chief Judge Henry Friendly engaged him in a heated colloquy about whether the Pentagon Papers were or were not "stolen." It was all downhill from there.

The Second Circuit ruled the following day (five to three) that the case should be remanded to Judge Gurfein for further hearings. The government's strategy on appeal—that insufficient time had been given to decide this momentous matter—clearly had convinced a majority of the Second Circuit; from the tone of the oral argument, the majority did not need much persuading.

In the meantime, the *Washington Post* had picked up the baton and had also begun to publish the Papers. To stop the *Post*, the government had gone to court in the District of Columbia before another Nixon appointee, Gerhard Gesell, with that judge making the same evidentiary determination as had Gurfein.

On June 23, while the *Times* was deciding what to do in response to the Second Circuit's ruling (it was looking at not being able to publish for weeks, at best), the D.C. Circuit affirmed Judge Gesell's decision.

Whether that tipped the *Times* to act is unclear, but the following day Abrams hand delivered a certiorari petition to the clerk of the U.S. Supreme Court. On Friday, June 25, the Court granted the petition and set oral argument down for the next day.

SATURDAY, JUNE 26

Oral argument began on Saturday with a good news/bad news announcement by Chief Justice Warren Burger: The government's motion to conduct part of the argument in secret had been denied.

This was bad news obviously for the government; it also meant that the government had submitted its motion *ex parte*—an incredible violation of every judicial and ethical protocol imaginable.

The good news for the *Times* was the vote: six to three—Justices Potter Stewart and Byron White had joined the four justices Bickel had identified as sure bets. An omen?

Solicitor General Erwin Griswold argued on behalf of the government. The former dean of the Harvard Law School, Griswold specifically declined to advocate the Nixon-Mitchell view (i.e., if the government classifies a document "top secret," such a

designation is dispositive); he also engaged in the following colloquy with Justice Hugo Black:

> Your construction of [the First Amendment] is well
> known, and I certainly respect it. You say that "no law"
> means "no law," and that should be obvious. I can only
> say, Mr. Justice, that to me it is equally obvious that "no
> law" does not mean "no law," and I seek to persuade the
> Court that that is true.

Abrams happily viewed Griswold's performance as "probably
the least persuasive challenge to Justice Black's views ever publicly
expressed."

Bickel, up next, forcefully put forward his separation of
powers argument. And just to make sure that there could be no
mistake, without prompting he conceded that "the prohibition
against prior restraint, like much else in the Constitution, is not
an absolute."

Justice William Douglas, about as much a First Amendment
absolutist as Justice Hugo Black, directly challenged the entire
premise of Bickel's argument; Bickel, however, knowing he did not
have to worry about Douglas's vote, brushed aside Douglas's observation that the *Times* was making "a very strange argument."

The key to Bickel's presentation lay in his colloquy with Justice Stewart.

Stewart posited as a hypothetical that publication would lead
to battlefield deaths. Bickel calmly responded: "Mr. Justice, I wish
there were a statute that covered [the situation].... I would only
say as to that it is a case in which in the absence of a statute, I
suppose most of us would say...."

At that point Stewart interjected: "You would say the Constitution requires that it be published, and that those men die, is
that it?"

Bickel famously responded: "No. I am afraid that my inclinations to humanity overcome the somewhat more abstract devotion to the First Amendment in a case of that sort."

WEDNESDAY, JUNE 30

Four days after the argument, the Supreme Court handed down its decision. By a vote of six to three, the Court, *per curiam*, held that the government had not met its burden to justify prior restraint, and thus, the *Times* would be allowed to continue to publish the Papers. Bickel's strategic approach, moreover, had been vindicated.

Predictably, the four justices Bickel had counted on as safe bets sided with the *Times*. Justices Black, Brennan, and Douglas each wrote separate concurring opinions stressing an absolutist First Amendment position.

Douglas, who had mocked Bickel's "very strange argument," also cited the absence of a "statute barring the publication by the press of the material which the *Times* ... seek[s] to use." And Justice Thurgood Marshall's concurring opinion was based entirely on the absence of congressional authorization for the injunctive relief sought by the government.

Justices Stewart and White, who did join the majority, demonstrated that they were no First Amendment "voluptuaries." Key to Stewart's concurring opinion was the fact that Congress had not passed a "specific law authorizing civil proceedings in this field."

In Stewart's view, the Court was therefore being pressed to perform an Executive, not Judicial, function under the Constitution. And notwithstanding that he was "convinced that the Executive is correct with respect to some of the documents involved," Stewart determined that the disclosure of them would not "surely result in direct, immediate, and irreparable damage to our nation or its people." (Echoing *Near v. Minnesota*.)

Justice White's concurring opinion also drew heavily on Bickel and further made clear what a close call it had been for the *Times*.

Rejecting First Amendment absolutism, White reviewed at some length the legislative history of the Espionage Act and demonstrated that Congress had contemplated giving the president broad injunctive power, but had then specifically declined to enact such authority. White also questioned the efficacy of prior restraint at that point (besides the *Times* and the *Post*, at least eight other newspapers had begun to publish the Papers). Nonetheless, White believed that publication would in fact do "substantial damage" to the nation and detailed alternative remedies available to the government—most notably, that proceeding criminally against those who disseminated the Pentagon Papers would be constitutional.

The three dissents (by Justices Warren Burger, Harry Blackmun, and John Marshall Harlan) mainly focused on the haste of proceeding on such weighty matters without a fully developed evidentiary record ("irresponsibly feverish," "frenetic haste," "frenzied train of events," "frenetic pace and character," etc.).

Justice Harlan observed (not unreasonably, and consistent with the Second Circuit): "I cannot believe that the doctrine prohibiting prior restraint reaches to the point of preventing courts from maintaining the status quo long enough to act responsibly in matters of such national importance as those involved here."

One can easily imagine, if Bickel had taken a different tack, those words being written as part of a majority opinion.

POSTSCRIPTS

The American Civil Liberties Union was so angry about Bickel's "no" answer to Justice Stewart that it took the highly unusual step of filing a post-argument amicus brief, disassociating itself from the legal position espoused by the *Times*.

Lord, Day & Lord lost the *New York Times* as a client forever. And whether or not there was a direct causal link, that venerable law firm is no more.

When President Nixon heard the Court's decision, he went into a tirade. Calling Justice Stewart "a weak bastard ...

overwhelmed by the Washington-Georgetown social set," he told aide Charles Colson: "We've got a counter government here and we've got to fight it. I don't give damn how it is done." Later that same day, Nixon told Haldeman that he wanted Howard Hunt (an ex-CIA official) to begin break-in operations at the Brookings Institute. He then railed against his own attorney general (and former law partner): "John [Mitchell] is always worried about is it technically correct. Do you think, for Christ's sakes, the *New York Times* is worried about all the legal niceties? Those sons of bitches are killing me.... We're up against an enemy, a conspiracy. They're using any means. We are going to use any means. Is that clear?!" This presidential ranting led directly to the creation of the White House Plumbers unit, designed initially to discredit Daniel Ellsberg (the man who leaked the Pentagon Papers). And the Plumbers' efforts led directly to Watergate.

Bickel subsequently failed to gain a fifth vote in *Branzburg v. Hayes*. Writing for the five-vote majority, Justice White rejected a reportorial privilege. This precedent played a key role in the subsequent litigation involving Valerie Plame, the "outed" CIA agent. *See* C.E. Stewart, "The Trials of Scooter Libby: Justice Run Amok?" *Federal Bar Counsel Quarterly* (November 2019).

There are many key sources for this subject. The starting point is Floyd Abrams's wonderful memoir *Speaking Freely: Trials of the First Amendment* (Penguin Books 2005). Other must-reads include H.R. Haldeman's *The Haldeman Diaries: Inside the Nixon White House* (Putnam 1994) and Richard Reeves's *President Nixon: Alone in the White House* (Simon & Schuster 2001). Perhaps not surprisingly, Herbert Brownell's memoirs make no mention of the Pentagon Papers: *Advising Ike: The Memoirs of Attorney General Herbert Brownell* (University Press of Kansas 1993).

CHAPTER XIV

A Switch in Time Saves Nine

C HARLES EVANS HUGHES, well before he became a Supreme Court Justice, once famously remarked: "We are under a Constitution, but the Constitution is what the judges say it is" (*see The Yale Book of Quotations* (ed. F. Shapiro) p. 374 (speech in Elmira, New York, May 3, 1907)).

That truism was never shown to be more true than when Hughes served as Chief Justice in the mid-1930s and the Court's repudiation of the Roosevelt administration's New Deal legislation resulted in an unprecedented constitutional crisis. One of the key litigated disputes that brought on that crisis arose in Brooklyn.

THE NEW DEAL THWARTED

After Franklin D. Roosevelt had been inaugurated as president on March 4, 1933, his administration quickly put together a laundry list of legislative programs to deal with the Great Depression. With broad public support (and wide majorities in Congress), virtually all of those programs were enacted into law.

Whether the programs did in fact "defeat" the Depression remains a subject of debate among historians to this day. What is not subject to debate is that much of the early New Deal legislation ran into tough sledding when it was challenged in the courts.

In fact, in 1935-36, the U.S. Supreme Court gutted the centerpieces of President Franklin D. Roosevelt's legislative agenda, striking down the National Industrial Recovery Act (NRA), the Agricultural Adjustment Act, the Railroad Retirement Act, as well as New York State's minimum wage law for women. Before getting to the constitutional crisis those decisions caused, a case arising out of Brooklyn deserves a look.

THE "SICK CHICKEN" CASE

In the 1930s, New York City was the largest live-poultry market in the United States; 96 percent of the poultry arrived from other states, was sold to slaughterhouse operators, who then killed the poultry and resold it to retail poultry dealers and retail butchers. Four brothers, Martin, Alex, Joseph, and Aaron Schecter ran two successful slaughterhouse markets in Brooklyn, which they operated in strict accordance with Jewish dietary law (*shochitim*).

For reasons that are not completely clear, NRA officials decided to make the Schecters a test case for the NRA's "Live Poultry Code" (the Code regulated prices, wages, hours worked, how and how many chickens could be purchased, etc.).

In the summer of 1934, NRA inspectors descended en masse upon the Schecters' slaughterhouses. The fruits of those investigatory efforts were presented to a federal grand jury, which handed down a 60-count indictment. Among the charges (which carried criminal penalties) were: (1) violations of NRA standards regarding work hours and pay, (2) threats of violence against NRA officials, (3) violating the "straight killing" rule (this meant customers could not select or purchase individual poultry), and (4) selling "unfit" (aka "sick") chickens. (At trial this boiled down to just one "egg bound" chicken—an internal condition the Schecters could not have detected prior to sale.)

Prosecuted by Walter Lyman Rice (a young Harvard Law graduate who was appointed as a special federal prosecutor), the trial was before Judge Marcus Campbell (an appointee of President Warren G. Harding) in the federal court based in Brooklyn (the Eastern District of New York). The Schecter brothers were defended by Joseph Heller (a Brooklyn Law graduate). One of the reasons that the Schecters chose to fight the charges was the "sick chicken" allegation, which they took to mean that their kosher slaughterhouses stood accused of being not kosher.

The trial was a mismatch of culture, education, experience, resources, and common sense. There was testimony that one NRA inspector did not know the difference between a chicken and a rooster; other NRA inspectors were said to have insulted and scared away a number of the Schecters' customers. Walter Rice and Martin Schecter fenced as to whether "keen" competition among business competitors was a good or bad thing.

The jury (with a little prod from Judge Campbell) returned convictions. The brothers were not only given very substantial monetary sanctions, but, more importantly, they were all sentenced to prison.

The Schecters appealed to the Second Circuit, unsuccessfully. They then turned to the Supreme Court. The Court agreed to hear the case, and oral argument took place on May 2-3, 1935. Donald Richberg, the NRA's general counsel (a progressive Chicago lawyer recruited to the New Deal), and Stanley Reed, the Solicitor General (and later a Supreme Court Justice), argued on behalf of the United States. Joseph Heller and Frederick Wood (of Cravath, DeGersdorff, Swaine and Wood) argued on behalf of the Schecters.

The government's basic argument was that the NRA was necessary to "protect against the evils of this unparalleled depression"; protecting liberty in the abstract constituted nothing more than "the liberty to starve."

Franklin Roosevelt and Political Advisor Louis Howe
(Author's Collection)

Heller, on the other hand, focused on the fact that the Schecters' business really was almost exclusively intrastate. He also emphasized that the Live Poultry Code was not only at odds with Jewish law and custom, but that it had the further effect of hurting small businesses generally and ran counter to all-American norms like consumer free choice. Wood's portion of the argument was on a more grandiose scale, comparing the New Deal's regulatory reach to that which Hitler or Mussolini would find comfortable.

Just weeks later (on May 27), Chief Justice Charles Evans Hughes delivered the unanimous Court ruling in open session (*A.L.A. Schecter Poultry Corp. v. United States*, 295 U.S. 495 (1935)). He first explicitly rejected the Roosevelt administration's overarching contention that the "grave national crisis" justified the NRA: "Extraordinary conditions do not create or enlarge constitutional power." He then moved on to eviscerate the NRA on two basic grounds: (1) the industrial "codes of fair competition" enshrined by the legislation impermissibly delegated congressional authority to the president, giving him "virtually unfettered" power to regulate business; and (2) the scope and breadth of the legislation ran afoul of Congress' power to regulate interstate commerce (Congress could only regulate where the effect upon interstate commerce was direct; "indirect" effects—e.g., here, an "unfit" chicken sold in Brooklyn was not subject to congressional power).

This decision sounded the death knell for the NRA, and perhaps the entire New Deal as well. Indeed, that same day, Justice Louis Brandeis told two powerful New Deal lawyers to tell FDR that "[t]his is the end of the business of centralization," and suggested that the "young men" of the New Deal go back to their respective states and "do their work" there.

FDR was furious at this shot across the bow, and his first public comment was to characterize the justices as living in "the horse and buggy age." The Schecter brothers, for their part, hoisted Heller on their shoulders in his Chambers Street office and repeatedly chanted "nine to nothing!"

FDR's Court-Packing Plan

Emboldened by his record reelection victory in 1936 over Kansas Governor Alfred "Alf" Landon (he carried all but Vermont and Maine), FDR decided to strike back at the Court. Shortly after his inauguration in January 1937, the president publicly announced that he would be sending over to Congress a bill to increase the size of the Court to as many as 15 justices—for each justice who stayed past 70 years of age, a new justice could be appointed. The public rationale for FDR's action was that the Court was so chockablock busy it was stressed to the point of overload.

No one was fooled by that, however, and the public reaction to FDR's Court-packing plan was sharply negative (and included a number of Democrats). But FDR kept on the attack, telling the nation that the justices were unable to deal with "our modern economic conditions," and that the Court required "new blood"; the country, he further asserted, needed to "save the Constitution from the Court and the Court from itself."

Members of the Court did not sit still for these ad hominems. Chief Justice Hughes, for example, wrote a letter to the Senate Judiciary Committee, in which he challenged every assumption underlying the president's plan. The Hughes letter had a significant impact on public opinion and the legislation's fate seemed uncertain (at best).

A SWITCH IN TIME SAVES NINE

In the midst of all this political brouhaha, the Court on March 29 handed down a decision in *West Coast Hotel v. Parrish*, 300 U.S. 379 (1937). Explicitly reversing its decision of just a year earlier on New York's minimum wage law (*Morehead v. New York ex rel. Tipaldo*, 298 U.S. 587 (1936)), as well as its decision on that same subject matter a decade earlier (*Adkins v. Children's Hospital*, 261 U.S. 525 (1923)), the Court (by a five-to-four margin) upheld Washington State's minimum wage law.

Chief Justice Hughes, writing for the majority, now took "judicial notice of the unparalleled demands for relief" caused by the Depression. The Court's prior precedent, which had been based on the concept of freedom of contract, was simply held to be inapt in light of the majority's "fresh consideration" of the subject.

The four dissenting justices (known in history as the "Four Horsemen") were furious, and not only to be on the losing side of the argument ("the meaning of the Constitution does not change with the ebb and flow of economic events."). Their fury was particularly directed at Justice Owen Roberts, who had suddenly switched sides. In a scathing attack on Justice Roberts, Justice George Sutherland (the author of *Adkins*) wrote:

[I]t is the duty of a member of the court, in the process of reaching a right conclusion, to give due weight to the opposing views of his associates; but in the end, the question he must answer is not whether such views seem sound to those who entertain them, but whether they convince him that the statute is constitutional or engender in his mind a rational doubt upon that issue. The oath which he takes as a judge is not a composite oath, but an individual one. And in passing upon the validity of a statute, he discharges a duty imposed upon *him*, which cannot be consummated justly by an automatic acceptance of the views of others which have neither convinced, nor created a reasonable doubt in, his mind. If upon a question so important he thus surrender his deliberate judgment, he stands forsworn. He cannot subordinate his convictions to that extent and keep faith with his judicial and moral independence. (Emphasis in original.)

Ouch! Two weeks later, the "new" majority on the Court made it clear that *Parrish* was not a fluke and that they were now playing on the same team with the president. In *NLRB v. Jones & Laughlin Steel Corp.*, 301 U.S. 1 (1937), Chief Justice Hughes, writing for the five-justice majority, upheld the National Labor Relations Act. The statute, which mimicked the NRA's industrial codes, was determined not to be an impermissible delegation of power to the Executive Branch, nor was it violative of the Interstate Commerce Clause.

In response to the argument that the law's scope was too broad, Hughes (again noting the "plainest facts of our national life") brushed that off (as well as his opinion in *Schecter Poultry*), saying that the legislation was in fact "limited"—merely to all things "affecting commerce." The Four Horsemen's dissent, written by Justice James McReynolds, had an exasperated/defeated tone to it, essentially asking into empty space: "Whatever happened to the *Schecter Poultry* 'direct/indirect' commerce test?!"

POSTSCRIPT

As a precedent, *Schecter Poultry* did not last long. But Mrs. Joseph Schecter did compose and publish a poem for posterity, entitled "Now That It's Over":

> No More excuses
> To hide our disgrace
> With pride and satisfaction
> I'm showing my face.
> For a long long time
> To be kept in suspense
> Sarcastic remarks made
> At our expense.
> I'm through with that experience
> I hope for all my life,
> And proud again to be,
> Joseph Schecter's wife.

FDR ultimately lost his Court-packing plan (the *Jackson* [Mississippi] *Daily News*' obituary: "dead as a salt mackerel shining beneath the pale moonlight."). But he not only got a majority of the Court to come into line, he soon thereafter got a chance to appoint new justices and began to replace the Four Horsemen.

Justice Owen Roberts never publicly conceded that he had switched his views based on political expediency. And in a note to Felix Frankfurter he insisted that "no action taken by the President ... had any causal relation to my action in the *Parrish* case."

An excellent overview of the historiography of the "switch in time saves nine" controversy can be found in Volume 110 (Number 4) of *The American Historical Review* (October 2005). Also highly recommended is Amity Shlaes's *The Forgotten Man: A New History of the Great Depression* (Harper Collins 2007).

CHAPTER XV

THE SUPREME COURT GRANTS THE PRESIDENT IMMENSE AND INDEFINITE POWERS (AND WHO KNEW?)

TODAY WE LIVE IN AN AMERICA WHERE everyone just presumes that presidential power over foreign policy is preeminent. Indeed, at least since the Cuban Missile Crisis, Americans have well understood that one person has the ability to destroy the world in a thermonuclear holocaust. But that was not always the case; and the constitutional underpinnings for the empowering of the president's on-steroids authority in foreign policy comes from three, little-known Supreme Court decisions.

IN RE NEAGLE

In 1890, the Supreme Court decided *In re Neagle*, 135 U.S. 1 (1890). The specific holding of *Neagle* is that federal officers acting as bodyguards to the justices are immune from state prosecution when they are acting within the scope of their federal authority.

David Neagle was a U.S. Marshall appointed by the attorney general to be Justice Stephen Field's bodyguard while Field was performing his circuit court functions in California. During the course of that tour of duty, Neagle killed a man he determined was about to harm Field. Although Neagle was arrested by a local sheriff, the U.S. Attorney in San Francisco filed a writ of habeas corpus for Neagle's release, which was granted by the circuit court. The sheriff appealed that ruling to the Supreme Court.

By a six-to-two vote (Field recused himself) the Court affirmed the circuit court's decision. In so doing, the Court held that the president (executive branch) could act in the absence of congressional authority (since there were no laws that provided for the protection of federal judges)—thus (and further), presidential duties are not limited to carrying out treaties and congressional acts according to their express terms; rather, those duties are based on broad implied powers: "the rights, duties, and obligations growing out of the Constitution itself, our international relations, and all the protections implied by the nature of the government under the Constitution." By that rationale, the Court thus recognized for the first time (in the words of one historian) "immense and indefinite presidential power." Even at the time of the Court's decision it was understood (at least by some) to be very significant. In his highly influential 1895 book *The American Commonwealth*, James Bryce wrote that, in foreign affairs, the president "is independent of the House, while the Senate, though it can prevent his settling anything, cannot keep him from unsettling everything." He can "embroil the country abroad or excite passion at home."

And presidents started to do just that. President William McKinley's war of choice with Spain in 1898 created an American empire, which the Court not only ratified in the *Insular Cases* (*see* Chapter X) but also allowed the federal government to rule the acquired territories unfettered by the Constitution. His successor, Theodore Roosevelt, went even further with his aggressive use of executive agreements. For example, having essentially taken over Santo Domingo in 1904-05, invoking unidentified "police" powers in order to protect U.S. interests, President Roosevelt signed a treaty giving U.S. naval officers control over the country's custom houses (its main revenue source). The Senate, however, rejected that treaty because it wanted no more American protectorates (beyond those it had taken on just a few years before). Undeterred, Roosevelt rejiggered the treaty into an executive agreement, citing a "stewardship" theory (that presidential power was "limited only by specific restrictions and prohibitions appearing in the Constitution or imposed by the Congress under its Constitutional powers.").

Curtiss-Wright Export

Fast forward to the 1930s, ironically at a time when the Supreme Court (at least initially) was rejecting wide-scale executive authority in domestic affairs (*see* Chapter XIV), the Court was expanding upon what it had written in *Neagle*. The first key decision came in *United States v. Curtiss-Wright Export Corp.*, 299 U.S. 304 (1936).

At issue in *Curtiss-Wright* was the president's authority to prohibit the sale of arms and ammunitions to belligerents in Latin America, pursuant to a joint resolution of Congress. In a seven-to-one vote, the Court upheld that authority. But Justice George Sutherland, writing for the majority, went well beyond the specific dispute at issue by (in the words of historian Walter LaFeber) "explicitly separating the Constitution's relationship to domestic policy from its relationship to foreign relations." Sutherland reached his conclusion of untethering foreign relations from the Constitution by three propositions:

1. that the federal government's "powers of external sovereignty" pre-dated the Constitution—that these powers were derived from and were "immediately passed" from Great Britain (and its king) to the Union at the time of the Revolution;

2. that, as a result of the foregoing, "federal power over external affairs [is therefore] in origin and essential character different from that of internal affairs"; and

3. that "in this vast external realm, ... the President alone has the power to speak or listen as a representative of a nation."

On this last point, Sutherland went on to declare that it is "the very delicate, plenary and exclusive power of the President as the sole organ of the federal government in the field of international relations—a power which does not require as a basis for its exercise an act of Congress." Sutherland added that this "exclusive power" had to be "exercised in subordination to the applicable provisions of the Constitution"; he did not, however, identify what "applicable provisions" he had in mind.

United States v. Belmont

Just one year later, Justice Sutherland authored another majority opinion in *United States v. Belmont*, 301 U.S. 324 (1937). That opinion held that an executive agreement was the equivalent of a treaty and that, in certain cases, a president's decision making could preempt state law.

After the Bolsheviks seized effective control of Russia during the Russian Revolution, one of the first things they did was to seize the assets of banks and corporations, some of which had assets in the United States. Who owned those assets was unclear until 1933, when President Franklin Roosevelt formally recognized the Soviet Union and, as part of that recognition, negotiated the Litvinov Assignment; that was an executive agreement whereby the U.S. government agreed to "assign" assets held by Americans in Russian companies to the Soviet government and the federal government agreed to do the same vis-à-vis assets held by Russians in America.

August Belmont & Co., a New York bank holding assets of a Russian company, legally challenged the Litvinov Assignment, arguing that only a treaty ratified by the Senate could constitutionally impair its property rights. The District Court for the Southern District of New York dismissed the government's case to seize the assets, and the Second Circuit Court of Appeals affirmed. These rulings were based on

- the fact that the bank deposits had been made in New York,
- title of such deposits was a matter of New York State law (not federal), and
- a judgment in favor of the United States for the assets would violate the public policy of New York State.

Justice Sutherland, writing for a unanimous Court, reversed the Second Circuit. He wrote that the president had the unfettered power to enter into executive agreements with foreign governments without the advice and consent of the Senate. And to the concerns of the lower courts, Sutherland added that the president's executive agreements are binding over and trump state constitutions, state laws, and state public policies.

By Sutherland's two rulings, in the words of Louis Henkin, in *Foreign Affairs and the Constitution* (Clarendon Press 1972), the Court had articulated "a singular constitutional history: the powers of the United States to conduct relation with other nations do not derive from the Constitution."

JUSTICE GEORGE SUTHERLAND

At first glance, Justice Sutherland was an unlikely architect of presidential power. He was, after all, a leading member of the "Four Horseman"—the group of "conservative" justices who eviscerated much of the New Deal's domestic legislation. Indeed, he was the author of the majority opinion in *Adkins v. Children's Hospital*, 261 U.S. 525 (1923), in which the Court, applying the "freedom of contract" theory of due process made famous/infamous in *Lochner v. New York*, 198 U.S. 45 (1995) (*see* Chapter IV), struck down the District of Columbia's minimum wage law for women. (Interestingly, Sutherland's analysis in *Adkins* sounds very much based in modern feminism—i.e., women are not frail, delicate individuals who need extra protection(s); rather they are the equal of men and thus can exercise the right to contract in the marketplace just as much as any man. Sutherland's feminist credentials were, in fact, real: As a U.S. Senator (from Utah), he introduced the Nineteenth Amendment in the Senate, campaigned for its passage, and helped draft the Equal Rights Amendment.) Besides his antipathy for the New Deal, Sutherland also had a very low opinion of President Roosevelt; Sutherland once called FDR an "utter incompetent."

So why did Sutherland create an extra-constitutional template for the president to exercise power in foreign policy seemingly without constraints?

While in the Senate, Sutherland had written an article in 1910, distinguishing between the "internal and external powers" of the federal government. After leaving the Senate (but before he was put on the Court by President Harding), Sutherland published a book in 1919 that expanded on that theme. While deferring to the states on domestic issues (e.g., child labor laws), Sutherland argued that in "external matters" the states had "no residuary power." And as to the government's obligation under the Constitution to "provide for the Common Defense," Sutherland contended that "[a]lways the end is more important than the means."

This last observation opened up Sutherland to criticism as advocating "executive totalitarianism." Notwithstanding, as Justice Sutherland, he (in the words of historian Walter LaFeber) "provided that most important historical and judicial justification for taking the critical step of separating foreign and domestic affairs."

Postscripts

President Franklin Roosevelt certainly felt empowered by Justice Sutherland's rulings. In 1941, when an American destroyer, the *U.S.S. Greer*, was attacked by a German submarine, the president issued a "shoot-on-sight" policy for any Axis submarines that "enter the waters the protection of which is necessary for American defense." The historic importance of the *Greer* incident and the "shoot-on-sight" policy cannot be understated. For example, Hitler deemed it to be a de facto "state of war" declaration by the United States, and it was a key factor in his decision to declare war against America after Japan attacked Pearl Harbor. For those who want to know more about the *Greer* incident, see C.E. Stewart, *Myron Taylor: The Man Nobody Knew* (Twelve Tables Press 2023).

President Harry S. Truman did suffer a rebuke from the Court when he seized the nation's steel mills during the Korean War to prevent a labor strike. *See Youngstown Sheet & Tube Co. v. Sawyer*, 343 U.S. 579 (1952). That there was no congressional declaration of war played a key role in that decision; moreover, that the presidential action was directed at domestic institutions—as opposed to actions/activities abroad—was an important contributor as well. Justice Robert Jackson, in his concurring opinion in *Youngstown Sheet*, identified three zones of presidential authority: (1) maximum authority—acting with express or implicit authority from Congress; (2) a "zone of twilight"—where Congress has been silent; and (3) the "lowest ebb"—acting "incompatible with the express or implied will of Congress." For other Court decisions reviewing presidential authority over foreign policy, see, e.g., *FEA v. Algonquin SNG, Inc.*, 426 U.S. 548 (1976) (presidential restrictions on oil imports upheld based on open-ended congressional delegation of authority); *Reagan v. Wald*, 468 U.S. 222 (1984) (presidential restrictions on travel to Cuban upheld given congressional authorization).

For those who want to get a better understanding of *Neagle* and Justice Sutherland's decisions in the broader context of American foreign policy, see Walter LaFeber's "The Constitution and United States Foreign Policy: An Interpretation," *The Journal of American History*, 695-717 (December 1987). For those who want to know more about Justice Sutherland, see Joel Francis Paschal's *Mr. Justice Sutherland: A Man Against the State* (Princeton University Press 1951).

CHAPTER XVI

THE SUPREME COURT DECIDES THE RIGHTS OF NATIVE AMERICANS: THE *CHEROKEE CASES*

INITIALLY, THE FOUNDING FATHERS believed that the Indians could be assimilated into American society as farmers. But the War of 1812 caused a sea change in that perspective; now, Native Americans were deemed to be "uncivilized," incapable of assimilation, and would have to be moved—by force, if necessary—to the western side of the Mississippi River (to Indian Lands Territory, later to be named Oklahoma). In the words of Andrew Jackson: "What good man would prefer a country with forests and ranged by a few thousand savages to our extensive Republic, studded with cities, towns, and prosperous farms ..., occupied by more than 12,000,000 happy people, and filled with all the blessings of liberty, civilization, and religion."

REMOVING NATIVE AMERICANS

Five Indian tribes were forced from Southern states in the 1820s and 1830s. The Choctaws and Chickasaws were moved from Mississippi. The Creeks were put in chains in Alabama (and not allowed to take weapons or cooking equipment). Initially, the

Seminoles did not cooperate and hid in the Florida Everglades; but the U.S. Army tracked them down with bloodhounds (approximately 40 percent of the tribe died during the process of being moved west). The Cherokees, based in Georgia, took a different approach: they decided to legally challenge being forced to leave their homes.

GEORGIA ON MY MIND

Unfortunately for the Cherokees, they lived in the northwestern part of the state; previously that was not an area of interest to Georgia citizens—until gold was discovered. That led to the Georgia legislature passing a series of laws in 1828 stripping the Cherokees of their rights and authorizing the removal of the tribe from any land sought by the state. Objecting to those laws, the Cherokees argued that, as an indigenous *nation*, they had negotiated treaties with the U.S. government that protected their land and their status as an independent nation (e.g., the 1791 Treaty of Holston signed by Cherokee leaders and William Blunt on behalf of the United States). The Cherokees (led by their Principal Chief, John Ross, tried to persuade President Andrew Jackson and the Congress in 1830 to live up to the existing treaties, but those efforts went nowhere.[1] They then turned to the courts.

CHEROKEE NATION V. GEORGIA

Urged on by prominent politicians opposed to President Jackson (e.g., Henry Clay, Daniel Webster) and a self-appointed lawyer championing their cause (Jeremiah Evarts), John Ross hired William Wirt (a former U.S. Attorney General) to bring a case to the Supreme Court. Although Wirt had issued an opinion as attorney

---

[1] Indeed, in May of 1930, Congress passed the Indian Removal Act, authorizing the president to set aside lands west of the Mississippi River in exchange for the lands of Indian Nations in the east.

general in 1824 denying the rights of the Cherokee's to impose a tax on American traders doing business with the Cherokee Nation, he later redeemed himself in the eyes of his new clients by issuing an opinion in 1828 recognizing the Cherokees as an independent nation, governed by their own laws.

In 1831, invoking Article III of the Constitution,[2] Wirt (and co-counsel John Sergeant) petitioned the Court for an injunction, seeking the Court "to restrain in the State of Georgia, the Governor, Attorney General, Judges, justices of the peace, sheriffs, constables and others, officers, agents, and servants of that State, from executing and enforcing the laws of Georgia, or any of these laws, or serving process, or doing anything toward the execution or enforcement of these laws within the Cherokee territory...." In support of that relief, it was argued that the Cherokees were a fully sovereign people and that the Georgia State laws violated Article VI of the Constitution (the Supremacy Clause), as well as being in breach of international treaties between the United States and the Cherokee Nation.

After a one-sided oral argument (Georgia did not send lawyers to participate), the Court handed down *Cherokee Nation v. Georgia*, 30 U.S. (5 Pet.) 1 (1831). Writing for the majority, Chief Justice John Marshall ruled that the Court lacked jurisdiction to determine the case. Because the framers of the Constitution did not consider the Indian Tribes to be "foreign nations"—they were, instead, "domestic dependent nation[s]"—there was no standing under Article III: "the relationship of the tribes to the United States resembles that of a 'ward to its guardian.'" Marshall evidenced sympathy for the Cherokee's situation and wrote that "in a proper case with proper parties" the relief sought might be possible.[3]

---

[2] The Court's "original jurisdiction" to hear "controversies ... between a state, or the citizens thereof, and foreign states, citizens or subjects."

[3] Justice William Johnson, in his concurrence, however, wrote that the "Indian tribes" were "nothing more than wondering hordes, held together only by ties of blood and habit, ... having neither rules nor government beyond what

YET ANOTHER GEORGIA LAW

While Ross and Wirt were planning their legal test case, the Georgia legislature was not idle. In 1830, it passed yet another law directed at the Cherokees—this one required "any white person" who wanted to live inside the Cherokee Nation to obtain a state license (and, in the process, swear allegiance to Georgia and Georgian law). In 1831, right before oral argument of *Cherokee Nation v. Georgia*, a group of 11 American missionaries—living inside the Cherokee Nation—defied the new law, decrying it as illegal. They were arrested on the order of George Gilmer, Georgia's governor.

After two trials, all 11 missionaries were convicted on September 13, 1831, and sentenced to four years of hard labor. Nine of the convicted men accepted pardons, but Samuel Worcester and Elizor Butler did not; those missionaries wanted to take another run at the U.S. Supreme Court. Wirt was again counsel of choice to argue the case (and, again, Georgia refused to be represented by counsel on the grounds that the Supreme Court did not have jurisdiction to hear and decide the case).

WORCESTER V. GEORGIA

On March 3, 1822, the Court handed down its decision. Chief Justice Marshall—seemingly at odds with his ruling of a year prior—now indicated that the relationship of the Indian Nations vis-à-vis the United States was the equivalent of nation-state to nation-state. Because the United Sates inherited the rights of the British Crown, it was necessary to consider the evidence that the Indian Tribes were viewed as "separate nations" back in Colonial America. Therefore, only the federal government could enter into

---

is required in a savage state." Justice Smith Thompson (joined by Justice Joseph Story) dissented, believing that there was Article III jurisdiction because of the nation of Cherokee "self-government" and the indisputable nature of the extant treaties with the United States.

treaties with them, and regulate the use of Indian lands. Thus, because the states lacked constitutional authority in such matters, Georgia's statute was invalid and Worcester and Butler could not be convicted of that invalid statute (31 U.S. (6 Pet.) 515 (1832)).[4]

THE AFTERMATH OF WORCESTER

Angered by Chief Justice Marshall's decision (which could well interfere with administration's aggressive steps to push the Indian Tribes west of the Mississippi River), President Jackson *allegedly* (and famously) said: "John Marshall has made his decision; now let him enforce it!"[5] What we know Jackson *actually* did say was "[t]he decision of the Supreme Court has fell still born, and they find that it cannot coerce Georgia to yield to its mandate."

All of the historical hubbub about the nonaction by the president is a little beside the point, however.[6] Under the Judiciary Act of 1789, Supreme Court decisions had to be remanded to the lower court; and only if the lower court failed to heed the Supreme

---

[4] Some historians believe that Marshall's pivot was caused by his regret over prior decisions about Georgia land decisions and rulings adverse to the Indian Nations (e.g., Fletcher v. Peck, 10 U.S. 87 (1810)). Justice Joseph Story, who concurred in Marshall's decision, wrote to his wife the day after the Worcester decision: "Thanks be to God, the Court can wash their hands clean of the iniquity of oppressing the Indians and disregarding their rights." Justice Henry Baldwin dissented on a procedural nicety, and also cited the Cherokee Nation decision as contrary to the substantive ruling by the Court.

[5] This quotation first turned up in 1865 in Horace Greeley's book *The American Conflict*.

[6] On March 10, 1832, Henry Clay wrote: "Our public affairs are evidently tending to a crisis. The consequences of the recent decision of the Supreme Court must be very great. If it be resisted, and the President refuses to endorse it, there is a virtual dissolution of the Union. For it will be vain to consider it and existing if a single state can put aside the laws and treaties of the U.S. and when their authority is vindicated by a decision of S. Court, the President will not perform his duty to enforce it."

Court's decision would the higher court then seek to invoke the federal government's enforcement powers. Given that the Court recessed right after *Worcester* and would not reconvene until January 1833, the federal government's enforcement mechanism was, in effect, only a hypothetical at this point.

What was not hypothetical was being played out—first in Georgia. On March 17, the trial court in Georgia was petitioned to release the two men; the court refused. When the now Georgia governor (Wilson Lumpkin) was then asked to issue pardons, he also refused (citing the overreach of the federal government).[7]

And if that were not enough, on November 24 South Carolina issued its Ordinance of Nullification—a direct repudiation of federal authority over that state's affairs (challenging the Tariff of 1828). Not only did President Jackson reject that threat to federal authority—on December 8, he issued his Nullification Proclamation, avowing that the federal government would use whatever force necessary to bring South Carolina to heel (also declaring that secession was unconstitutional)—prominent administration members delicately began lobbying Lumpkin to give pardons to Worcester and Butler; these unsuccessful efforts came at the same time the administration feared tipping Georgia into South Carolina's secession camp.

On December 22, the Georgia legislature repealed the 1830 law under which Worcester and Butler had been convicted. Pardon negotiations then picked up again, but then floundered because Governor Lumpkin wanted an admission that the two men had broken Georgia law. Ultimately, on January 14, 1833, Lumpkin

---

7 On November 6, 1832, Lumpkin told the state legislature: "The Supreme Court of the United States ... have, by their decision, attempted to overthrow the essential jurisdiction of the State in criminal cases.... I have, however, been prepared to meet this usurpation of federal power with the most prompt and determined resistance."

issued not a pardon but a proclamation, freeing Worcester and Butler from prison.[8]

On December 29, 1835, under enormous pressure from the Jackson administration, certain dissident members of the Cherokee Nation signed the Treaty of New Echota; that treaty—which provided for the tribe's removal from Georgia—was extremely unpopular with most of the tribe. Yet, under a forced march (overseen by the U.S. Army), approximately 18,000 Cherokees left Georgia in 1838 for the Indian Territory; of that number, approximately 4,000 people died on the infamous "Trail of Tears." By 1839, Jackson's successor, Martin Van Buren, was able to report: "it affords me sincere pleasure to be able to apprise you of the entire removal of the Cherokee Nation of Indians to their new homes west of the Mississippi."

POSTSCRIPTS

The starting point for knowing more about these decisions is Jill Norgen's *The Cherokee Cases: Two Landmark Federal Decisions in the Fight for Sovereignty* (University of Oklahoma Press 1996). *See also* Edwin Miles, "After John Marshall's Decision: *Worcester v. Georgia* and the Nullification Crisis," *The Journal of Southern History* (1973); Joseph Burke, "The Cherokee Cases: A Study in Law, Politics, and Morality," *Stanford Law Review* (1969). For those wanting a broader context for how American expansionism came into conflict with *Worcester* and the Indian Tribes, see Walter LaFeber's *The American Age: U.S. Foreign Policy at Home*

---

[8] On January 16, 1833, President Jackson asked Congress for military authority to crush the South Carolina rebellion, which Congress did via the Force Bill (on March 1). On that same day, Congress also passed the Compromise Tariff of 1833—an economic measure that satisfied South Carolina. With the Nullification Crisis now dialed down, South Carolina citizens convened a convention and repealed the Nullification Ordinance on March 15 (three days later the convention also nullified the Force Bill!).

and Abroad (W.W. Norton 1989). For those who want to read the leading treatise on the Van Buren presidency, see Joel H. Silbey's *Martin Van Buren and the Emergence of American Popular Politics* (Rowman & Littlefield Publishers 2002).

While the *Worcester* decision recognized Indian sovereignty, it had no effect on the executive branch's extinguishment of Indian land title. Even today Supreme Court jurisprudence vis-à-vis the rights of Native Americans continues to be controversial. In 2020, the Court decided *McGirt v. Oklahoma*, 591 U.S. ___, 140 S. Ct. 2452 (2020), in which it ruled that Congress had never technically disestablished the Five Civilized Tribes' reservation when Oklahoma was granted statehood; as such, all that land was legally Native American land. The effect of that ruling was that crimes committed on the tribes' land could *only* be prosecuted under federal law.

That led to a judicial mess in Oklahoma state courts, as numerous past criminal conviction were vacated. Then an Oklahoma court ruled that state law did not apply when a non–Native American committed a crime against a Native American on Native American land. The Supreme Court agreed to take that case and, on June 29, 2022, it ruled (five to four) that there was joint federal and state jurisdiction to prosecute non–Native Americans for such crimes. *Oklahoma v. Castro-Huerta*, 597 U.S. ___, 2022 WL 2334307 (2022). Writing for the majority, Justice Brett Kavanaugh opined that *Worcester*'s presumption that states had no jurisdiction over tribal lands had been weakened by subsequent decisions (e.g., *United States v. McBratney*, 101 U.S. 621 (1881); *United States v. Kagama*, 168 U.S. 375 (1886); *Lone Wolf v. Hitchcock*, 187 U.S. 553 (1903)) ("the *Worcester*-era understanding of funding country as separate from the State was abandoned later in the 1800s"). Justice Neil Gorsuch, who wrote the *McGirt* majority opinion was now writing in dissent. He was of the view that *Worcester* was still good law: "Where this Court once stood firm, today it wilts."

CHAPTER XVII

Nobody's Perfect: Lincoln, the Constitution, and Civil Liberties During the Civil War

As Mark Neely so aptly put it in his Pulitzer Prize–winning book, *The Fate of Liberty: Abraham Lincoln and Civil Liberties* (Oxford University Press 1991): "War and its effect on civil liberties remain a frightening unknown." The presidency of Abraham Lincoln is, of course, justly famous for many things, such as saving the Union and emancipating the slaves. Less well known (and certainly not well celebrated) is his administration's track record vis-à-vis constitutional rights during the prosecution of the Civil War. This chapter highlights two judicial decisions—one by the Chief Justice of the United States and another by an Associate Justice of the Supreme Court—that serve as Supreme bookends to help better understand Lincoln's record.

Ex Parte Merryman

Before the Civil War started in earnest, the most dangerous state in the Union was clearly Maryland. Lincoln, faced with numerous well-documented assassination plots awaiting him there on his 1861 trip from Illinois to Washington, had to take a secret train through Baltimore to ensure his safe arrival. Maryland, a border state surrounding the U.S. Capitol, was also a slave state; Lincoln had received only 2,294 votes there in the 1860 election and many of its citizens were decidedly not in favor of the incoming administration (and, conversely, more sympathetic to the Deep South states that had already seceded).

After Fort Sumter was fired upon in Charleston Harbor and shortly thereafter had surrendered, Lincoln on April 15, 1861, called for the states to send 75,000 militiamen to Washington to help suppress the rebellion. Unfortunately, the only railroad access to the District of Columbia from the north came through Maryland.

On April 19, a Baltimore mob attacked the Sixth Massachusetts Regiment as it attempted to get to the U.S. Capitol; many deaths and injuries resulted. As a result, Maryland's governor and other state officials implored the president not to have any more troops sent through the state. Maryland citizens thereafter destroyed the railroad bridges in Baltimore and cut the city's telegraph lines linking it (and the District of Columbia) to the north.

On April 26, the Maryland legislature met to consider secession. The following day, Lincoln authorized the suspension of the writ of habeas corpus for the area between Philadelphia and Washington. The president's order was directed to military authorities only, giving them the right to arrest people aiding the rebels or threatening to overthrow the government (with any arrestee not eligible for release under a writ of habeas corpus).

On May 25, John Merryman was arrested under an order issued by Brigadier General William Hugh Klein. Merryman, a lieutenant in a secessionist drill company in Cockeysville, Maryland, was accused of destroying railroad bridges and planning to take his company south to join the Confederate army. Merryman was imprisoned in Fort McHenry, overlooking the Baltimore harbor.

Merryman's lawyers sought out Chief Justice Roger Taney, author of the odious *Dred Scott* decision (*see* Chapter I), whose judicial circuit encompassed Maryland; they asked Taney to issue a writ of habeas corpus, which Taney did on May 26. Taney ordered General George Cadwalader, whose jurisdiction covered Fort McHenry, to produce Merryman before Taney in Maryland federal court on May 27. That day, Cadwalader instead sent an Army colonel with a written explanation stating that he was acting under presidential authority, detailing the facts underlying Merryman's arrest, and asking for an extension to get more guidance from the president.

Taney, upset that there had been "no official notice" given to the courts or the public of the presidential claim of power, refused the request and held Cadwalader in contempt. On May 28, three things happened:

1. Cadwalader received express instructions from the U.S. Army ordering him, under the president's authority, to continue holding Merryman in custody;
2. A U.S. Marshal appeared at Fort McHenry, attempting (unsuccessfully) to execute on Taney's writ of attachment to seize Cadwalader for purposes of enforcing the contempt order; and
3. Taney issued an oral opinion, which ultimately became *Ex Parte Merryman*, 17 F. Cas. 144 (C.C.D. Md. 1861).

As is clear from the citation, Taney's opinion—issued from his Supreme Court chambers—was filed in federal court in Maryland on June 1, 1861. Nonetheless, legal historians continue to debate its jurisdictional basis—some argue it was merely a circuit court decision, while others argue that Taney, as Chief Justice, was acting pursuant to Section 14 of the Judiciary Act of 1789, which grants certain authority to federal judges. Following up on his oral ruling, Taney wrote that Lincoln had clearly violated the Constitution. More specifically, the problem was that only Congress had suspension authority, pursuant to Article I, Section 9, where the specific language about habeas corpus is located:[1] "This article is devoted to the Legislative Department of the United States, and has not the slightest reference to the Executive Department." Also citing English law (whereby the Parliament, not the King, has that power), Taney further cited Justice Story's "Commentaries," as well as Chief Justice John Marshall's opinion in *Ex Parte Bellman*.[2]

Having found the president in violation of the Constitution, however, Taney did not order Merryman's release; rather, he directed that a copy of his opinion be transmitted to the president, where it would "remain for that high officer, in fulfillment of his constitutional obligation, to 'take care that the laws be faithfully executed,' to determine what response he will take to cause the civil process of the United States to be respected and enforced."

Lincoln, faced with this direct judicial rebuke to his authority and actions, did nothing—at least initially. On May 30, with Merryman remaining in Fort McHenry, Lincoln privately asked Attorney General Edward Bates to prepare "the argument for the suspension of the Habeas Corpus." At the same time, he broadened the suspension to cover the area between New York City and Washington, and placed Secretary of State William Henry Seward in overall charge of the process (under whom it would remain until February 1862, when its oversight shifted to the War Department).

On July 4, with Congress now in session, Lincoln sent on a formal message defending his actions in Congress' absence. Its reasoning was not airtight and its words and tone were defensive (to say the least). He wrote that "extraordinary measures" had been undertaken post-Sumter, but trusted the Congress would ratify them. Acknowledging that some acts might not have been "strictly

---

[1] "The Privilege of the Writ of Habeas Corpus shall not be suspended, unless when in Cases of Rebellion or Invasion the public Safety may require it."

[2] 8 U.S. 75 (1807). "If at any time the public safety should require the suspension of the powers vested by this act in the courts of the United States, it is for the Legislature to say so."

legal," Lincoln first assured Congress that while the suspension of habeas corpus "might [be] deem[ed] dangerous to the public safety ... [it had] purposely been exercised but very sparingly."[3] Responding to Taney's taunt that one charged to "faithfully execute" the laws "should not himself violate them," Lincoln offered the following rhetorical question:

> [A]re all the laws, but one, to go unexecuted, and the government itself go to pieces, lest that one be violated? Even in such a case, would not the official oath be broken, if the government should be overthrown, when it was believed that disregarding the single law, would tend to preserve it?

Then, having posed that question "directly," Lincoln added (in the passive voice): "But it was not believed that this question was presented. It was not believed that any law was violated." Why not? Because there was obviously a case of rebellion, Congress was absent, the Constitution was silent as to whether Congress or the president could exercise the power, and "it cannot be believed that the framers of the [Constitution] intended that in every case the danger should run its course until Congress could be called together, the very assembling of which might be prevented, as was intended in this case by the rebellion."

In 1861, Congress did not pass legislation ratifying Lincoln's past suppressions or authorizing future ones. Nonetheless, and notwithstanding Lincoln's less than confident arguments for bis authority and actions, that did not dissuade him from issuing another order to the military on October 14, 1861. By that order, the area in which the habeas suspension covered now spanned Washington to Bangor, Maine.

---

[3] That was not quite true—besides Merryman, among those also arrested and imprisoned at Fort McHenry included the mayor of Baltimore, the entire city council, the police commissioner, and the entire police board.

RUNNING THE "MACHINE".

1864 Cartoon Depicting Lincoln's Cabinet (and Seward's Little Bell)
(Author's Collection)

On August 8, 1862, the suspension was expanded to cover the entire country. That order (issued by the Secretary of War, pursuant to presidential authority) also added a new provision: those arrested would be "tried before a military commission." Subsequently, on September 24, Lincoln issued a proclamation, publicly announcing the nationwide scope of the suspension.

Congress ultimately got in on the matter with the Habeas Corpus Act of March 3, 1863. That statute gave prospective legal cover, but did not clear up whether the presidential actions prior thereto had always been legal, or were legal now only because of congressional approval. Later that year came another presidential proclamation, this one issued on September 15. Now the suspension would "continue throughout the duration of the said rebellion."

With that "legal" chapter on civil liberties seemingly closed, attention would now turn to the issue of military commission trials.

First, Vallandigham

The first prominent military trial of a civilian was that of leading Copperhead politician Clement Vallandigham. Since that episode will be detailed in the next chapter (*see* Chapter XVIII), it will not be covered here. One thing the Vallandigham imbroglio did do was to give Lincoln a chance to present a far more effective public defense of his administration.

In response to what has come to be known as the "Corning letter" (a June 12, 1863, public letter by a group of Albany Democrats, led by Erastus Corning, head of the New York Central Railroad, condemning the Vallandigham arrest and trial as being "against the spirit of our laws and Constitution ... the liberty of speech and of the press, the right of trial by jury, the law of evidence, and the privilege of habeas corpus."), Lincoln published a reply. Because the legislative-executive issue was no longer in play, Lincoln started on stronger footing: obviously the Constitution provided for a suspension of the writ in "cases of Rebellion or Invasion, [when] the public Safety may require it." That the United States faced a rebellion was "clear, flagrant, and gigantic." Then, addressing what had led to Vallandigham's arrest (a vitriolic speech, denouncing the war as an effort to liberate African-Americans and enslave Whites), Lincoln—worried about the effect such inflammatory speeches would have on the military draft—wrote that the speaker was arrested "because he was damaging the army, upon the existence, and vigor of which, the life of the nation depends."

Lincoln then posed a rhetorical question that long resonated with the public: "Must I shoot a simple-minded soldier who deserts, while I must not touch a hair of the wily agitator who induces him to desert?" (Thereafter, Vallandigham's well-accepted nickname was the "wily agitator"!)

Next, Milligan

Lambdin P. Milligan, a Huntington, Indiana, lawyer and disappointed office seeker, joined an organization named Sons of

Liberty; its avowed purpose was to open Northern prison camps and foment an insurrection in the Midwest. In October 1864, he (and four co-conspirators) were arrested by the U.S. Army. A military trial followed and, on December 10, 1864, Milligan was found guilty and sentenced to death by hanging.

On May 10, 1865, nine days before Milligan's scheduled execution, his lawyer petitioned the federal court in Indianapolis for a writ of habeas corpus. Importantly, part of that petition included the fact that a federal grand jury had met in January 1865 and had refused to indict Milligan.

Two different judges reviewed the Milligan petition: Supreme Court Justice David Davis, whose circuit court jurisdiction included Indiana, and Judge David McDonald, a federal district judge in Indianapolis. Because they reached different conclusions—McDonald was against granting the writ and Davis was in favor—the case was certified to be reviewed by the U.S. Supreme Court, with three specific questions to be addressed:

1. Should the writ be issued?
2. Should Milligan be released from custody?
3. Did the military commission that conducted Milligan's trial had jurisdiction to do so?

Lengthy arguments before the Court concluded on March 13, 1866. On April 3, Chief Justice Salmon Chase orally ruled that the military commission did not have jurisdiction over Milligan and ordered that a writ be issued for his release. But it was not until December 17, 1866, that the Court issued a written decision(s). *Ex Parte Milligan*, 71 U.S. 109 (1866).

Justice Davis, an old friend and political ally of Lincoln (he had been his campaign manager at the 1860 Republican convention), wrote the majority opinion. It began by emphasizing that "the importance of the main question presented ... cannot be overstated; for it involves the very framework of the government and the fundamental principles of American liberty." At issue were "the rights of the whole people; for it is the birthright of every American citizen when charged with a crime, to be tried and punished according to the law."

Drawing upon the Fourth, Fifth, and Sixth Amendments, Davis used the Bill of Rights for the first time to expand civil liberty, ruling that the Constitution prohibited the trial of citizens by a military commission when civil courts were open and available (as they were in Indiana).

Chief Justice Chase issued a concurring opinion, joined in by two other justices. Chase agreed that Milligan was entitled to an Article III civil court trial, but disagreed with respect to the relevance of Congress' 1863 legislation. Davis's opinion took the view that the habeas corpus statute overstepped Congress' reach by authorizing trials by military commission. In Chase's view, Congress did have that authority, but the 1863 law had not, in fact, authorized such trials.

Immediate reaction to the Court's decision—a direct repudiation of Lincoln's wartime stewardship—was decidedly mixed.

In the North, especially among those seeking post-war retribution against the South (enforced by the military), there was great consternation, with a number of critics calling Davis's decision "the new *Dred Scott*."

On the other hand, Southern editorial writers, hoping for a quick end to military trials in their jurisdictions (President Andrew Johnson had ordered them to cease in 1866; in fact, the last one took place in 1869), took a different tack: they viewed the opinions far more favorably ("the Democracy of the nation has now been vindicated.").

While many legal scholars and historians have hailed *Milligan* as "a great triumph for civil liberties in time of war," Mark Neely dismissed the opinion as "irrelevant" and having had "little effect on history."

He has a point.

It was of no moment in stopping President Woodrow Wilson from engineering thousands of domestic arrests and subsequent trials during World War I (under the Espionage Act of 1917, the Sedition Act of 1918, and the Alien Enemies Act of 1798).

It did not stop President Franklin D. Roosevelt's imprisoning 120,000 American citizens of Japanese descent in World War II, with the Supreme Court's subsequent approval of that terrible act—the *Korematsu* decision (*see* Chapter III).

During that same period, the Court also decided *Ex Parte Quirin*, 317 U.S. 1 (1942) (a military trial of eight Nazi saboteurs arrested in the United States—two were U.S. citizens—was upheld; *Milligan* was ruled not applicable because the German spies were considered unlawful enemy combatants). And in more recent times, with respect to individuals "detained" during the never-ending war against terrorism that began after 9/11, *Milligan* has not seemed to have had much relevance. *See Rasul v. Bush*, 542 U.S. 466 (2004); *Hamdi v. Rumsfeld*, 542 U.S. 507 (2004); *Hamdan v. Rumsfeld*, 548 U.S. 557 (2006); *Boumodiene v. Bush*, 553 U.S. 723 (2008).

POSTSCRIPTS

No one knows with certainty just how many civilians were arrested, held without habeas corpus, and ultimately subjected to military trials during the Civil War. Mark Neely, who has done extensive work in the historical archives, puts the number well north of 10,000.

During the period that this process was under the jurisdiction of Secretary William Henry Seward, he is reputed to have told the British ambassador: "I can touch a bell on my right hand, and order the arrest of a citizen of Ohio; I can touch a bell again, and order the imprisonment of a citizen of New York; and no power on earth, except that of the President, can release them. Can the Queen of England do so much?" This quotation (which was widely referred to as "Seward's Little Bell") first appeared in anti-administration newspapers in 1863, but there is little evidence that Seward in fact said these words to anyone, let alone to the British ambassador. Notwithstanding, as one historian has written, "Seward had more arbitrary power over the freedom of individual American citizens all over the country than any other man has ever had, before or since."

For those wanting to read more on these subjects, in addition to Neely's excellent book (*The Fate of Liberty: Abraham Lincoln and Civil Liberties* (Oxford University Press 1991)), there is a wonderful compendium of essays in *Ex Parte Milligan Reconsidered: Race and Civil Liberties from the Lincoln Administration to the War on Terror* (ed. Stewart Winger & Jonathan White) (University Press of Kansas 2020); *see also* Frank Williams, "Abraham Lincoln, Civil Liberties, and Maryland," in *The Civil War in Maryland Reconsidered* (Louisiana State University Press 2021) (ed. Charles Mitchell & Jean Baker). The best one-volume biography on Lincoln is David Donald's 1995 book *Lincoln* (Simon & Schuster); the best multi-volume biography on Lincoln is Michael Burlingame's magisterial *Abraham Lincoln: A Life* (Johns Hopkins University Press 2008).

CHAPTER XVIII

Nobody's Perfect: Lincoln, the Constitution, and Civil Liberties During the Civil War (Part II)

THE PREVIOUS CHAPTER gave a (teasing) hint into President Abraham Lincoln's political and legal persecution of Clement Vallandigham, a figure lost to history. Even to many American historians he rates—at most—a footnote. But Vallandigham was an important political figure during the Civil War era (albeit not in a positive vein), and his trials during that time period provide us with important (and interesting) lessons.

His Early Political Career

Born and raised in Ohio, Vallandigham briefly practiced law in Dayton before being elected to the Ohio legislature in 1845. Losing races for a variety of elective posts thereafter, he tried again in 1856, running for Congress, but he was narrowly defeated. Claiming illegal voting, Vallandigham challenged the result before the House of Representatives and was successful (he was seated on the penultimate day of the congressional term). Vallandigham was reelected in both 1858 and 1860. In that latter year, the Ohio congressman also labored hard to elect Stephen Douglas to the presidency, believing that Douglas's doctrine of "popular sover-eignty" was the only way out of the growing sectional conflict over the expansion of slavery. Indeed, he prophesied that if the Demo-cratic Party could not unite behind and elect Douglas, "the result will be the disruption of the Union, and one of the bloodiest civil wars on record, the magnitude of which no man can estimate."

After Lincoln's election, Vallandigham made various attempts to find ways to prevent what he had prophesied. For example, he traveled to Richmond to urge Virginians not to follow South Car-olina out of the Union. Later, in February 1861, he gave a speech in the House of Representatives entitled "The Great American Revolution"; in it he blamed the "belligerent" Republican Party for the sectional crisis and proposed three Constitutional amend-ments as a means to avoid civil war: a thirteenth amendment that would divide the country into four sections—North, South, West, and Pacific (a majority of the electorate from each section would be required to elect the president); a fourteenth amendment that would address the issue of secession (no state could secede unless all of the states in its geographical section approved); and a fif-teenth amendment that would guarantee equal rights to all cit-izens in the territories (thereby authorizing popular sovereignty and enabling slave owners to bring their "property" anywhere they chose to do so). Those proposals garnered Vallandigham a lot of publicity, most of it highly negative (the proposals were "pure and simple treason," he was "the biggest fool in America," perhaps he believed "the hair of the dog would cure his bite," etc.). With his (and others') proposals for compromise proving unworkable as the polarized debate became even more hardened, Lincoln was inau-gurated as President on March 4, 1861. After the firing upon Fort Sumter, Douglas pledged his support to his long-time rival, Lin-coln, and urged Northern Democrats to follow his lead: "There are but two parties, the party of patriots and the party of traitors. We belong to the first." Shortly thereafter, Douglas was felled by typhoid and he died on June 3, 1861. Vallandigham did not wait for his political patron to die, however, before parting ways.

From his home in Dayton (Congress was not in session), Vallandigham publicly blamed the war on Lincoln and opposed the North's attempting to coerce the seceding states to rejoin the Union by military force: "It is too late for anything except peaceful separation." These well-circulated sentiments were quickly branded as "dastardly treason," and Vallandigham was soon the most hated member of Congress. Not dissuaded, when Congress was back in session by the summer of 1861, Vallandigham introduced seven resolutions in the House, seeking to censure Lincoln for a host of "unconstitutional acts." They went nowhere. Another resolution, seeking a "Convention of the States" at which "all controversies" would be addressed, also went nowhere. By now, many subscribed to the view of one of Vallandigham's former, close friends: "He is more than a Judas; he is a damned traitor!"

Vallandigham, however, thought he was right and refused to budge. And when the second session of the 37th Congress convened in December 1861, he put his foot down on the pedal.

Initially, he tried to make political hay by criticizing Lincoln's defusing of a foreign policy crisis with England (done to discourage England from recognizing the Confederacy as a legitimate nation state under international law). Then, he proposed legislation to arrest and imprison Lincoln if the President were to continue to arbitrarily arrest people considered to be hurting the war effort. Warning that "[w]e are in the throes of revolution," Vallandigham also fought various efforts aimed at the emancipation of slaves and the abolition of slavery.

LEADER OF THE COPPERHEADS

Although viciously attacked by many in Congress (around this time the term "Copperhead" came into the political lexicon; it was used against Vallandigham and his fellow peace Democrats; it is not only a snake in the grass, but a poisonous one to boot), Dayton's congressman lined up 35 fellow Democratic representatives behind his pro-peace, anti-administration screed and he wrote to ex-President Franklin Pierce that he believed his efforts would pay off at the polls in 1862.

Unfortunately for Vallandigham two things made his own prospects for reelection in that year not optimal. First, the Ohio legislature (dominated by Republicans) redrew his district, adding a large swatch of Republican votes (and he had won in 1860 by only 134 votes). Second, his Republican opponent was Robert Schenck, a Union general wounded at Second Battle of Bull Run whom Lincoln had personally recruited to run against the hated Copperhead. The incumbent fought as best he could, whipping up a virulent, race-baiting vision: "The Constitution as it is, the Union as it was, and the N[***] where they are." But it was not enough. In an election year where the Democratic Party made strong gains across the North, Vallandigham went down to defeat by more than 600 votes.

The Republicans, with little else to boast, rejoiced in his electoral downfall:

> [T]hat pimp of Jeff. Davis and standing disgrace to his State, Clem Vallandigham, is laid out cold and stark in the embrace of political death.... He is dead, dead, dead—and a loyal people will bury him so deep in the mire of his own infamy, that the stench from his putrid carcass will never offend the nostrils of good men, nor the recollection of his treason and perfidy tarnish the fair name of the State he has long misrepresented and dishonored.

But Vallandigham, believing it was only gerrymandering that defeated him, was unbowed. In fact, he was emboldened by the Democrats' general electoral successes, and undertook something of a victory lap of speaking engagements before Northern, war-weary audiences. This experience would soon lead him to a constitutional confrontation that ultimately the U.S. Supreme Court would have to pass on.

With his congressional career over, Vallandigham turned his sights on the Ohio governor's seat. Facing opposition from within his party, he devised a somewhat unusual strategy: to become a martyr to the war effort. Major General Ambrose Burnside, the War Department's commander of the Department of the Ohio, had issued General Order No. 38, on April 13, 1863; that document (with a supplemental order issued a week later) boldly declared that anyone "declaring sympathies for the enemy" would be arrested, tried as a spy or traitor by a military tribunal, and if convicted put to death. On May 1, 1863, Vallandigham, speaking for almost two hours before a large audience assembled to celebrate the democracy of Knox County (and knowing Burnside's agents were present and taking detailed notes), not only directly attacked Burnside and his attempts to stifle free speech but also decried "King Lincoln" and urged his listeners to use the "ballot box" to dethrone him. Four days later, at two a.m., Vallandigham was arrested (forcibly) at his Dayton home, leaving behind his "sobbing, hysterical wife."

A Military Trial

To his supporters, Clement Vallandigham was indeed a martyr, falsely "kidnapped" by "cowardly, scoundrelly abolitionists." And a number of them rioted and burned down the *Dayton Journal,* which was the local Republican paper. Nonetheless, Burnside went ahead with a military trial on May 7 before eight Union officers. With Vallandigham protesting the authority of the tribunal and declining to have counsel represent him, the trial went forward and the specific charges were laid out against him; they included:

- he had called the conflict "a wicked, cruel, and unnecessary war";
- he had called the conflict "a war not being waged for the preservation of the Union";

- he had called the conflict "a war for the purpose of crushing out liberty and erecting a despotism";
- he had called the conflict "a war for the freedom of the blacks, and the enslavement of the whites";
- he had called General Order No. 38 "a base usurpation of arbitrary authority," urging his listeners to disobey the directive; and
- he had vowed "to do what he could to defeat the attempts now being made to build up a monarchy upon the ruins of our free government."

Asked how he pleaded to these charges, Vallandigham tried to filibuster; the presiding officer cut him off and entered a not guilty plea.

After a brisk two-day trial, the inevitable guilty verdict was rendered. But what to do with the treasonous, former congressman? Rejecting execution, the penalty was determined that he be "placed in dire confinement in some fortress of the United States, . . . there to be kept during the [duration] of the war."

On May 11, former Ohio Senator George Pugh moved for a writ of habeas corpus on Vallandigham's behalf in the U.S. District Court for the Southern District of Ohio. Judge Humphrey Leavitt denied the motion; basically ignoring Chief Justice Roger Taney's decision in *Ex Parte Merryman*,[1] Leavitt ruled that the arrest and trial were validly conducted pursuant to the president's authority as commander-in-chief.

EXILE

Although Burnside swiftly chose a suitable prison (Fort Warren) for Vallandigham, the political heat that this brouhaha generated caused Lincoln to intervene. The president, who considered

---

[1] 17 F. Cas. 144 (C.C.D. Md. 1861) (sitting as a federal circuit judge, Taney held that only Congress could suspend habeas corpus),

the Copperhead leader to be a "wily agitator" (but, who also, in the words of his Secretary of the Navy, "regret[ted] what ha[d] been done" by Burnside), came up with an inspired thought: he ordered Vallandigham out of the Union, and (with safe passage) deported him into the hands of the Confederate army.

Not surprisingly, the Southern states did not want Vallandigham (he publicly declared himself "a prisoner of war"); and after he bounced back and forth between a number of Dixie states, the Copperhead was allowed to board a ship that evaded the Union blockade and made its way to Bermuda. From there, Vallandigham was able to get to Canada.

While on his odyssey, Vallandigham's machinations seem to pay off. On June 11, the delegates to the Ohio Democratic State Convention voted 411 to 11 to nominate the former congressman to run for governor. Once he reached Canada, Vallandigham formally accepted his party's nomination. He campaigned in abstentia, with prominent Ohio Democrats trekking instead to visit the candidate in Canada.

On October 13, 1863, the citizens of Ohio went to the polls. Vallandigham's opponent was John Brough, a pro-war Democrat who ran on the Republican-sponsored Union ticket. Vallandigham lost by a landslide: 288,374 to 187,492. In his diary, Secretary of the Navy Gideon Welles reported on Lincoln's reaction the following day:

> I stopped in to see and congratulate the President, who is in good spirits and greatly relieved from the depression of yesterday. He told me he had more anxiety in regards to the election results of yesterday than he had in 1860 when he was chosen. He could not, he said, have believed four years ago, that one genuine American would, or could be induced to vote for such a man as Vallandigham, yet he has been made the candidate of a large party—their representative man, and has received a vote that is a discredit to

1864 Cartoon Depicting Lincoln's Administration Burying the Constitution
(Author's Collection)

the country. The President showed a great deal of emotion
as he dwelt on this subject, and his regrets were sincere.

One important lesson Lincoln and his Republican Party
operatives learned from this experience for 1864 was the importance of the soldier vote, which broke approximately 95 percent
for Brough. The governor-elect subsequently visited Lincoln at
the White House and expressed regret that he had not won by a
greater margin. Lincoln later remarked that he was reminded of
a "man who had been greatly annoyed by an ugly dog [and] took
a club and knocked the dog on the head and killed him; but he
still continued to whack the animal, when a passer-by cried out
to him, 'Why, what are you about, man? Don't you see the dog
is dead? Where is the use of beating him now?' 'Yes,' replied the

man, whacking away at the dog, 'I know he is dead, but I wanted to teach the mean dog that there is punishment after death.' Poor Val was dead before the election, but Brough wanted to keep on whacking him, as the man did the dog, after death."

In the meantime, Vallandigham's legal challenge to his prosecution continued, with George Pugh applying for a writ of certiorari to the U.S. Supreme Court. On January 22, 1864, the Court heard argument on the application (although Chief Justice Taney was too ill to attend). Less than a month later, on February 15, 1864, a unanimous Court (per Justice James Wayne) rejected the arguments put forward by Vallandigham's counsel (*Ex Parte Vallandigham*, 68 U.S. (1 Wal.) 243 (1864)). The Court determined that it did not have the power to "originate a writ of certiorari to review ... the proceedings of a military commission." Because it ruled on jurisdictional grounds, the Court took no position on whether Vallandigham's arrest, trial, and sentence were illegal. No mention was made of Chief Justice Taney's prior *Merryman* decision; in fact, Taney was listed as being in favor of the outcome (although he confided to friends that he was despondent over the future of the Court and the Constitution). Public opinion on the Court's ruling was predictably mixed: the Republicans were pleased, the Copperheads were not.

The 1864 Election

Undeterred, Vallandigham was determined to play a key role in the 1864 presidential race, hoping to defeat Lincoln and put in his place a successor committed to peace. To assist him, his Ohio friends snuck him across the border and back into Ohio, where he attended the Third District Democracy's Convention on June 15, 1864; he was chosen as a delegate to the party's National Convention in Chicago. The Lincoln administration learned of the Copperhead's return to the United States and his growing political visibility. Concerned that any action by the government would only help to promote Vallandigham's popularity, Lincoln decided to do nothing. That hands-off policy allowed Vallandigham to travel to Chicago in August and play a critical role in the drafting and adoption of a "peace plank" in his party's platform; it proclaimed that the war was a failure and "immediate efforts [must] be made for a cessation of hostilities, with a view to an ultimate convention of the States, or other peaceable means, to the end that, at the earliest practicable moment." When the party's nominee, General George McClellan formally accepted the nomination, however, he repudiated the "peace plank": "I could not look in the face of my gallant comrades of the army and navy, who have survived so many bloody battles, and tell them that their labors and the sacrifices of so many of our slain and wounded brethren had been in vain; that we had abandoned that Union for which we have so often periled our lives."

This exposed schism between the two wings of the Democratic Party, together with an improving economy and a surge in Union victories on the battlefield (e.g., Atlanta), took away any chance of McClellan prevailing. In November, Lincoln won reelection easily.

After the War

With the North victorious six months later, one would think that Vallandigham would have finally packed it in and retreated from public life with dispatch. But he did not. He publicly (and repeatedly) advocated an easy peace with the South, with no vindictive acts to be taken against individuals; he also argued against the emancipated peoples receiving full political and social rights. In addition, Vallandigham, with visions of political rehabilitation, plotted to become one of Ohio's U.S. Senators; but those efforts did not work out as he had hoped. He was drafted in 1868 to run against Robert Schenck again for his old congressional seat. "Waving the bloody shirt," the Republicans made the contest a choice between patriotism and treason. Patriotism won, although Vallandigham did run ahead of the national ticket.

He still had politics in his veins and had not given up hope of someday getting to the Senate, but Vallandigham had to earn a living. In December 1869, he started a law firm with Daniel Haynes, a prominent local jurist. In short order, the firm prospered.

In 1871, Vallandigham took over the defense of a man charged with murder. He was attempting to prove that the victim had in fact accidentally shot himself, and during a break in the trial Vallandigham showed his colleagues how he would demonstrate this before the jury. Unfortunately, he chose to pick up a loaded pistol. Pressing it close to his body and pulling the trigger, Vallandigham cried out: "My God, I've shot myself!" Twelve hours later, he died; he was 50 years old.

POSTSCRIPT

The definitive biography of Vallandigham is by Frank L. Klement, *The Limits of Dissent: Clement L. Vallandigham and the Civil War* (University Press of Kentucky 1970). In addition to the two works on Lincoln identified in Chapter XVII, readers may also want to consult Edward L. Widmer's *Lincoln on the Verge: Thirteen Days to Washington* (Simon & Schuster 2020); *Our Lincoln: New Perspectives on Lincoln and His World* (W.W. Norton 2008) (ed. Eric Foner); William C. Harris's *Lincoln and the Border States: Preserving the Union* (University Press of Kansas 2011); and Michael Burlingame & John R. Turner Ettlinger (eds.), *Inside Lincoln's White House: The Complete Civil War Diary of John Hay* (Southern Illinois University Press 1997). The seminal work on the Democratic Party during this period in American history is by Joel H. Silbey, *A Respectable Minority: The Democratic Party in the Civil War Era, 1860-1868* (W.W. Norton 1977).

CHAPTER XIX

Did William Rehnquist Lie?
First to Become a Supreme Court
Justice, and Later to Become
Chief Justice

In December of 1952, William H. Rehnquist wrote a memorandum to his boss, Supreme Court Justice Robert H. Jackson. It likely was written just after the first set of oral arguments on the legendary case *Brown v. Board of Education*, 347 U.S. 483 (1954). The title of the memorandum was "A Random Thought on the Segregation Cases." To many legal historians it is the most "notorious" memorandum ever written by a Supreme Court clerk.

A Random Thought (or Two)

Rehnquist's memorandum is a brief, six-paragraph document. The bulk of the memorandum deals with cases that caused the Supreme Court to get into "hot water"—e.g., *Dred Scott* (*see* Chapter I), *Lochner* (*see* Chapter IV), and the Court's decisions invalidating the first set of New Deal legislation (*see* Chapter XIV).

The document then turns to parts of the oral argument recently proffered—by John W. Davis and by Thurgood Marshall. Davis (of Davis Polk & Wardwell) represented the state of South Carolina; he had argued that the resolution of the issue must be left to Congress, and that the Justices' personal views should not play a decisive role in the outcome. In response, Rehnquist wrote:

> [T]he Court is, as Davis suggested, being asked to read its own sociological views into the Constitution. Urging a view palpably at variance with precedent and probably with legislative history, appellants seek to convince the Court of the moral wrongness of the treatment they are receiving. I would suggest that this is a question the Court need never reach; for regardless of the Justice's individual views and the merits of segregation, it quite clearly is not one of those extreme cases which commands intervention from one of any conviction. If this Court, because its members individually are "liberal," and dislike segregation, now chooses to strike it down, it differs from the [Anti–New Deal Court] only in the kinds of litigants it favors and the kinds of special claims it protects. To those who would argue that "personal" rights are more sacrosanct than "property" rights, the short answer is that the Constitution makes no such distinction.

Marshall (of the NAACP) had famously based much of his argument on sociological evidence. Indeed, before the Court, he asked that it take judicial notice of Gunnar Myrdal's *An American Dilemma: The Negro Problem and Modern Democracy* (Harper 1944), which detailed the causes and consequences of segregation (the Court in fact took Marshall up on his request; see note 11 in the *Brown* decision). To that point, the Rehnquist memorandum replied: "If the Fourteenth Amendment did not enact Spencer's *Social Statios* [sic] [a reference to Justice Holmes's famous dissent in *Lochner*], it just as surely did not enact Myrdal's *American Dilemma.*"

If that had been the totality of Rehnquist's memorandum, it is highly unlikely it would have become so famous/infamous. It is the penultimate sentence that has caused the big kerfuffle: "I realize that it is an unpopular and unhumanitarian position for which I have been excoriated by "liberal" colleagyes [sic], but I think *Plessy v. Ferguson* was right and should be re-affirmed." *Plessy*, of course, is one of the *worst* cases in the Court's entire jurisprudence, where the Court (with one dissent) embraced the "separate but equal" doctrine (*see* Chapter II).

NOMINEE TO THE SUPREME COURT

William Rehnquist joined the Nixon administration as an assistant attorney general, in charge of the Office of Legal Counsel. The president's first meeting with him did not go well; Nixon told his White House Counsel (John Dean) that Rehnquist "dressed like a clown" (pink shirt, psychedelic tie, etc.). Nonetheless, in 1971, the president nominated Rehnquist, along with Lewis F. Powell, to fill the vacant seats of Justices Hugo Black and John Marshall Harlan II.

Rehnquist's nomination was opposed by many Democratic senators, but it looked like he would nonetheless be confirmed (the Senate Judiciary Committee voted out his nomination 12 to 4). On December 6, 1971, however, just as the Senate was ready to debate his appointment, *Newsweek* magazine released the text of the Rehnquist memorandum, written 19 years before. At first, Rehnquist stood silent on the document and whether he was even its author (his initials, WHR, are at the bottom of the memorandum).

Two days later, he delivered a letter to the Chairman of the Senate Judiciary Committee, James O. Eastland (D-MS). In his letter, Rehnquist wrote:

> As best I can reconstruct the circumstances after nineteen years, the memorandum was prepared by me at Justice Jackson's request; it was intended as a rough draft of a statement of *his* views at the conference of the Justices, rather than as a statement of my views.... He expressed

concern that the conference should have the benefit of all of the arguments in support of the constitutionality of the "separate but equal" doctrine, as well as those against its constitutionality.

* * *

I am satisfied that the memorandum was not designed to be a statement of *my* views on these cases. Justice Jackson not only would not have welcomed such a submission in this form, but he would have quite emphatically rejected it and, I believe, admonished the clerk who had submitted it. I am fortified in this conclusion because the bald, simplistic conclusion that "*Plessy v. Ferguson* was right and should be re-affirmed" is not an accurate statement of my own views at the time.

I believe that the memorandum was prepared by me as a statement of Justice Jackson's tentative views for his own use at conference. The informal nature of the memorandum and its lack of any introductory language make me think that it was prepared very shortly after one of our oral discussions of the subject. It is absolutely inconceivable to me that I would have prepared such a document without previous oral discussion with him and specific instructions to do so.

* * *

In view of some of the recent Senate floor debate, I wish to state unequivocally that I fully support the legal reasoning and the rightness from the standpoint of fundamental fairness of the *Brown* decision. (Emphasis in original.)

Rehnquist's 1952 memorandum and his 1971 written explanation of it were debated by the Senate. After a week (and with Christmas looming), the nomination was approved by a vote of 68 to 26.

A Second Time Around (Under Oath)

In 1986, Chief Justice Warren Burger announced his retirement and President Ronald Reagan nominated William Rehnquist to succeed him. Now Rehnquist's opponents would get to ask him—under oath—what they had not been able to do in 1971; to wit, they could interrogate him on his 1952 memorandum.

Rehnquist began his testimony before the Judiciary Committee by reaffirming his 1971 letter to Senator Eastland: "[I] have absolutely no reason to doubt its correctness now." He then tried to mitigate the discordant sentiments voiced in his memorandum. First off, he declared that he had always "thought Plessy against Ferguson was wrong," even when he had clerked for Justice Jackson. (This reiterated an assertion previously written in his 1971 letter to Senator Eastland.) At the same time, however, he noted that Plessy "had been on the books for 69 years, [that Congress had not acted in the interim, and] that the same Congress that promulgated the 14th Amendment had required segregated schools in the District [of Columbia].... [Accordingly, he (and Justice Jackson)] saw factors on both sides." Rehnquist also pledged his fealty to Brown—both as to its outcome and reasoning. (This also tracked an assertion that had been made in his 1971 letter to Senator Eastland.) Rehnquist next attempted to put the historical portions of his memorandum into the context of Justice Jackson's own previously expressed views:

> Justice Jackson was a great believer in the idea of whatever you want to call representative democracy, the Court having made mistakes in the past by reading its own moral views into the Constitution. And much of the theme of this one and a half page memo is along those ideas that the Court has run afoul in the past by reading into the Constitution what it felt were the morally right views, only to find that it had made a mistake. And this apparently was an effort to apply those ideas to the Brown case.

* * *

[T]he thesis which is very roughly and very shortly, certainly developed in the memo that most of the Court's mistakes up to that time had been reading its own moral notions into the Constitution was a view that Justice Jackson was a champion of. His entire book, *Struggle for Judicial Supremacy*, is devoted to that thesis.

And lastly, he (and Senator Orrin Hatch (R-UT)) noted that the justices' notes from the initial, December 1952 conference—directly after the first oral argument (about the time of Rehnquist's memorandum)—show a very uncertain set of justices perplexed about how best to move forward (of whom Jackson was but one).

Then came the attacks, the harshest of which came from Democratic Senators Howard Metzenbaum (Ohio), Ted Kennedy (Massachusetts), and Joe Biden (Delaware). Both Kennedy and Metzenbaum drilled in on the repeated use of "I" in the document. Kennedy: "Do the 'I's' refer to you, Mr. Rehnquist?" Rehnquist: "No, I do not think they do." Kennedy: "You maintain that the 'I's' refer to Justice Jackson?" Rehnquist: "Yes. Obviously something for him to say."

To Metzenbaum's incredulous questioning on the "I's," Rehnquist offered these answers:

Yes, I suppose one could read it either way. The "I's" in it certainly could have been mine rather, just looking at it as a text, rather than Justice Jackson's.

* * *

I think the reconstructing again on the basis of this memo, I would suspect that a logical interpretation in the last paragraph is I perhaps imagined this was the way Justices spoke in conference.

When Biden questioned him on the part of the sentence that referenced being "excoriated by 'liberal' colleagies [sic]," Rehnquist testified that he was referencing the likelihood of Jackson being "excoriated" at some future conference of the justices; at the same time, he did not deny that he had had hard-fought policy arguments on this subject with his fellow clerks: "Again, it is hard to remember back, but I think it probably seemed to me at this time that some of the others simply were not facing the arguments on the other side, and I thought they ought to be faced.... I thought there were good arguments to be made in support [of the other side]."

Ultimately, the Judiciary Committee voted out the nomination 13 to 5 (besides the aforementioned no-voting senators, Paul Simon (D-IL) and Patrick Leahy (D-VT) also voted no). Thereafter, the Senate confirmed Rehnquist by a vote of 65 to 33. He served as Chief Justice until his death on September 3, 2005. Rehnquist was succeeded by John Roberts, who had served as his law clerk in 1980-81.

Evidence Supporting Rehnquist's Testimony

The most direct evidence in favor of Rehnquist's explanation of the memorandum is his uncontradicted sworn testimony. Justice Robert Jackson, having died on October 9, 1954 (after joining the Court's initial, unanimous decision, but before its "remedies" decision—*Brown v. Board of Education*, 349 U.S. 294 (1955) ("all deliberate speed")), was not in a position to dispute his former clerk's version.

Rehnquist's fellow clerk, Donald Cronson, also weighed in on this subject, first in a telegram sent from London three days after the *Newsweek* article. Cronson had also written a memorandum for Justice Jackson at the same time as Rehnquist (more about that later). As for Rehnquist's memorandum, Cronson recalled collaborating on it with Rehnquist; indeed, he claimed "a great deal of the content was the result of my suggestions ... and it is probable that the memorandum is more mine than [Rehnquist's]." Cronson further stated that Jackson had asked for a memorandum "supporting the proposition that *Plessy* was correct." At the same time, however, Cronson also told the *New York Times* that both he and Rehnquist "personally thought at the time [1952] that the 1896 decision, *Plessy v. Ferguson*, was wrong."

Finally, it seems clear from Justice Jackson's prior decisions, writings, and contemporaneous evidence, especially at the time of the first set of oral arguments on *Brown*, that he was troubled by how to adequately deal with *Plessy*, Congress' role/responsibility to desegregate schools and public accommodations, Marshall's sociology arguments (which he never found persuasive), and how to effect an appropriate remedy (if the Court were to step in where Congress had failed to act). The fact that Jackson himself drafted six versions of a separate (but never published) opinion on *Brown* (long after Rehnquist's clerkship had ended—starting on December 7, 1953, ending on March 15, 1954) is further evidence that Jackson was struggling with how best to articulate a constitutional basis for the Court making a "political decision" against segregated schools.

EVIDENCE AT ODDS WITH REHNQUIST'S TESTIMONY

First and foremost, at no point in his career did Justice Jackson ever say or write *anything* indicating that *he* thought *Plessy* "was right and should be re-affirmed." Indeed, both in 1971 and 1986, Jackson's long-serving secretary accused Rehnquist of "smear[ing]" a great man: "Justice Jackson did not ask law clerks to express his views. He expressed his own and they expressed theirs. That's what happened in this instance."

And it was not only partisan Democrats who were not buying Rehnquist's story. Years later, John Dean wrote: "I thought he lied. His explanation was so at odds with the style and contents of his memo to Jackson that it did not pass the smell test.... To say I was disappointed is an understatement."

Almost as implausible as Rehnquist's explanations (under oath) as to the "I's" not being him was his explanation of Jackson being "excoriated by 'liberal' colleagyes [sic]." First of all, there is no evidence of Jackson ever being excoriated by his Supreme Court colleagues. And while Jackson believed in judicial restraint, he was in fact a political liberal, having served FDR in a number of capacities before joining the Court (e.g., solicitor general, attorney general). Finally, not only did other contemporaneous clerks (e.g., Alexander Bickel, Donald Trautman, John Fassett) recall contentious, lunch-time debates with Rehnquist, so did Donald Cronson, who later wrote: "Bill Rehnquist defended the [pro-*Plessy*] position with gusto and cogency. His virtuoso performance [at the lunch-time debates] on the subject of *Plessy* may have led to the composition of the WHR memorandum."

And Cronson also proved unhelpful to Rehnquist in other ways as well. First off was his own 1952 memorandum, "A Few Expressed Prejudices on the Segregation Cases." Based on Jackson's constitutional and jurisprudential views, not only did it offer numerous alternative ways to deal with *Brown* (including the one the Court ultimately chose: not overruling *Plessy* per se, but holding that "separate but equal" violated the Constitution when applied specifically to public schools), it also set forth Cronson's view that "*Plessy* was wrong." Perhaps more important was its use of pronouns, where Cronson consistently referred *not* to "I," but to Jackson's prerogative(s) (e.g., "One of the main characteristics to be found in *your* work on this court is a reluctance to overrule existing constitutional laws...." (emphasis added); "*You* are still the justice."). In sum, the approach, tone, and style of Cronson's memorandum stands in fairly stark contrast to Rehnquist's.

Even more problematic was the fact that Cronson's memory got more refreshed as he thought more about his interactions with his co-clerk. In 1975, Cronson prepared another memorandum ("A Short Note on an Unimportant Memorandum"), which he sent on to Rehnquist; he expected that it would cause "the basically trivial episode of the WHR Memorandum [to] soon be allowed to obtain the obscurity that it deserves." It is in this document that Cronson first undercut Rehnquist's "excoriated" explanation (he also later did so in a 1986 *Washington Post* story). Cronson then posited that Rehnquist's attribution of the "I's" to Jackson "was a trivial error, and an entirely honest one." He went on to attempt to reconcile inconsistencies between his version of what happened in 1952 with Rehnquist's, but those attempts only highlighted that the circle could not be squared. In reply, Rehnquist asked Cronson not to publish his memorandum, suggesting that this was "a case where it is best to let sleeping dogs lie."

Another memorandum written by Rehnquist for Jackson during his clerkship also hurts his "I's" explanation. Before the Court in *Terry v. Adams*, 347 U.S. 461 (1953), was the issue of whether White-only pre-primary elections were constitutional. Rehnquist's memorandum first states:

> I have a hard time being detached about this case, because several of the Rodell school of thought among the clerks began screaming as soon as they saw this that "Now we can show those damn Southerners," etc. I take a dim view of the pathological search for discrimination, a la Walker White, Black, Douglas, Rodell, etc., and as a result I now have something of a mental bloc against this case.

Rehnquist then went on to write:

> If you are going to dissent, I should think you might combine the ideas which you expressed last week with an attack on the reasoning of the two "majority opinions.
>
> * * *
>
> Your ideas—the Constitution does not prevent the majority from banding together, nor does it attaint [sic] success in the effort. It is about time the Court faced the fact that white people on [sic] the South don't like the

colored people; the Constitution restrains them from effecting this dislike through state action, but it most assuredly did not appoint the Court as a sociological watchdog to rear up every time private discrimination raises its admittedly ugly head.

When questioned about this memorandum by Senate Judiciary Committee members in 1986, Rehnquist was very clear in delineating that the "I's" meant him and the "you"/"Your" references meant Jackson.

(Interestingly, Jackson first drafted a dissenting opinion, in accord with Rehnquist's memorandum. Later, however, he changed his mind and joined Justice Clark's opinion, which concurred in the majority ruling that White-only pre-primaries violated the Fifteenth Amendment.)

Then there is the history of Rehnquist's views about *Brown*. While he pledged fealty to its holding and reasoning in 1971 and 1986, he was careful not to testify that he agreed with it at the time it was handed down. And that is because he did *not*.

After clerking, Rehnquist moved to Phoenix and began practicing in a small firm that had (in his words) "very little to do with either past or current decisions of the Supreme Court of the United States." But that did not quiet his interest in those subjects or his desire to engage in public debate thereon. In 1957, for example, Rehnquist spoke at a local bar association and railed against, among other things, the Warren Court's "Black Monday" decisions (*Brown* was widely referred to throughout the South as "Black Monday"). In that same year, Rehnquist published the first of two articles in *U.S. News & World Report*. While the thrust of both articles was on the influence of the Supreme Court's "liberal" clerks, Rehnquist also threw in a critique of the Court's "expansion of federal power at the expense of State power"—a coded phraseology many Southerners were leveling at the Warren Court in the wake of *Brown* ("Impeach Earl Warren").

Then, in 1959, Rehnquist penned an article for the *Harvard Law Record.* Finding it appalling that no senator had questioned Justice Charles Whittaker in his confirmation hearings about the *Brown* decision "decided three years before and implementing decisions [that] had been handed down in the interim," Rehnquist let Harvardians know how he really felt:

> There are those who bemoan the absence of *stare decisis* in constitutional law, but of its absence there can be no doubt. And it is no accident that the provisions of the constitution which have been most productive of judicial law-making—the "due process of law" and "equal protection of the laws" clauses—are about the vaguest and most general of any in the instrument. The Court in *Brown v. Board of Education* ... held in effect that the framers of the Fourteenth Amendment left it to the Court to decide what "due process" and "equal protection" meant. Whether or not the framers thought this, it is sufficient for this discussion that the present Court thinks the framers thought it.

In 1964, Rehnquist continued in a similar vein, opposing a proposed Public Accommodation Ordinance for Phoenix. In 1967, he published a letter defending *de facto* segregation in Phoenix's public schools; in that letter, Rehnquist posited that the elimination of such segregation was "distressing to me," as well as to many who "would feel we are no more dedicated to an 'integrated' society than we are to a 'segregated' society."

When he testified at his 1971 confirmation hearings, Rehnquist was very careful in what he said about *Brown.* Repeatedly, he testified that *Brown* represented settled constitutional law because a unanimous Supreme Court had ruled on the initial decision and it had been "repeatedly reaffirmed by a changing group of [justices]"; "that, to me, is very strong evidence that the Constitution does, in fact, require that result." (*See* 1971 Senate Hearing Transcript at pp. 55, 76, 161, 167-69.)

In 1985 (the year before he was nominated to become Chief Justice), Rehnquist gave an interview to the *New York Times*. In it, he repeated his view that *Brown* now constituted well-settled constitutional law. But he candidly acknowledged that his views had changed about *Brown* since his clerkship: "I think they probably have.... I think there was a perfectly reasonable argument the other way.... Whatever I wrote for Justice Jackson was obviously a long time ago, and to kind of integrate it into something I'm telling you now, I find rather difficult."

* * *

So, did William Rehnquist lie, misrepresent, dissemble to the Senate Judiciary Committee? I will let the reader(s) decide.

Postscripts

The starting points for readers who want to know more on this subject (beyond the 1971 and 1986 hearing transcripts) are Richard Kluger's *Simple Justice: The History of* Brown v. Board of Education (Alfred A. Knopf 1975); David M. O'Brien's *Justice Robert H. Jackson's Unpublished Opinion in* Brown v. Board: *Conflict, Compromise, and Constitutional Interpretation* (University Press of Kansas 2017); James F. Simon's *Eisenhower v. Warren: The Battle for Civil Rights and Liberties* (Liveright 2018); Brad Snyder & John Q. Barrett, "Rehnquist's Missing Letter: A Former Law Clerk's 1955 Thoughts on Justice Jackson and Brown," 53 *Boston College Law Review* 631 (2012).

It was not only conservatives and Southerners who found *Brown* to be a troubling decision. Learned Hand, for example, in his famous 1958 lectures at the Harvard Law School, attacked, in general, the Court as having become "Platonic Guardians," and—as to *Brown* specifically—it being a decision not based in law. In other words, if equal protection meant anything, *Plessy* had to be expressly overruled and *all* racial discrimination had to be found unconstitutional. *See also* Herbert Wechsler's "Toward Neutral Principles of Constitutional Law," 78 *Harvard Law Review* 1 (1959). But that would mean, among other things, all public accommodations would have to become nondiscriminatory and various states' antimiscegenation statutes would also have to be struck down; those equal protection advances would not come until the Civil Rights Act of 1964 and *Loving v. Virginia*, 388 U.S. 1 (1967).

Many believe that *Brown* was a seismic break from *Plessy v. Ferguson*. But let us allow Chief Justice Earl Warren to put that notion to rest: "Some people think *Brown* was revolutionary, ... [but] I see it as evolutionary in character. Just look at the various cases that had been eroding *Plessy* for so many years [*e.g.*, *Smith v. Allwright*, 321 U.S. 649 (1944) (striking down a Texas primary law disenfranchising Blacks); *Shelly v. Kraemer*, 334 U.S. 1 (1948) (striking down restrictive covenants in real estate contracts); *Sweatt v. Painter*, 339 U.S. 629 (1950) (the University of Texas Law School required to admit a Black student; creating an alternative all-Black law school did not provide equal facilities, resources, or opportunities)].... It was natural, the logical and practically the only way the case could be decided."

CHAPTER XX

Filling Justice Baldwin's Seat

W E HAVE RECENTLY WITNESSED three bruising nominations to the U.S. Supreme Court. First came President Barack Obama's 2016 nomination of Merrick Garland, upon which the Senate never took action (Garland is now President Joe Biden's attorney general). Next came President Donald Trump's nomination of Neil Gorsuch, who was confirmed (after the "nuclear option" was invoked) by a 54-to-45 vote in the Senate on April 7, 2017. And then came Trump's nomination of Brett Kavanaugh; he was confirmed (after the "nuclear option" was invoked) by a 50-to-48 vote on October 6, 2018. There have been lots of other contentious nominations, of course (*see, e.g.*, Chapter XXVII: "The Battle Over Brandeis"). One such battle—about which little is known—concerns the seat of Justice Henry Baldwin.

Baldwin was nominated to the Court by President Andrew Jackson and confirmed by the Senate on January 6, 1830. Previously, he had been a prominent Philadelphia lawyer, a congressman, and a trusted political ally of Jackson. As for his jurisprudential legacy, G. Edward White and Gerald Gunther have labeled Baldwin an "incoheren[t] ... jurist." With his death on April 21, 1844, a vacancy on the Court needed to be filled.

Because Baldwin's seat was considered a "Pennsylvania" seat, President John Tyler sought to replace Baldwin with another Keystoner. Tyler, the first vice president to succeed to the presidency after the death of his predecessor, William Henry Harrison, was wildly unpopular with both the Whig and Democratic parties. So how did "his Accidency" do in getting someone through the Senate? Not so well. Tyler first offered the seat to Pennsylvania Senator James Buchanan, who declined. Tyler then nominated Edward King, the presiding judge of the Philadelphia Court of Common Pleas, on June 5, 1844. After the Senate postponed considering King's nomination (for, among other reasons, deference to Buchanan, who a number of senators thought wanted a seat on the Court), King withdrew his name. Undeterred, Tyler nominated King again on December 4; after the Senate once again postponed consideration of King's nomination, Tyler pulled the plug on February 7, 1845.

In the weeks remaining in the Tyler administration, the lame-duck president put forward a second candidate: John M. Read, yet another prominent Philadelphia lawyer. Perhaps this would get through because Read was a friend of Buchanan (and Buchanan was widely reviewed as a likely cabinet member of the next president). Since nothing happened by the end of Tyler's term, however, the nomination was stillborn when James Polk ("Young Hickory"—so named as Andrew Jackson's protégé) took the presidential office on March 4, 1845.

Buchanan became Polk's Secretary of State, but the vacant seat just sat there, as the president took no action (with Congress not meeting in session until December of that year). In September of 1845, Thomas Ritchie, editor of the *Washington Union* (the Democratic Party's national organ), informed Polk that Buchanan wanted to go on the Court. Shortly thereafter, Buchanan met with the president to discuss the vacant seat. Buchanan played political

Cassandra with Polk, acknowledging that he had long been interested in being on the Court, while at the same time emphasizing his importance to the new administration in overseeing the
nation's foreign affairs. Two months later, he opted to stay in the
Cabinet, which suited Polk just fine. That left the issue of what
to do with the vacant seat. Buchanan "was most anxious" to have
Read appointed to the Court, and urged his nomination on Polk.
But Polk was not buying. Why? Although Polk told another colleague that the reason was because he was "determined to have a
first rate man there," the real reason was that Read, at an earlier
point in his political career, had been a Federalist (the predecessor
party to the Whigs). As Polk confided in his diary:

> I have never known an instance of a Federalist who after
> arriving at the age of 30 professed to change his opinions,
> who was to be relied on in his constitutional opinions. All
> of them who have been appointed to the Supreme Court
> Bench, after having secured a place for life[,] became
> very soon broadly Federal and latitudinarian in all their
> decisions involving questions of Constitutional power....
> I resolved to appoint no man who was not an original
> Democrat & strict constructionist, and who would be less
> likely to relapse into the Broad Federal doctrines of Judge
> Marshall & Judge Story.

Instead, based on the advice of Buchanan's rival Pennsylvania Democrats (including Vice President George Dallas, Andrew
Beaumont ("with whom I served in Congress and in whom I have
great confidence"), and Congressman David Wilmot (author of the
famous Wilmot Proviso in 1846)), Polk sent George Woodward's
name to the Senate on December 23, 1845. Woodward, who had
been a Wilkes-Barre lawyer before becoming a judge on the Fourth
Judicial District Court of Pennsylvania, was (in Polk's words) "a
sound, original, & consistent democrat, of the strict construction

school, ... [and] a man of fine talents & well qualified." But that was not really the complete story.

The Complexities of Pennsylvania's Democratic Party

Polk's public announcement that he would serve only one presidential term was intended to free him to unite the Democratic Party; it had the opposite result, as likely and unlikely competitors for the 1848 nomination proliferated and caused no shortage of headaches. This was particularly true when it came to making patronage decisions—with fractured groups under the party's tent, any decision favoring one would upset the other(s). As Polk confided to one party leader, the process cost him so much "labor and trouble" that "I sincerely wish I had no office to bestow." And of all the states, Pennsylvania was most problematic in this regard.

On the one hand, Polk's vice president, George Dallas, was a Keystoner; and he was an obvious contender for 1848, who wanted as many friends taken care of as possible. On the other hand was Buchanan, who now held the premier cabinet position, but who also eyed the presidency and was ever vigilant about his Pennsylvania power-base. There was also a third "hand" who needed to be factored in as well: Simon Cameron.

Cameron had been a successful businessman in Pennsylvania for over two decades and, prior to 1845, had also been active in the Pennsylvania Democratic Party. When Buchanan vacated his Senate seat on February 17, 1845 (in anticipation of becoming Polk's Secretary of State), Cameron threw his hat into the ring to succeed him. Cameron's opponent? None other than George Woodward. Woodward, in fact, was the party establishment's candidate. But he lost out to Cameron when the state legislature voted: 16 Democrats, together with 44 Whigs and 7 Native Americans (the nativist party), supported Cameron, who defeated Woodward 67 to 55.

Woodward, Dallas, and Polk (and many other party elders) were very upset with the result. Polk (and Dallas) were thus determined not to be helpful to Cameron on patronage matters, in which the new senator was a skilled operator (he once observed that patronage served either of two objectives: "love or fear"). Buchanan played a somewhat more cagey patronage game with the new senator, who in frustration blurted out to Buchanan in September of 1845: "I wish you would tell me whether there is to be peace or war." To the president, Cameron professed to be eager to work with the administration on its priorities; in reality, however, he was lying in wait to deliver a body blow to Young Hickory.

Dallas was obviously pleased with the Woodward selection. Buchanan was not, and made clear his views to Polk on Christmas day. Visibly agitated, Buchanan told Polk he had not slept the two nights since the nomination. His complaints were (1) that Polk "had not informed him of [Polk's] intention to nominate" Woodward, and (2) "his friends in Pennsylvania" believed that Polk was wielding patronage to his disfavor.[1] Polk was rather dismissive of Buchanan's concerns, stating it was his prerogative to make such a nomination, that he had heard Buchanan out on his preference (Read), but he—the president—preferred Woodward. As for patronage matters generally, Polk went on to review his other Pennsylvania appointments, a review that (according to Polk) "entirely satisfied" the Secretary of State.

Not surprisingly, that was not the case; and to make matters worse, a fuming Cameron was waiting to meet with Buchanan to discuss how to block Woodward's elevation to the Court. Buchanan, however, took the position that he would take no part in the nomination, pro or con. At the same time, Buchanan did nothing to dissuade Cameron from using every tool in his political

---

[1] One politician opined that "Dallas ... [had] prevail[ed] over 'Pennsylvania's favorite son,' yet the ass bears his burden & still shakes his ears, & is Secy of State!"; another wrote that "We hear that the Secretary of State was not advised of the nomination of Woodward until after it was sent to the Senate! Modern politicians are like spaniels; the more they are beaten, the more they love their masters."

THE GREAT AMERICAN STEEPLE CHASE FOR 1844.

1844 Cartoon Depicting the Competing Candidates for the Presidency
(Author's Collection)

toolbox to hurt the Dallas wing of the party (and obviously Polk as well).

The local media in Pennsylvania was mobilized to dredge up Woodward's nativist remarks from his formative political days; also highlighted was Woodward's wobbly tariff record—Woodward had vacillated between tariff support (an important state issue) and espousing free trade (a position widely viewed as pro-South). More troubling for the nomination was the fact that he had no senatorial rabbi. Without a Pennsylvania Democratic Senator to lead the charge, Woodward tried to get Massachusetts Whig, Daniel Webster, to help out; but that did not work. Indeed, the entire Whig senatorial caucus was determined to vote en masse against the nominee; that would not be a problem, however, assuming the Democratic majority held steady for the president's nominee.

Polk knew that Cameron was "active in his exertions to have Mr. Woodward's nomination ... rejected." And he suspected that Buchanan was also working to that end: "It will be deeply painful to me, if I ascertain that my suspicions are correct, but if I do so ascertain, I will act with promptness and energy towards Mr. Buchanan, whatever the consequences to myself or my administration may be."

THE SENATE'S ADVICE AND CONSENT
ON WOODWARD'S NOMINATION

On January 20, 1846, the Senate (in closed session) began debate on Woodward's nomination. Two days later, Woodward was rejected by a vote of 29 to 20—6 Democrats defected to join 23 Whigs in denying Woodward a seat on the Court. That night, Polk was told the bad news, and he reflected on what had gone wrong in his diary. His first focus was on Buchanan—perhaps Buchanan had helped deep-six the nomination because he wanted the seat for himself: "This I hope is a mistaken impression."

Then, together with Dallas and other political intimates, Polk reviewed how they had lost the six Democratic senators. Polk dismissed Senator James Wescott of Florida with his ultimate put-down—he was "a Whig in disguise" (Senator David Yulee (Florida) was a "pseudo-Democrat," and he termed Cameron "at heart a Whig"). Polk also thought that because Buchanan was "intimate" friends with Cameron, Ambrose Sevier (Arkansas) (he "almost lived at Buchanan's"), and Wescott, the secretary of state, could have prevented those senators (and Thomas Hart Benton (Missouri) as well) from voting against Woodward. The president continued to suspect Buchanan's hand was behind Cameron's open and notorious activities; and if he could prove it he "would instantly dismiss him." Buchanan subsequently sent on an emissary (John Mason, the attorney general) to Polk (1) to deny that he had played any role in the rejection of Woodward, and (2) to re-change his mind about wanting to be appointed to the Court. This last bit of news only confirmed Polk's worst suspicions of Buchanan's motivations and behind-the-scenes actions. Polk told his attorney general that "Mr. Buchanan had brought all his troubles on himself; that I would take my own time, and receive further developments before I made another nomination." Polk also told Mason that if "any member of my cabinet" is found to be working with the Whigs to reject his nominations, he would find "a lion in his path."

Polk's "further developments" mainly related to the president's nomination of his friend and former Congressman Henry Horn to be the Collector of the Port of Philadelphia. Were Horn to receive a similar fate, the president told Thomas Ritchie that "the chain would be snapped."

And if the president were not angry enough at his secretary of state and the defection of the six Democratic senators, Congressman Wilmot visited him at the White House on January 28 to report on hearsay from one of his congressional colleagues. According to Wilmot's colleague, Cameron had quoted Wescott as saying, vis-à-vis Polk's nomination of Woodward: "the only way to treat an ugly Negro who was unruly, was to give him a d__n drubbing at the start and he would learn to behave himself." It was further reported to Polk that Wescott had not only subsequently affirmed he made this "low and vulgar" remark, but he also repeated it. The next day, Wilmot wrote the president to correct his hearsay report: Wescott had made the remark *only* in the context of "dealing with obstinate negroes" generally; it was Cameron who had appropriated the remark as to how to deal with presidential nominations. Polk's ultimate verdict? "I consider both [Cameron and Wescott] ... guilty of gross rudeness & vulgarity."

THE IMMEDIATE AFTERMATH OF WOODWARD'S DEFEAT

While Buchanan moped around in a "melancholy and dissatisfied manner," Cameron was actively plotting to humiliate the president again—this time on Horn's nomination. The Keystone senator decided to make no pretense at playing possum. Instead, Cameron called on Polk and told the president he would withdraw his opposition to Horn if Polk would tell Horn to play patronage ball with him. An obstinate Polk refused. Rebuffed, Cameron chose to bide his time until seven Democratic senators were absent from the Capital attending a funeral on May 25, 1846; he then called up Horn's nomination and, with a unanimous Whig voting bloc and a handful of Democrats, it went down to defeat.

A furious Polk resubmitted Horn's nomination to the Senate. Cameron, however, was able to peel away a larger number of Democrats and the Senate rejected Horn for a second time on June 24, 1846. Polk cussed out Cameron in his diary as "a managing tricky man, in whom no reliance is to be placed, ... I consider him little better than a Whig."

Yet Another Nominee, Eventually

Having seen how effective Cameron had been in cobbling together a handful of Democrats with a unified Whig bloc in the Senate, Polk decided that he would not do anything vis-à-vis the open seat for a while. Then, upon concluding that Buchanan had *not* in fact "taken affirmative action" against Woodward's nomination, the president on June 10, 1846, offered the seat (once more) to his Secretary of State (having been told that Buchanan really did want a seat on the Court). Two and one half weeks later, Buchanan accepted. But he wanted to be nominated immediately, fearing that his political foes (e.g., Dallas and Cameron) would be able to generate sufficient opposition if given enough time. Polk, however, wanted to wait until just before Congress adjourned. After weeks of fretting, Buchanan went to the president on August 1, 1846, and said (once again) he would pass on the Court, wishing instead to "remain in the Cabinet" until the end of Polk's term.

Polk now turned to yet another Pennsylvania state court judge, one who had been considered (and passed over) during the run-up to Woodward's nomination: Robert C. Grier, a Jacksonian Democrat who wore judicial robes in Allegheny County. Perhaps out of fatigue, but more likely because Grier had not chosen sides in fractious/tribal state politics, both Cameron and Buchanan blessed the president's nominee. On August 3, 1846, the president submitted Grier's name to the Senate; and the next day a unanimous Senate approved Grier as an Associate Justice of the Supreme Court. The 28-month odyssey to find a replacement for Henry Baldwin was over.

POSTSCRIPTS

Robert Grier's tenure on the Court (1846-70) is mainly known for his infamous concurrence in *Dred Scott v. Sanford*, 60 U.S. (19 How.) 393 (1857) (agreeing with Chief Justice Roger Taney's ruling that, because the Missouri Compromise of 1820 violated fundamental property rights "found" in the Fifth Amendment, the statute was unconstitutional—thus, creating the doctrine of substantive due process). Grier had perhaps foreshadowed his sympathies with his Southern judicial brethren when he co-presided over a trial in 1851 (with U.S. District Court Judge John K. Kane) that dealt with criminally enforcing the terms of the Fugitive Slave Act: *United States v. Hanway*. Because of Grier's charge to the jury regarding the legal definition of "treason," the jury (after 15 minutes) acquitted the defendant. Nonetheless, during the proceeding Grier had also referred to abolitionists as "infuriated fanatics and unprincipled demagogues" who "denounced the constitution, the laws, and the Bible." *See also Moore v. Illinois*, 55 U.S. (14 How.) 13 (1852) (upholding Illinois law that made it a crime to hide runaway slaves). More importantly and problematic, Grier engaged in *ex parte* communications with President-Elect James Buchanan prior to the release of the *Dred Scott* decision; not only did Grier accede to Buchanan's lobbying for Grier to concur in Taney's odious opinion, but Grier also tipped off Buchanan as to the decision itself, which enabled Buchanan to reference the "likely" outcome in his inaugural address on March 4, 1857 (*Dred Scott* was handed down on March 6, 1857).

Interestingly, Grier later upheld the constitutionality of President Abraham Lincoln's naval blockade of Southern ports in the *Prize Cases*, 67 U.S. 635 (1863). Notwithstanding the fact that Congress had never declared war on the states that seceded, Grier wrote that "[a] civil war is never solemnly declared," and held that Lincoln's power(s) as commander-in-chief allowed him to use the army and navy as he saw fit to ensure the survivability of the Union.

President Polk's criticism of Cameron's fealty to the Democratic Party was spot-on. When he ran for reelection to the Senate, Cameron sought the nomination of the Know-Nothing Party (which he did not secure). Thereafter, he joined Pennsylvania's People's Party, which morphed into the Republican Party. With that party's backing, Cameron was returned to the Senate in 1857. Three years later, he was a favorite son candidate for the Republican presidential nomination (one of my ancestors, William M. Stewart, was pledged to him on the first ballot, and (as instructed) switched to support Abe Lincoln on the second and third ballots). In exchange for Cameron's support for Lincoln on those later ballots, the Keystone senator was nominated to serve as Secretary of War in the new president's cabinet. Cameron was a poor choice, however, and in 1862 he was moved out of the cabinet and shipped off to Russia as the American minister. His tenure in Russia was also short-lived. After the Civil War, Cameron was once more sent to the Senate in 1867, where he served for another ten years (he was succeeded by his son).

The starting point for those who want to understand the Polk presidency is his four-volume presidential diary: Milo Quaife, ed., *Diary of James K. Polk* (A.C. McClurg & Co. 1910). Probably the best (but limited) biography of Polk is Charles Sellers's *James K. Polk Continentalist, 1843-1846* (Princeton University Press 1966); and the best biography of Buchanan (our *worst* president) is Philip Klein's *President James Buchanan: A Biography* (Pennsylvania State University Press 1962). The starting point for understanding more about the Senate's rejection of Woodward's nomination is Daniel

Curran's "Polk, Politics, and Patronage: The Rejection of George W. Woodward's Nomination to the Supreme Court," *The Pennsylvania Magazine of History and Biography* (July 1997). Finally, the best compendium of current, scholarly work on this era of American history can be found in Joel Silbey's *A Companion to the Antebellum Presidents 1837-1861* (Wiley-Blackwell 2014).

CHAPTER XXI

How Lincoln Outsmarted and Fired Salmon Chase, and Then Appointed Him Chief Justice

IT IS NOT DEFAMATORY TO NOTE that manipulation is an important tool in the hands of a skilled politician. When politicians are elevated to statesmen, however, manipulation to some becomes a dirty word—statesmen would never lower themselves to such shenanigans. The opposite is true, of course. Statesmanship and manipulation go hand in hand, and an episode in Abraham Lincoln's presidency shows this well.

Lincoln's always ambitious and often duplicitous Secretary of Treasury Salmon P. Chase was an ongoing challenge of political management throughout Lincoln's first term. Chase, like many in Lincoln's cabinet, thought he was better suited than Honest Abe to be the nation's chief magistrate. And as the 1864 campaign started to heat up, Chase began to position himself to challenge Lincoln for the Republican nomination.

Intrigue

In February 1864, political pamphlets designed by his followers (in the main, the so-called Radical Republicans) took the

Chase strategy public. The most famous of them came out under the signature of Senator Samuel C. Pomeroy (the "Pomeroy Circular"), arguing that Lincoln's reelection was "practically impossible," and promoting Chase as a "statesman of rare ability," and the best "available candidate." Recognizing (in the words of Navy Secretary Gideon Wells) that the document could well be "more dangerous in its recoil than its projectile," Chase immediately wrote to Lincoln, contending that he had been merely a passive observer of the efforts of others on his behalf, and that (given his "respect and esteem" for Lincoln) he did not want to stay on without Lincoln's "entire confidence."

Lincoln's first response was merely to acknowledge that he had received Chase's letter and that he would "answer a little more fully when I can find the leisure to do so." Six days later, after letting Chase twist slowly in the wind, Lincoln wrote again to say he did "not perceive occasion" for relieving Chase from his position.

Lincoln's political associates were not so restrained, however. Chase's disloyalty was savaged in the press and on the floor of Congress, and Lincoln partisans quickly moved to shore up support in various state nominating committees for Lincoln's renomination. With respect to those latter efforts, the Republican caucus in Ohio (Chase's home state) met five days after the Pomeroy Circular and enthusiastically endorsed Lincoln; Ohio Congressman James Garfield (a Chase supporter and a future president) thereafter advised Chase to stand down because "the people desire the reelection of Mr. Lincoln." Outflanked and outmaneuvered, Chase publicly withdrew from presidential consideration on March 5.

By the time of the June convention (of the now-named National Union Party), Lincoln had cleared the field of all opposition, and was easily renominated. This emboldened him, politically as well as in his prosecution of the war. When a patronage problem in the Treasury Department arose later that month, Chase (who had twice before submitted his resignation) tendered it again; Lincoln accepted immediately ("You and I have reached a point of mutual embarrassment in our official relations which it seems cannot be overcome, or longer sustained"). According to Chase's own journal, Lincoln's action dumbfounded him; in fact, he learned the news of the acceptance of his resignation while in conference at the Senate (ironically with Senator William P. Fessenden, his successor). Yet, even as he was in denial and expressing his shock to his own journal ("I have found a good deal of embarrassment from [Lincoln] but what he found from me I could not imagine."), Chase reflected on a third party's report that Lincoln had earlier said that he would be favorably disposed to appoint Chase to the Chief Justiceship "in case of [a] vacancy," and recalled an earlier conversation he had had with Lincoln where he told the president that he would rather be "Chief Justice of the United States than hold any other position that could be given to me."

Chief Justice Roger Taney (who was 87 years old and had been in failing health for some time) was the subject of much speculation. Chase, after flirting with the notion of becoming a Democratic candidate (if they would "cut loose from Slavery and go for freedom") or lining up with Republican splinter groups, now saw that office as his best and last chance to become president. In a September visit to Washington, he met twice with Lincoln, finding him "indifferent but cordial," and admitting to his daughter that "I feel I do not know him." But that aloofness did not cool Chase's plan—he set off on the campaign trail to hawk Lincoln's reelection in the critical states of Ohio, Michigan, Kentucky, Missouri, and Pennsylvania.

TANEY IS DEAD

On October 12, Taney died. And with his death, the lobbying of Lincoln began immediately and in earnest, not only on behalf of Chase but also on behalf of noted New York lawyer William M. Evarts, Justice Noah Swayne of Ohio, Montgomery Blair of Maryland, and Attorney General Edward Bates of Missouri (on October 13, Bates asked Lincoln for the post "as the crowning retiring honor of my life"). Chase, however, had the most persistent champions.

Charles Sumner, who was the powerful Chairman of the Committee on Foreign Relations, is illustrative of this campaign. He fired off numerous letters of support to Lincoln, and kept Chase apprised of his efforts. On October 12, Sumner asked Lincoln to appoint Chase, calling Taney's death "a victory for Liberty and the Constitution." Getting no positive reaction, Sumner wrote the president again on October 24, citing "feverishness in the public mind with regard to the Chief Justiceship." He urged Chase's nomination ("the sooner it is made the better"), arguing that his nomination "would cause a glow of delight ... among all the best supporters of the Administration." Gilding the lily, Sumner passed on a sycophantic communication he had received from Chase (which he had persuaded Chase to send on to him so he could pass it on to Lincoln); it included the following passage: "Happily it is now certain that the next Administration will be in the hands of Mr. Lincoln from whom the world will expect great things. God grant that his name may go down to posterity with the two noblest additions historians ever recorded—Restorer & Liberator."

Lincoln did nothing, however. He saw only political downsides in naming any of the contenders before the November election. He also saw only political upsides to having Chase redouble his speaking efforts on his behalf in the key swing states. Chase, catching the not so subtle hint, did just that. On October 31 in Cleveland, for example, he spoke on behalf of Lincoln's reelection and claimed that George McClellan, the Democratic presidential candidate, would, if elected, permit the continued existence of slavery. Chase kept up his speaking tour until the very end; his journal entry on election day was simply: "voted for Lincoln & Johnson."

A POLITICAL NOMINATION

With his reelection secured Lincoln still did not act. On November 20, Sumner wrote to Lincoln yet again, observing that "the country is anxious" by the president's inaction. Then suddenly, on December 6, just as Congress was reconvening and Lincoln was reconfiguring the cabinet for his second term, he sent a terse note to the Senate: "I nominate Salmon P. Chase of Ohio, to be Chief Justice of the Supreme Court of the United States vice Roger B. Taney, deceased."

The weaknesses (political and otherwise) of the other candidates had played a role in Lincoln's decision. Chase's obvious legal talents had also played a role. But the political calculus, even after securing reelection, had been the decisive factor. As Lincoln explained to an aide: "His appointment will satisfy the Radicals and after that they will not dare kick up against any appointment I may make." Even so, Lincoln was not without his qualms: "If [Chase] keeps on with the notions that he is destined to be President of the United States, and which in my judgment he will never be, he will never acquire that fame and influence as a Chief Justice which he would otherwise certainly attain."

Chase's nomination was approved by the Senate the same day. Also on December 6, Chase wrote to Lincoln, thanking him effusively "for the manner in which the nomination was made," and pledging that Lincoln would "never regret" his decision.

Postscripts

President Abraham Lincoln's judgment of Salmon Chase proved accurate. While Chase did lead the Court through the difficult period of Reconstruction, and handled President Andrew Johnson's impeachment trial with acuity,[1] the presidential bug

---

[1] He also dissented from the majority decision in the *Legal Tender Cases*, 79 U.S. 457 (1871), which reversed his ruling in *Hepburn v. Griswold*, 75 U.S. 603 (1869). Pursuant to the Legal Tender Act of 1862 (which Chase, as Secretary of the Treasury, had been instrumental in its passage), the U.S. government had issued paper money, known as United States Notes during the Civil War. In *Hepburn*, Chase (and a majority of the Court) ruled that the 1862 statute violated the Fifth Amendment's Due Process Clause. Two years later, a majority of the

never did leave him. Chase openly (and unsuccessfully) sought the Democratic nomination in 1868. In the words of one of his biographers, Chase "let the dark side of his character overwhelm his proper political instincts. In the end he found himself identified as a weak and contradictory person before the public. His reputation suffered badly."

An excellent starting point to understand the complexities of cabinet politics during Lincoln's presidency is Doris Kearns Goodwin's *Team of Rivals: The Political Genius of Abraham Lincoln* (Simon & Schuster 2005). The best biography of Chase is Walker Spahr's *Salmon P. Chase: Lincoln's Vital Rival* (Simon & Schuster 2022).

Court ruled that the issuance of paper money did not conflict with Article I of the Constitution. Some scholars believe the *Legal Tender Cases* rank with the Court's worst decisions.

CHAPTER XXII

Why Judge Learned Hand Was Never Appointed to the U.S. Supreme Court

LEARNED HAND IS ONE of the undisputed giants of American jurisprudence. His judicial career covered more than a half century, beginning as United States District Judge in the Southern District of New York in 1909. Although he was elevated to the Second Circuit Court of Appeals in 1924 and subsequently became chief judge of that court, Judge Hand never fulfilled the destiny so many believed was inescapable: becoming a Supreme Court Justice. Hand came close to the prize on three occasions.

The first Supreme Court vacancy for which Hand was considered opened up in President Warren G. Harding's administration. Notwithstanding Judge Hand's growing reputation, however, he did not make the final cut. This was principally because Chief Justice William Howard Taft blackballed him. Taft had never forgotten, nor forgiven, Judge Hand's breaking off from the Republican Party to join the Bull Moose Party's effort in support of Taft's 1912 rival, ex-President Theodore Roosevelt (this was especially galling to Taft because he had put Judge Hand on the federal bench during his presidency).

Citing Hand's disloyal past, Taft counseled Harding: "If [Judge Hand were] promoted to our Bench, he would most certainly herd with Brandeis and be a disaster. I think it would be risking too much to appoint him."

SECOND CIRCUIT

Interestingly, two years later, Taft supported Judge Hand's elevation to the Second Circuit. And, in fact, Taft reported to Hand that he had personally lobbied for the appointment.

With the retirement of Chief Justice Taft in 1930, Judge Hand was seriously considered for the Court. But to understand why it did not happen we must consult the controversial "Joe Cotton story."

JOE COTTON

Cotton was a prominent New York lawyer (he had been a partner at the Cravath law firm and then left to start his own firm, the predecessor of Cahill, Gordon) who became quite active in public affairs. In the Hoover administration, he served as Under Secretary of State and was reputed to be one of President Herbert Hoover's closest advisers.

When Taft's retirement plans became known, Cotton was meeting with Hoover. Cotton told the president that he had "a great opportunity": he could elevate Justice Harlan Stone to be Chief Justice, appoint Judge Hand to Stone's seat, "and thus put on the Supreme Court the most distinguished federal judge on the bench today."

Hoover, however, felt he owed Charles Evans Hughes (a former Justice, the Republican presidential nominee in 1916, and former Secretary of State) the right of first refusal. Cotton responded that Hughes would not even consider the post because his son was Hoover's Solicitor General and Hughes obviously would never force his own son to step down to avoid the clear conflict. Hoover acknowledged Cotton's point, and said that if Hughes declined "that solves the problem" and he could then go ahead with the Stone/Hand package.

STARTLED REACTION

Hoover thereupon picked up the phone and called Hughes in New York. Hughes, rather than rejecting the idea outright, booked a seat on the train to Washington that night; at breakfast with Hoover the next morning he accepted the appointment. Cotton's startled reaction (which he widely retold) was: "The son-of-a-bitch never even thought of his son!"

CLEARLY DISAPPOINTED

Learned Hand, who believed he had a realistic shot, was clearly disappointed and suspected that Taft may have again poisoned the well. Regardless of the reason(s), the only person to whom he truly expressed his disappointment was his wife, writing: "That damned thing was in my thoughts all the time; it made a kind of coward of me."

In 1942, President Franklin D. Roosevelt persuaded James F. Byrnes to step down from the Court to become head of the Office of Economic Stabilization. Justice Felix Frankfurter (himself an FDR appointee) launched a blitzkrieg to persuade the president to appoint Hand to the Court; he also directed his prodigious efforts at people he thought had FDR's ear on such matters (e.g., Attorney General Biddle). Frankfurter even went so far as to draft a public statement for the president announcing Judge Hand's designation.

Notwithstanding, FDR nominated Wiley Rutledge, a judge on the Court of Appeals for the District of Columbia Circuit. Some viewed the age issue as dispositive—Riley was 48, Hand was 70 (ironically, Riley died in 1949, while Hand continued on the Second Circuit for 12 years thereafter).

Another reason may have been that FDR, the master politician, resented Frankfurter's relentless attempts to limit FDR's freedom of movement. Biddle, in fact, later told Judge Hand that "if Felix hadn't pushed, pushed, pushed, you'd have had a better chance."

A related and fascinating vignette into FDR's decision-making process came from Justice William O. Douglas's memoirs. In it, Douglas recounts a poker game at the White House during which the subject of Byrnes's successor came up. Douglas asked FDR who was *not* going to be appointed, and the president (after the characteristic gesture of throwing back his head and laughing) replied: "Learned Hand is not going to be appointed." When Douglas observed that he would be "passing by a fine man," FDR responded: "Perhaps so. But this time Felix overplayed his hand ... Do you know how many people asked me today to name Learned Hand? ... Twenty, and every one a messenger from Felix Frankfurter.... [B]y golly, I won't do it."

Learned Hand, although again disappointed, expressed a keen insight as to why he had not been nominated. Age, he thought, was a factor; but Judge Hand also thought there was "a deeper difficulty"—FDR did not know him personally, he was not a Democrat, there were two New Yorkers on the Court, and, most important, Judge Hand had a well-deserved reputation for having a judicial mind that was skeptical of ideology of any stripe (let alone that of the New Deal). As Hand concluded: "[FDR] has a sensitive nose for people, and my ways of going at things are so different from his that he may well have felt me alien; I fancy he did."

POSTSCRIPT

The best biography of Learned Hand is by Gerald Gunther: *Learned Hand: The Man and the Judge* (Knopf 1994). For those who want to see a selection of Hand's papers and addresses, see *The Spirit of Liberty* (Knopf 1952) (ed. Irving Dilliard). In 1958, Hand gave the Oliver Wendell Holmes Lectures at the Harvard Law School; these were Hand's last major critique of judicial activism—a position he had first articulated in 1908 when he was critical of *Lochner* (*see* Chapter IV). *See* Learned Hand, *The Bill of Rights* (Harvard University Press 1958).

CHAPTER XXIII

LBJ AND THE SUPREME COURT

L YNDON B. JOHNSON, at first, liked the nickname "Landslide Lyndon," which reflected his narrow victory over Coke Stevenson in the 1948 Texas Democratic primary runoff for the Senate. In time, however, he grew to dislike the moniker immensely because it reinforced widespread notions that his victory was due to less than honorable political shenanigans.

The politics of that incredible race—a race that had he not won would likely have had an immense impact on this nation's polity (e.g., Vietnam, Civil Rights legislation, the Great Society, NASA)— are told well in Ronnie Dugger's *The Politician: The Drive for Power from the Frontier to Master of the Senate* (W.W. Norton 1982) and Robert Dallek's *Lone Star Rising: Lyndon Johnson and His Times, 1908-1960* (Oxford University Press 1991). This chapter will highlight a lesser known part of that political drama: how the brilliant legal maneuvering of Abe Fortas made Johnson's victory possible.

87 VOTES

Six days after the primary election, George Parr, the "Duke" of Duval County, delivered the famous, just discovered votes from

Precinct 13 in Alice, Texas. The final tally ended with Johnson receiving 494,191 votes and Stevenson getting 491,104. A week later, the State Democratic Executive Committee endorsed Johnson's 87-vote victory by a single vote margin. The next day the party's convention ratified that decision.

Stevenson was not to be put off so easily, however. Following an all-night drive to the federal district judge his supporters believed would be most favorably disposed, Stevenson's attorneys arrived at Judge Whitfield Davidson's private home near the border of Louisiana and petitioned for a temporary restraining order, barring the putting of Johnson's name on the November ballot. Davidson (a Stevenson friend and conservative anti–New Dealer) issued the order at 6:25 that morning, and scheduled the hearing on Stevenson's claims under the federal civil rights statute for the following week (September 21) in claims under the federal civil rights statute for the following week (September 21) in Fort Worth. The hearing went as Stevenson and his attorneys had hoped, with Davidson on September 22 rejecting Johnson's argument that the court was without jurisdiction to intervene in a state election and keeping the temporary injunction in place until investigations were completed into the allegations of voting fraud.

Time was now a critical factor. The deadline under Texas law for placing names on the printed ballot was October 3. And although Davidson had ordered the investigators to report back to him on October 2, from Johnson's perspective (especially given the likely findings of the investigators) that provided only a small technical chance for getting his name on the ballot, and an even smaller realistic one. The question on the table was: What to do?

WHERE'S ABE?

In Fort Worth, Texas, a roomful of top legal talent debated the possible options on the evening of September 22. While the object was clear—dissolve the injunction and get Johnson's name on the ballot—no one, in the words of one of Johnson's lawyers, "could agree on how to do it." Johnson, frustrated but knowing instinctively what he needed to do, asked: "Where's Abe?"

Abe Fortas, it turned out, was in Dallas taking depositions in an antitrust case. He immediately came to Fort Worth and joined the discussions of Johnson's options. After listening to various descriptions of what had taken place and possible avenues of legal attack, Fortas told the group what he thought should be done. What he proposed was a risky gamble that ran counter to the collective wisdom Johnson had heard up to that point.

The key to Fortas's plan was to get the matter up to the Supreme Court Justice who had administrative responsibility for the Fifth Circuit Court of Appeals—Hugo Black—as quickly as possible.

Thus, rather than exhaustively pursuing all available legal remedies, which was the seeming consensus of the assembled lawyers (which, Fortas believed, would achieve ultimate victory as a matter of law, but would come far too late to get Johnson's name on the ballot), Johnson's legal case would promptly be put in front of that court of appeals judge least likely to be persuaded by Johnson's jurisdictional argument, to lose there, and then press the appeal immediately to Justice Black, who (presumably/hopefully) would agree to hear the matter as a single Justice and then rule in favor of Johnson.

Fortas outlined his plan to the assembled group, acknowledging that it was a "one-shot" strategy and that, if it was unsuccessful, "[y]ou lose everything." But, in Fortas's mind, this was the only legal strategy available to achieve the desired result before October 3.

When Fortas finished outlining his plan, none of the assembled lawyers spoke. As Fortas later recalled: "Everyone was delighted to have me take the responsibility." It was at that point Johnson—in true riverboat gambler style—weighed in: "Let's do what Abe says."

Fortas left the group and went into a separate room with a secretary. He shortly returned with a single-page document, stating:

Lyndon Johnson and Barry Goldwater Dolls
from the 1964 Election
(Author's Collection)

"That's all you need." One of the other Johnson lawyers years later observed that "[i]t was a thing of beauty to watch the way he handled it."

The following day Fortas's document was put into a brief-like format, and a Johnson lawyer was dispatched by plane to New Orleans, where the Fifth Circuit was located. Johnson's legal team had decided that the circuit judge least likely to be helpful was Joseph C. Hutcheson; Hutcheson in a prior case had held that to lift a lower court injunction would require the concurrence of at least three circuit court judges. The Johnson team thus applied to Hutcheson for relief, and he agreed to hear the matter.

A four-hour hearing was held on Friday, September 24. At first, Hutcheson told the parties he would take the matter under advisement; that threatened to deep-six Fortas's strategy. Fortunately, however, Hutcheson's period of indecision lasted only five hours. The judge called both sides into chambers and announced that he did not believe he could act independent of the other members of the court and was thus forced to rule that he had "no power and ought not to set aside or stay the injunction."

The next day, Johnson's legal team phoned Justice Black at his home in Virginia. He agreed, *ex parte*, to hear their application for a stay of the injunction; Tuesday, September 28, was set as the hearing date (allowing Stevenson's lawyers a chance to prepare and appear).

Jurisdiction and Procedure

At 9:30 on Tuesday morning, lawyers for Johnson and Stevenson assembled in Justice Black's chambers. Former Texas Governor Dan Moody, on behalf of Stevenson, stressed the facts (i.e., the alleged fraud); Fortas stressed jurisdiction and procedure (such primary elections were "irrevocably and incontestably vested" in Texas state law, beyond the purview of a federal court). Another Johnson lawyer brought in the possible political ramifications of allowing the injunction to stand: "There will be no name of a Democratic nominee. The republican nominee ... will be the only candidate on the ticket." (Black had been a fiercely partisan Democratic senator prior to his elevation to the Court, and control of the Senate was a major political consideration in 1948.)

The session in front of Justice Black went on for more than three and one-half hours, with Black then retiring to consider the matter. A short time later he reconvened the group of lawyers to announce his decision, ruling in Johnson's favor: "It would be a drastic break with the past, which I can't believe Congress ever intended to permit, for a federal judge to go into the business of conducting what is to every intent and purpose a contest of an election in the state." He went on to tell Moody that his client had options beyond the federal courts, including the Senate itself, as well as the criminal justice system (i.e., to prosecute fraud). The following day, September 29. Justice Black signed an order directing that all proceedings be stayed "until further order of the Supreme Court." That signed order had two immediate effects: first, it stopped in mid-hearings the judicial fact-finding proceedings ordered by Judge Davidson (indeed, with only minutes to spare before all the ballot boxes would be opened and/or examined, including the box containing the "votes" from Precinct 13); and second, Johnson's name was allowed to be placed on the printed ballot.

Fortas's plan had worked!

On October 5, the full Supreme Court refused to hear Stevenson's petition to review Justice Black's decision. Johnson went on to defeat the Republican candidate (Jack Porter) by a vote of 702,985 to 349,665, and was sworn in as the junior senator from Texas on January 3, 1949. The Supreme Court, on January 31, 1949, rejected Stevenson's petition for a trial on the merits. And the Senate's Subcommittee on Privilege and Elections—in response to Stevenson's challenge—declared on June 21, 1949, that "no evidence has been disclosed which would establish Stevenson's allegations," concluding that Johnson was "a duly elected Senator of the United States from the State of Texas."

POSTSCRIPTS

During the period Lyndon Johnson liked to joke about his nickname (see page 229), he enjoyed telling a story about a young Mexican boy who lived in Alice, Texas. A passerby, seeing that the boy was crying, stopped and asked him, "Son, are you hurt?" The boy said, "No, I no hurt." "Are you sick?" "No, I no sick." "Are you hungry?" "No, I no hungry." The passerby then asked: "What's the matter? What are you crying for?" The boy replied, "Well, yesterday, my papa, he been dead four years, yesterday, he come back and voted for Lyndon Johnson, and he didn't come by to say hello to me."

Sharped-eyed readers will note that omitted at the outset of this chapter was any reference to Robert Caro's book on the 1948 election: *The Years of Lyndon Johnson: Means of Ascent* (Knopf 1990). Unlike Caro's first LBJ book, *The Years of Lyndon Johnson:*

The Path to Power (Knopf 1982), which is one the great political biographies extant (and worthy of the National Book Critics Circle Award it received), Caro's book on the 1948 election is almost cartoonish in depicting good (a Christ-like Stevenson) versus evil (a Satanic LBJ); Stevenson was, in fact, a troglodyte, racist reactionary. And while LBJ was no saint, even Caro (in his first book) acknowledged that Johnson had had the senatorial primary of 1941 stolen from *him*. Furthermore, while the evidence of stolen votes in 1948 is pretty much not in dispute, what is also not in dispute is (1) Stevenson also stole votes, and (2) the "Duke" of Duval County delivered votes for LBJ because he hated Stevenson, not because of some Faustian bargain with Johnson.

CHAPTER XXIV

NIXON AND THE SUPREME COURT

L EONARD GARMENT'S MEMOIR, *Crazy Rhythm: My Journey from Brooklyn, Jazz, and Wall Street to Nixon's White House, Watergate, and Beyond* ... (Random House 1997), is a wonderful book. In addition to the many interesting vignettes he shared about his multi-dimensional life, Garment also gave his readers two episodes of legal history that not only have some grounding in the Supreme Court but also reveal fascinating insights into Richard Nixon.

DESPERATE HOURS

The first episode relates to a case Garment worked on with Nixon when they were colleagues at Nixon, Mudge, Rose, Guthrie & Alexander.

Garment represented the Hill family in a lawsuit against Time Inc., charging an invasion of the family's privacy. Time's publication *Life* had run an article about a Broadway play called *The Desperate Hours* (later a movie starring Humphrey Bogart), and depicted it as a reenactment of a real-life hostage crime by escaped convicts against the Hills (which it decidedly was not).

Garment won a large money damage award at trial, and the verdict was upheld throughout the New York State appellate process.

After Time appealed to the U.S. Supreme Court, Garment enlisted Nixon to handle the oral argument. It was to be his first argument in any appellate court, and Nixon's preparation for the argument was monumental. He literally left no stone unturned. (Nixon later told a journalist: "I locked myself up in my office for two weeks. No phone calls. No interruptions. It takes a tremendous amount of concentration.") The case was not only important as part of Nixon's public/political recovery, but it also was significant in that it would be the first Supreme Court case after *New York Times v. Sullivan*, 326 U.S. 254 (1964), to weigh the relative merits of individual privacy and media freedom.

Nixon was up to the task. The *Washington Post's* view was that Nixon's presentation on April 27, 1966, was "one of the best oral arguments of the year." And Justice Abe Fortas—not a political fan of Nixon's, to say the least—was later quoted as saying that Nixon had made "one of the best arguments that he had heard since he had been on the Court" and that he had the potential to be "one of the great advocates of our time."

Garment and Nixon, thinking a majority of the Court had been won over, flew back to New York on the shuttle. One man was exhausted, and went home to sleep. The other returned home to dictate a five-page, single-spaced memorandum critiquing the argument and the applicable constitutional law;[1] the document was sitting on Garment's desk waiting for him when he got in the next morning. That memorandum "remains the most instructive example of Richard Nixon's tenacity and discipline that [Garment

---

[1] Among the things critiqued in Nixon's memorandum was his regret at not giving more emphasis on the recent right of privacy ruling in the *Griswold* decision and the fact that Justice William O. Douglas's "emanations" and "penumbras" were not well grounded in constitutional law; as Nixon foresaw, that "was going to get the Court into deep and dangerous constitutional waters." *See* Chapter V.

had] ever read, including the papers he produced in his presidential and post-presidential years."

Nixon's post-mortem was not in vain, because the case was held over for reargument in the Court's next term. And though Garment thought Nixon did an even better job the second time he argued (October 18 and 19, 1966), they both concluded that the Court's sympathies had shifted dramatically against their clients' position. And they were right—the Court (five to four) reversed and remanded the case for a new trial. (385 U.S. 374 (1967).)

BLACK'S MACHINATIONS

Years later, Leonard Garment learned the details underlying the Court's decision making.

After the first argument, Chief Justice Earl Warren assigned Justice Abe Fortas to write the majority opinion (six to three) upholding the Hills' victory. Fortas's draft, however, brought numerous comments and allowed his bitter rival, Hugo Black, to petition (successfully) for more time to craft his dissent—a delay that pushed the case into the next term. During that period, Black used his formidable political skills to lobby his colleagues (at one point calling Fortas's draft "the worst First Amendment opinion he had seen in a dozen years"). He also unleashed a written broadside intra-Court against the Fortas position the day before reargument. That document included the following line: "After mature reflection I am unable to recall any prior case in this Court that offers a greater threat to freedom of speech and press than this one does."

In the end, Black's attacks were enough to ensure a five-to-four victory for Time. Writing for this new majority was Justice William Brennan, the author of *New York Times v. Sullivan*. Building on that decision, Brennan wrote that Time Inc. should be permitted to have a new trial to determine whether the magazine's article was reckless or willfully inaccurate. Because the Hills were not public figures (the issue in *Sullivan*), Brennan stressed that there needed to be a balance between First Amendment/Freedom of Speech concerns versus inaccurate media reporting on private individuals. The dissenting opinions (the former majority) thought this "balancing" skewed too heavily in favor of the media, creating a problem of "unchallengeable truth" for private individuals who had little or no way to rebut the false information.

According to Garment, Nixon's reaction upon hearing the decision was: "I always knew I wouldn't be permitted to win a big appeal against the press. Now Len, get this absolutely clear: I never want to hear about the *Hill* case again."

The *Hill* case also may have been significant in the role it played in Fortas being forced to leave the Court. To the day he died, Fortas believed that a *Life* article in May of 1969, which revealed his financial arrangement with an individual under investigation by the Securities and Exchange Commission (which in turn led to his resignation as an Associate Justice), had been a direct payback from Time for his siding with the Hills.

WATERGATE TAPES

The second episode of legal history relates to Leonard Garment's role as White House counsel in the dark days of Watergate. (After Nixon's election, Garment joined the White House staff. After John Dean was fired, he became White House Counsel.)

Once a presidential aide had revealed the taping system in the Oval Office to the Senate Watergate Committee in July of 1973, Garment and his colleagues were compelled to address the question of whether the tapes could and/or should be destroyed. Garment's client (the president) was then at the Bethesda Naval Hospital with viral pneumonia, and it was there the issue was vetted.

Notwithstanding "urgent destroy-the-tape advice we were getting from a number of men—including Nelson Rockefeller, Henry Kissinger, and John Connally," Garment's legal advice was that destroying the tapes could be obstruction of justice (the Senate

Committee had publicly made clear its intention to seek the tapes) and thus constitute a ground for impeachment.

The key decision underlying Garment's conclusion was the 1956 opinion of Judge Edward Weinfeld in the Southern District of New York: *United States v. Solow*, 138 F. Supp. 812. Weinfeld, who Garment rightly called "one of the most respected jurists in the country," had held that the destruction of documents, when it was known that a governmental body intended to issue a subpoena for them, was obstruction of justice. The Second Circuit affirmed Weinfeld's ruling, and there was no contrary judicial precedent.

Perhaps not surprisingly, Garment's legal analysis was not the decisive factor governing the tapes' fate. After getting Garment's legal advice, President Nixon called H.R. "Bob" Haldeman for guidance. Haldeman, prior to having been forced to resign as Chief of Staff in April of 1973, had listened to a number of the tapes (including some of the "worst").

His advice to Nixon was that the tapes should be preserved because they constituted "Nixon's best defense."

Oops!

Ultimately, the Watergate Special Prosecutor subpoenaed a number of presidential tapes, and the Supreme Court unanimously ruled that the White House had to comply with the subpoena. *United States v. Nixon*, 418 U.S. 683 (1974). Within a matter of days of that ruling, Nixon's defense was in ruin and he was forced to resign the presidency.

POSTSCRIPTS

Courtesy of the Nixon Presidential Library, his April 27, 1966, oral argument in the Supreme Court can be accessed (and listened to) via the Internet.

Also available via the Internet are approximately 30 hours of extremely interesting Nixon interviews from the 1980s, conducted by his one-time aide (and principal architect of the Nixon memoirs), Frank Gannon.

To say there are a plethora of books about Nixon is to grossly understate the case. Any starting point has to be *The Haldeman Diaries* (G.P. Putnam's Sons 1994). Other great Nixon books include Evan Thomas's *Being Nixon: A Man Divided* (Random House 2015); Mark Freeney's *Nixon and the Movies: A Book about Belief* (University of Chicago Press 2004); Robert H. Ferrell, ed., *Inside the Nixon Administration: The Secret Diary of Arthur Burns, 1969-1974* (University Press of Kansas 2010); and Pat Buchanan's *The Greatest Comeback: How Richard Nixon Rose from the Dead to Create America's New Majority* (Crown Forum 2014).

In 1989, Garment wrote an article for *The New Yorker* about the *Hill* case (an article that formed the basis of that portion of his later published memoir). I wrote Garment a letter, complementing him on the "perspective of [his] article, as well as the insights [he had] brought to the personalities involved, [which] made it a fascinating piece for lawyers, as well as a most accessible history for those outside our profession (not an easy thing to do!)." He wrote me back the following: "Thanks for taking the time to say nice things about the *Hill* case article. Writing is a bloody business, but a few words like yours help redeem it."

CHAPTER XXV

BORK AND THE CONSTITUTIONAL CRISIS OF 1973

ROBERT BORK IS A LITMUS TEST for most folks over 50 years of age. Either he was a brilliant law professor and jurist who was unfairly denied a seat on the U.S. Supreme Court, or he was a rabid, right-wing ideologue who, if put on the Court, would have created an America "in which women would be forced into back-alley abortions, blacks would sit at segregated lunch counters, rogue police could break down citizens' doors in midnight raids...." (Senator Edward M. "Ted" Kennedy, June 23, 1987). Less well known is his service to America as Solicitor General and his role in the Saturday Night Massacre.

GETTING HIRED BY NIXON

At a 1972 meeting in the White House to discuss possible legislation relating to busing children to school, Bork first met President Richard Nixon. Being a bearded law professor from Yale, Bork could see Nixon "visibly recoil a step or two" when Nixon was introduced to him (Nixon professed to loathe Ivy League professors). But when Bork was allowed to weigh in on the proposed

243

bill—stating that the Supreme Court authority upon which it was premised was "corrupt constitutional law"—Nixon immediately reacted: "I believe the same thing, but I didn't know there was a law professor anywhere in the United States who agreed with me."

The month after Nixon's landslide reelection, Bork was called at his New Haven home by U.S. Attorney General Richard Kleindienst: Would Bork accept the job of solicitor general if it were to be offered? Bork quickly replied "most certainly." The next day, John Dean, the White House Counsel, followed up, requesting that Bork come to Camp David for an interview with Nixon. Without any irony, Dean also asked Bork whether he had any skeletons in his closet.

Bork's interview with Nixon was a pleasant session, with Nixon holding forth on a wide range of subjects. At one point the president said it was too bad Bork had gone to Yale; Bork responded that in fact he was a Chicago graduate. Nixon replied: "That's almost as bad." When the interview ended, the two men had not talked about the solicitor general position, and Bork left clueless as to why he had been selected by the president.

On June 26, 1973, after noncontentious confirmation hearings (and having allowed for his predecessor to stay until the end of the Supreme Court's term), Bork was sworn in as Solicitor General. "On top of the world," with what he deemed a "real plum" of a job, Bork had no idea of the tsunami into which he had walked.

ON THE JOB

No sooner had Bork settled into his office at the Department of Justice than Spiro Agnew, Nixon's vice president, scheduled a meeting with the new solicitor general. Bork, intellectually acute but politically naive, had no idea what to expect. After a 20-minute conversation that was "desultory, leading nowhere," the meeting ended and Bork returned to the Justice Department "rather confused about the whole episode."

The fog began to clear a bit when Nixon's chief of staff, Alexander Haig, asked Bork to the White House a few weeks later. The primary purpose of the meeting was to entreat Bork to leave his new post and take charge over Nixon's legal defense team dealing with the Watergate mess. At the same time, Haig told Bork that Agnew was under investigation by the U.S. Attorney in Baltimore for taking bribes when he had been governor of Maryland. Bork ultimately talked his way out of accepting Haig's offer (Bork: "I'll have to hear the tapes." Haig: "You can't hear the tapes.").

As for Agnew, the evidence against him convinced everyone at the Justice Department that Agnew was a common criminal (he also had taken bribes while vice president). Nixon's new attorney general, Elliot Richardson, brought Bork to a high-level powwow at the White House with Haig and the entire Nixon defense team (now led by Texas law professor Charles Alan Wright) to see how Agnew's "situation" could or should be resolved. The team wanted (at least) a delay in any indictment. When that did not get anywhere, Haig bumped up the pressure: "Let's go see the President."

In route to the Oval Office, Richardson and Bork ducked into a men's room. Fearing it was bugged, Richardson turned on all the water faucets; both men agreed that this was a "resignation issue" (i.e., neither could stay at the Justice Department if Agnew was not indicted). In the Oval Office, Nixon was "totally relaxed" as he heard the pros and cons debated before him. After 45 minutes of back and forth, Nixon spoke up: "I guess you have to indict him." As the Agnew indictment became imminent, the vice president played what he thought was a trump card: vice presidential immunity—no one in that post could be indicted and tried before Congress had impeached and removed him from office. Agnew's lawyers moved on that basis to close down the Baltimore grand jury, adding as an additional ground the prejudice that flowed from alleged Justice Department press leaks. Bork was assigned by the attorney general to respond. The latter ground was easy to address; the immunity issue, however, was much trickier: not only

Nixon and Agnew Puppets
(Author's Collection)

was there no definitive law on that point, any position taken could have an impact on Nixon's increasing legal difficulties (e.g., Was there presidential immunity? If so, what was the nature and scope of said immunity?).

While finalizing the Justice Department's brief (which, among other things, differentiated between the presidency and the vice presidency—the latter essentially a nonfunctional post that only becomes important if the president leaves office, dies, or is impeached), Bork had to prepare for and then make his first oral argument before the Supreme Court. After the argument "went smoothly enough," Bork learned he would not have to travel to Baltimore to argue Agnew's motions—the vice president had that day taken a plea deal and resigned. Richardson reported to Bork that his brief was one of the reasons Agnew had thrown in the towel.

BORK AND THE SATURDAY NIGHT MASSACRE

Initially, the solicitor general had nothing to do with the work Special Prosecutor Archibald Cox was doing vis-à-vis

Watergate. Soon, however, Attorney General Richardson began to task Bork with discrete assignments in that area: meeting with Cox and his staff regarding how to deal with national security matters, rewriting Cox's open-ended charter to make clear it covered only Watergate-related subjects, and negotiating with Cox and his staff regarding the "proper" role of executive privilege. Then came Nixon's plan to deal with the tapes: the venerated John Stennis (the *very* senior senator from Mississippi) would review Nixon's recordings and present authenticated versions to Cox. Stennis was not only very old, he was also in poor health and had bad hearing. Recognizing his limitations (but bowing to the president's patriotic implorings), Stennis told the White House he would take on the job, but would need help to actually do it. No problem, said the White House, Fred Buzhardt—Nixon's Special Counsel (and political fixer)—would be happy to pitch in! Would Cox agree to Nixon's "take it or get fired" deal?

Bork went to work Saturday morning (October 20, 1973) with "no inkling that the dispute would in any way involve [him]." In a televised press conference later that day (which Bork watched at the Justice Department), Cox announced that he could not in good conscience agree to the president's "compromise." Directly thereafter, Richardson summoned Bork to his office.

Bork arrived to find the attorney general, the deputy attorney general, William Ruckelshaus, and a number of Richardson's staff. Richardson and Ruckelshaus—both of whom had assured the Senate Judiciary Committee they would only fire Cox for "extraordinary improprieties"—quickly affirmed they could not axe Cox. Richardson then asked Bork: "Can you fire him, Bob? The gun is in your hand—pull the trigger!"

Bork would later write that, at that moment, he "was in a welter of contradictory impulses, unable to see clearly what the results would be of a firing or a refusal to fire." Clearly, Nixon had the legal authority to fire Cox, and the public defiance of the president by a constitutionally inferior officer of the executive branch (on television yet) was grounds in and of itself. Bork also worried that if he took the same tack as Richardson and Ruckelshaus, the Justice Department might be reduced to chaos, with mass resignations and a White House operative like Buzhardt being put in place as acting attorney general. After trying to sort out his "contradictory impulses," Bork announced: "I can fire him, but then I will resign." Both Richardson and Ruckelshaus urged him not to take the latter step (fearing the same chaos at Justice), assuring him that they would publicly make clear they had urged Bork to stay.

Ultimately Richardson resigned and Ruckelshaus tried to (Nixon refused his resignation and fired him instead). Bork was driven to the White House, and with Charles Wright as the principal draftsman, produced this letter to Cox:

October 20, 1973

Dear Mr. Cox:

As provided by Title 28, Section 508(b) of the United States Code and Title 28, Section 0.132(a) of the Code of Federal Regulations, I have today assumed the duties of Acting Attorney General.

In that capacity I am, as instructed by the President, discharging you, effective at once, from your position as Special Prosecutor, Watergate Special Prosecution Force.

Very Truly Yours,

Robert H. Bork
Acting Attorney General

Bork then was ushered in to meet with Nixon in the Oval Office. Bork thought the president was "distraught," having not anticipated the consequences of his "compromise." In a disjointed conversation about what might happen next, Nixon suddenly blurted out: "You're next when a vacancy occurs on the Supreme

Court." As Bork would later write: "I hadn't the courage to tell him that I didn't think he could get anyone confirmed to the Supreme Court, and particularly not the person who fired Cox."

That night, Bork and his wife hosted a dinner party for Ralph Winter (a colleague from Yale Law School) and his wife. All over the rest of Washington (and throughout the nation), the political world was in an upheaval and the impetus for Nixon's impeachment took on a whole new momentum.

Bork was now a national figure; on Monday a crowd stood outside a local diner, pressed against a window, staring at him having breakfast. One of the first things he did when he returned to the Justice Department was to meet with Cox's deputies and assure them that their work could (and would) continue without interference. What about the tapes, they asked. Bork replied: "I'll back you up. Go to court for any tapes and documents you need."

With the political firestorm ignited throughout the country, and with a warning from a White House official that a cornered Nixon "might take desperate actions of which I might not approve," Bork did his best to ensure that the Justice Department continued to function. One way he accomplished that was to select a successor to Cox. All roads quickly led to Leon Jaworski, a former president of the American Bar Association, prosecutor at the war crime trials after World War II, and head of a prominent Texas law firm (Fulbright & Jaworski). With Jaworski in place, and once the president nominated Ohio Senator William Saxbe to be the Attorney General in December 1973, Bork was able to transition back to his old job.

That did not end Bork's interplay with Watergate, however. With the tapes dispute going up to the Supreme Court, Bork was called into a White House meeting where he was told by Alexander Haig that Nixon wanted Bork to argue on his behalf before the Court. Bork replied that that was an impossibility, given that the special prosecutor was a branch within the Justice Department. Haig was incredulous, calling Bork's position a "technicality." Bork replied: "They hang people on technicalities!" (James St. Clair, Nixon's latest lawyer, whispered to Bork: "I think you're right." Bork: "Tell him that!" St. Clair: "Maybe I will . . . someday.")

After the Court ruled against the president, Haig called Bork to report that the White House was debating whether to obey the Court. Bork's advice: "If you don't, it is instant impeachment." Shortly thereafter the tapes were produced to Jaworski.

POSTSCRIPTS

Before he died in December 2012, Robert Bork wrote a memoir of his experiences as solicitor general. Published in 2013 as a result of his wife's efforts, *Saving Justice: Watergate, the Saturday Night Massacre, and Other Adventures of a Solicitor General* (Encounter Books) is a great book for lawyers and non-lawyers interested in the Watergate era.

Bork's principal academic work was in antitrust, and in 1978 he published what many believe to be the seminal work in that field: *The Antitrust Paradox: A Policy at War with Itself* (Simon & Schuster). Oddly, he created a paradox of a different sort two decades later when, as a hired expert on behalf of Netscape in the litigation wars with Microsoft, he took positions 180 degrees different from those he advocated in *Antitrust Paradox* (e.g., profits are not evidence of a monopoly, bundling and restrictive contracts are okay; vertical integration is okay, dominant market share achieved by internal growth is okay). One might suppose, as Ralph Waldo Emerson once opined, that "[a] foolish consistency is the hobgoblin of little minds."

CHAPTER XXVI

THE SENATE'S ADVICE AND CONSENT OF CLEMENT HAYNSWORTH

MANY READERS REMEMBER contentious hearings of potential Supreme Court Justices (e.g., Robert Bork, Neil Gorsuch, Brett Kavanaugh). Little remembered today is President Richard M. Nixon's first nominee to the Court, Fourth Circuit Judge Clement Haynsworth.

Nixon submitted Haynsworth's name to the Senate on April 18, 1969. That nomination cannot be understood outside of the blazing trajectory—and ultimate flameout—of the judicial career of Abe Fortas. As we know, Fortas played a critical role in saving Lyndon Johnson's political career (*see* Chapter XXIII), and thereafter was heavily relied upon by LBJ in crises big and small. When Johnson was president, he prevailed upon a very reluctant Fortas to leave his lucrative law practice to become an Associate Justice on the Court.

In 1968, Earl Warren decide to retire as Chief Justice; LBJ promptly nominated Fortas to be elevated to that post. But the president was a lame duck at that point, with Republicans smelling political victory in the November elections and not wanting to lose the chance of nominating a very different type of jurist to succeed the liberal icon Warren. Senate Republicans were able to filibuster the Fortas nomination over the summer months of 1968; with the election looming, Fortas (who understood Washington politics almost as well as LBJ) then felt obliged to withdraw his name from consideration (which, of course, still left him as an Associate Justice). Unfortunately, that was not the end of problems for Fortas.

Life magazine, which had begun an investigation into Fortas's finances in 1968, uncovered financial/legal ties between Fortas and a businessman who had legal problems with the Securities and Exchange Commission and the Department of Justice—problems that ultimately led to a felony conviction. *Life* had not only disclosed these ties to the Justice Department but it had also published a sensational article on May 4, 1969, detailing the underbelly of what seemed (at least) to be an association that reflected very bad judgment by Fortas. He then made it worse by a poorly conceived (and incomplete) media response.

More important was a May 7, 1969, meeting between Attorney General John Mitchell and still Chief Justice Earl Warren, which Mitchell followed up on a few days later with a set of materials the Justice Department had assembled—material that did not place Fortas's conduct in a favorable light (some in the DOJ believed the conduct was prosecutable). At that same time, political figures and editorial writers began calling for Fortas's scalp (or at least his resignation). Fortas, who seems to have consulted only with Justice William Douglas and Washington "Wise Man" Clark Clifford as to his plans, ultimately threw in the towel on May 14, defending his conduct as completely aboveboard, while at the same time recognizing it was his "duty ... to resign in the hope that this will enable the Court to proceed with its vital work free from extraneous stress."

By that action, newly elected President Richard Nixon now had an opportunity to replace both Warren and Fortas. For Chief Justice, Warren Burger was selected, and his nomination went smoothly. That would not be the case for the empty Fortas seat, however.

CLEMENT HAYNSWORTH: THE PLUSES

There was little doubt in 1969 (and even less doubt today) that Clement Haynsworth was a well-qualified candidate for the U.S. Supreme Court. A *summa cum laude* graduate of the famous Southern Baptist institution, Furman University, Haynsworth went on to the Harvard Law School, from which he graduated in 1936. He returned to his Southern roots, where he developed a successful law practice. President Dwight D. Eisenhower nominated him to the Fourth Circuit in 1957, and he was confirmed by the Senate with little fanfare.

His record as an appellate judge between 1957 and 1969 was a distinguished one, and he ultimately became chief judge of the Fourth Circuit. A number of his opinions were highly praised and influential (e.g., *Rowe v. Peyton*, 383 F.2d 709 (4th Cir. 1967); *United States v. Chandler*, 393 F.2d 920 (4th Cir. 1968); *Wratchford v. S.J. Groves & Co.*, 405 F.2d 1061 (4th Cir. 1969)), and his administration of the Fourth Circuit was considered exemplary.

Beyond the monastic confines of judicial life, Judge Haynsworth's record had become well-known in political circles. South Carolina Senator Ernest Hollings was a big booster, and Maryland Senator Joseph Tydings—a former U.S. Attorney who had appeared before Judge Haynsworth—thought him to be "thoughtful, fair and open minded ... innovative and, indeed, dynamic." Attorney General Mitchell, who as Nixon's 1968 campaign manager had been a principal architect of the "Southern" and "Law and Order" strategies, became acquainted with the Haynsworth record, and quickly added him to the Justice Department's Supreme Court short list (an FBI report prepared at Mitchell's request identified the judge as the "foremost jurist in the area, very conservative and definitely in favor of law and order").

Upon Haynsworth's nomination by the president, a huge outpouring of support and best wishes ensued. Charles Alan Wright wrote the judge, quoting Judge Charles Wyzanski:

> Being asked to serve on the Supreme Court would be like being invited to spend the night with Cleopatra. First, of course, you would accept. Second, you would have doubts about your ability to perform. And third, after you had done it you would find that it wasn't nearly as much fun as you thought it would be.

Supreme Court justices and other federal judges weighed in with their support. Retired Justice Tom Clark, for example, wrote Haynsworth that "[w]e read of your appointment and were elated." And the American Bar Association rated Haynsworth as "highly qualified" to join the Court.

Clement Haynsworth: The Minuses

The fact that Haynsworth fit neatly into Nixon's political calculations was not a positive to many liberals in the media and the Senate. Scrutiny of his 12 years of opinions, moreover, showed that he was not a judicial leader in the field of civil rights (for example, in one case he ruled that the action of a local school board in Virginia, in response to *Brown v. Board of Education*, should first be reviewed by the Virginia Supreme Court) (in fairness, it should be noted that Haynsworth had written a number of pro–civil rights decisions); and his decisions in a number of cases involving organized labor immediately drew that group's disfavor (George Meany, head of the AFL-CIO, would opine that Haynsworth was not "fit to be an Associate Justice of the Supreme Court").

One particular labor case tangentially involved a small company named Vend-a-Matic, of which Haynsworth had been a vice president prior to going on the bench. Haynsworth remained as a Vend-a-Matic director until he resigned in 1963, when the Federal

Judicial Conference determined that no judge should serve as a corporate officer or director. That same year, Haynsworth joined a majority Fourth Circuit decision that a corporation named Darlington had the right to shut down an individual operating unit for anti-union purposes;[1] it would turn out that Vend-a-Matic did an immaterial amount of business with Darlington. This case would prove to be pivotal for Haynsworth's opponents.

SENATE HEARINGS

Mississippi Senator James Eastland, chair of the Judiciary Committee, set hearings on Haynsworth's nomination to begin on September 9. In advance thereof, various interest groups (principally, labor and civil rights) organized in opposition. Bypassing Massachusetts Senator Edward "Ted" Kennedy (as quoted in *Newsweek* magazine, a labor leader said, "We couldn't use Teddy to wage a fight on an ethical issue"), the opposition selected Indiana Senator Birch Bayh to lead the fight. The sudden death of Senate Republican Leader Everett Dirksen of Illinois pushed off the hearings for a week. That event had profound consequences for the nomination, for several reasons: (1) Haynsworth (and Nixon) lost a very tough and disciplined Senate insider to lead the fight; (2) Dirksen was replaced by Pennsylvania Senator Hugh Scott, with Scott's replacement as assistant leader going to Michigan Senator Robert Griffin—both of whom initially said they would support Haynsworth; (3) in the time prior to September 9 (and during the week's delay), there was little of the intensive preparation of judicial candidates that is now undertaken (the principal session was a one and one-half hour "moot court" with Deputy Attorney General Richard Kleindienst); and (4) the delay gave the media, interest groups, and Haynsworth's Senate foes additional

---

[1] The Supreme Court ultimately would rule that an employer could shut down its entire operations for those purposes, but could not pick out just one for closure.

time to organize more systematically and raise a number of questions about Haynsworth's past.

On September 16, the hearings finally began, and questioning of Judge Haynsworth quickly centered on the Darlington case. The senators seemingly accepted Haynsworth's sworn explanation of his status with respect to Vend-a-Matic (especially prior to the Judicial Conference's determination) and, in any event, appeared to have concluded that Haynsworth had never decided a case in which he had a financial interest.[2] An expert on ethical rules governing judges, moreover, testified that Judge Haynsworth—under the rules that existed in 1963—had no choice but to hear and decide the Darlington litigation.

At that point, Senator Bayh then introduced another case involving the Brunswick Corporation; Bayh revealed that Haynsworth had owned $17,500 of Brunswick stock when the case had been decided. This fact had been uncovered by scores of opposition worker bees during the one week's delay. Initially, this caught the Haynsworth Justice Department team off guard, because no one had looked at the Brunswick decision. It turned out that the case had been argued and decided in conference on November 10, 1967, with Judge Harrison Winter writing the decision and circulating it to Judges Haynsworth and Woodrow Wilson Jones on December 27; the two judges joined in Judge Winter's decision shortly thereafter. Just before Christmas, Haynsworth's broker had recommended to many of his customers that they buy Brunswick stock; upon that solicitation, Haynsworth agreed to buy 1,000 shares (out of 18 million outstanding). Ultimately, all of the forgoing came out at the Senate hearings.

Other attacks followed, first from organized labor and then from various civil rights leaders. The former charged that

---

[2] North Carolina Senator Sam Ervin, citing Edmund Burke ("the cold neutrality of the impartial judge"), declared that this obviously applied to Haynsworth and that he knew "of no higher tribute that can be paid to any occupant of judicial office."

Haynsworth's decisions "prove him to be anti-Labor." The latter asserted that his nomination was "a deadly blow at the image of the U.S. Supreme Court," because Haynsworth was merely "for the status quo or for inching along." These frontal assaults were met by formidable defenders, but the overarching thrust was clear— Haynsworth was not going to be a supporter of the Warren Court's judicial philosophy (as had been Abe Fortas).

The Senate in Action

On September 26, the hearings finally came to an end; they had been the longest in memory (by far). The Judiciary Committee then voted out the nomination, 10 to 6 in favor. The majority called Haynsworth "extraordinarily well qualified," and addressed in detail each of the substantive issues raised by Haynsworth's critics. Substance, however, had begun to have little to do with reality; politics became paramount. When the Court opened for business in October (with only eight justices), it looked like the Senate would confirm Haynsworth by a vote of 56 for and 40 against. But Nixon's new Senate leadership had abandoned Haynsworth, with Robert Griffin becoming a leading critic. And senators from Northern industrial states started pealing off under political pressure, with some Republicans from those states urging Nixon to withdraw the nomination. In response, the White House stepped up its lobbying efforts, but it was both a bit ham-handed and behind the political wave building against the unethical, anti–civil rights caricature Haynsworth's opponents had created. Relationships in and among senators became estranged as the Senate vote approached, in large measure as a "backlash from Fortas."

Days before the Senate began debate, a young Justice Department lawyer who had been delegated responsibility for the nomination, William Rehnquist, reported to the White House that the trends from the Senate were all negative. The debate that ensued on the Senate floor was superficial and long-winded; it also became quite personal among the senators, with Bayh being attacked for campaign contributions and Southern senators accusing their colleagues of regional bias.

Ultimately, the Senate voted 45 yeas and 55 nays. Only one Northern Democrat supported the nomination; Republican Senators Scott, Griffin, Javits, Brooke, Percy, Case, Smith, Williams, and Mathias—all representing Northern states—voted against Haynsworth. Haynsworth—the "extraordinarily well qualified" nominee—had lost. How and why?

LESSONS FROM HAYNSWORTH'S DEFEAT

There were many reasons for Haynsworth's defeat. First, the Democrats' lingering bitterness of the 1968 filibuster of Abe Fortas and the next year's forcing him off the Court were definite factors. Second, the Nixon administration's "Southern Strategy" made it a lot easier for Northern politicians from both sides of the aisle to be receptive to the anti-Haynsworth forces. Third, while the White House's lobbying efforts were not very effective (and late in getting started), more problematic was the lack of Department of Justice preparation of Haynsworth and ongoing support throughout the process; William Rehnquist later apologized to Haynsworth on that score, adding that "[m]y one gain from the whole process was a chance to become acquainted with you." Fourth, internal Senate politics played a key role: the death of Everett Dirksen, the leadership replacements by the Republicans, the choice of Bayh to lead the opposition, the senators who ultimately championed the nomination—all of these (and more) were critical. Bayh's skillful leadership was of particular importance—he was able to weave together a whole host of disparate threads to suggest ethical "questions" and "insensitivities," while at the same time showing personal respect and deference to Judge Haynsworth; and to the extent these "questions" and "insensitivities" had resonance with individual Senators, they had a lot to do with the experience Fortas had gone through.

The last lesson comes from Lewis Powell, one of Haynsworth's strongest public supporters. In correspondence with Haynsworth after the Senate vote, Powell (a former American Bar Association president) rejected Haynsworth's prophecy that Powell might himself be nominated to the Court, believing that he (also a Southern lawyer who had spent "most of my professional career ... devoted to business and corporate clients") would receive a similar fate. Powell ultimately did join the Court, but it would take the 1976 election to the presidency of the first true Southern politician since before the Civil War, and the realignment of the Republican Party—with the South as a key base—to erase the regional biases Haynsworth experienced first hand.

POSTSCRIPTS

After Clement Haynsworth's defeat came the nomination of Judge G. Harrold Carswell, which few defended then (and even fewer today). The high/low point of that process was when Nebraska Senator Roman Hruska defended Carswell as follows: "Even if he were mediocre, there are a lot of mediocre judges and people and lawyers. They are entitled to a little representation, aren't they, and a little chance? We can't have all Brandeises and Frankfurters and Cardozos and stuff like that there."

After Carswell came Judge Harry Blackmun of the Eighth Circuit, who was ultimately approved by the Senate. Initially dubbed one of the "Minnesota twins" because his long-standing association with Chief Justice Warren E. Burger, Justice Blackmun once on the Court came to distance himself from his "twin," and ultimately proved to be a very different justice than the Nixon White House anticipated.

During the course of the blistering attacks by his senatorial opponents, Haynsworth said to his wife: "You know, my dear, the more I read about this man, the more I've convinced he simply will not do."

Haynsworth, after much soul searching, responded affirmatively to his judicial brethren (and other supporters) and decided to remain on the Fourth Circuit (where he served with distinction until his death in 1989). Justice Lewis Powell would later write: "He accepted his defeat with grace and without bitterness." Haynsworth's own view was that "I went through an experience which I think was searing at the time, but I think I'm not less a man for that; I hope I am a bigger man for it." Others agreed. While still a sitting judge, by a unanimous vote of both houses of Congress, the federal courthouse in Greenville, South Carolina, was named in Haynsworth's honor.

Subsequently, Senate Majority Leader Mike Mansfield and a number of other Democrats publicly stated they made a mistake in voting against Haynsworth.

As a matter of full disclose, Haynsworth's Harvard Law School roommate was my father-in-law.

Readers interested in the definitive history of the Haynsworth nomination should consult John Frank's *Clement Haynsworth, the Senate, and the Supreme Court* (University of Virginia Press 1991).

CHAPTER XXVII

THE BATTLE OVER BRANDEIS

B Y NOW, READERS OF THIS BOOK know that American history is replete with difficult/vicious confirmation hearings/battles over U.S. Supreme Court nominees. Now let us examine one such battle concerning one of the country's greatest justices.

ONE FRIDAY AFTERNOON

In the afternoon of Friday, January 28, 1916, a clerk rose on the floor of the U.S. Senate to read a message from the President of the United States, Woodrow Wilson. Breaking weeks of suspense as to whom would succeed Justice Joseph Lamar, the clerk revealed that Wilson's nominee was Louis D. Brandeis of Massachusetts. It did not take long for all hell to break loose.

Editorial reaction ran strongly against the "attorney for the people." *The New York Times* accused President Wilson of a "flagrant breach of trust" by attempting to "'pack' the Court" with an "avowed partisan" against corporate interests, which had a slew of important cases pending before the Court.

On the other side voicing quick approval were such disparate politicians as Benjamin "Pitchfork Ben" Tillman (senator from South Carolina), James Michael Curley (the model for *The Last Hurrah*), and John F. "Honey Fitz" Fitzgerald (the grandfather of John F. Kennedy Jr.). Brandeis's reaction was to tell the press that "I have nothing to say, nothing at all." It was a position he stuck with throughout the entire process.

Tangled Issues

Initial reactions aside, as historian A.L. Todd has noted, the Brandeis nomination was beset by "three tangled issues: the fact that Brandeis was a Jew, his fitness for a place on the Court, and election year politics."

With respect to the latter, the conundrum in which Senator Henry Cabot Lodge found himself was the most interesting: although he had numerous personal, professional, and political reasons for openly opposing Brandeis (that likely would have aborted the nomination), Lodge also would be facing Massachusetts voters in 1916 directly for the first time and did not want to arouse to be enmity of Brandeis's political friends; this political whipsaw engineered by Wilson made even his enemies respectful of his Machiavellian qualities.

As to the "fitness" issue, numerous corporate entities (e.g., U.S. Steel) believed that the "radical" Brandeis had repeatedly shown himself unsuited to be a dispassionate arbiter of justice.

And as to the religious and ethno-cultural issues implicated by the nomination, no Jewish person had ever been a Supreme Court Justice, and many of those whose ancestors had immigrated to America from Western Europe (as opposed to Eastern Europe) were simply bigots, deeming Brandeis's background to be an unsurmountable barrier for high office.

Added to those three obstacles was a fourth—the individual ambitions of men.

William Howard Taft Mug from the 1908 Election
(Author's Collection)

Former President William Howard Taft obsessively coveted a seat on the Supreme Court. He not only believed that he should have been the nominee but also held the firm conviction that Brandeis was "a socialist, ... a hypocrite, a man ... who is utterly unscrupulous ..., a man of infinite cunning, of great tenacity of purpose, and, in my judgement, of much power for evil." That Brandeis had inflicted a damaging political blow to Taft's presidency and his attorney general in 1910 (the "Ballinger" affair), further served as a catalyst for Taft and his former attorney general (George Wickersham) to organize members of the establishment bar in the Washington-New York-Boston corridor in opposition to Brandeis.

Hearings

A subcommittee of the Senate Judiciary Committee was quickly empaneled to conduct hearings on the Brandeis nomination. Those proceedings dragged on for more than a month, mainly because practically anyone who had an opinion, pro or con, was allowed to participate.

Witnesses, letters, and petitions ranged from the absurd (one witness was a New York lawyer whose principal objection to Brandeis stemmed from his pique that Brandeis had made condescending margin notes on a brief the lawyer had prepared!) to those who testified about Brandeis's roles in a variety of high-profile cases; as to the latter, the detailed minutiae was numbing (with each side citing portions in support or opposition). Certain elderly Bostonians prominent at the bar were allowed to present their understanding as to Brandeis's reputation (this testimony, which usually concluded with such words as "unsavory," "untrustworthy," or "unscrupulous," was admittedly never based on firsthand knowledge). The anti-Brandeis effort was quarterbacked by a New York attorney named Austen George Fox (hired by a large group of mainly Harvard alumni); and Fox was given a wide swath by the subcommittee to stage-manage the opposition.

Just as the hearings were coming to a close, Fox unveiled a surprise: a petition in opposition to the nomination signed by six former presidents of the American Bar Association, as well as the incumbent, Elihu Root. This group, which had been put together by Wickersham could not be lightly dismissed. In addition to Root (former senator, secretary of war, secretary of state), the signers included Taft, Joseph Choate (former Ambassador to England and U.S. Representative to the Hague), Moorfield Storey (once secretary to Senator Charles Sumner and former president of the NAACP), and Simeon Baldwin (former chief justice of the Connecticut Supreme Court and governor of that state).

While the subcommittee deliberated on what action it would take, the president of Harvard publicly weighed in, writing that "I have long believed [Brandeis to be] untrustworthy." Lengthy analyses by the *Nation* and the *New Republic* of the "evidence" produced at the hearings led each to disparate conclusions as to Brandeis's worthiness for the Court (the *New Republic*'s piece, it should be noted, was penned but unsigned by Brandeis's close friend, Felix Frankfurter).

When two weeks had passed and the subcommittee had done nothing, a member of Wilson's political family, Henry Morganthau, met with Brandeis to sound him out as to (1) withdrawing his name, and (2) running for the Senate against Lodge (whether this was done at Wilson's behest is not clear). Brandeis, after much persuasion, agreed to take the proposal "under prayerful consideration." That he shortly thereafter decided not to take the political bait was propitious because, two days later, the subcommittee approved (on a pure party vote) the nomination up to the full committee.

THE JUDICIARY COMMITTEE

The vote by the Judiciary Committee was the key to Brandeis's nomination. The White House was confident it had the votes in the Senate at large, but Brandeis had to have the backing of a majority to get the nomination out of committee and avoid a filibuster on the floor. The committee was made up of ten Democrats and eight Republicans; if all the Republicans opposed Brandeis, not one Democrat could be lost.

On the Democratic side, only five "aye" votes were a given; the other five, for a variety of reasons (e.g., strained relations with Wilson), could not be counted on. Principally because of that uncertainty, committee members from both sides of the aisle kept putting off addressing the nomination head on.

These delays at first seemed to be of benefit to the anti-Brandeis forces, allowing them to move outside the Senate to whip up public opinion; one mailing was headlined "Brandeis and the Dynamiters," linking Brandeis to radical labor union officials who had bombed the *Los Angeles Times* in 1911.

The growing frustration caused by the delays and such attacks resulted in a pro-Brandeis senator venting his rage on the Senate floor against Republican filibustering on April 28. This had the unfortunate consequence of causing one of the wavering Democratic senators to defend the Republicans and to state "there has never been a time that I have been ready to vote for a report favorable to Mr. Brandeis. I have voted to postpone the consideration of the nomination because I have not reached a conclusion and I wanted a further investigation and more information."

With the nomination thus hanging by a thread, the forces on Brandeis's side redoubled their efforts, and the White House finally started to use the presidency's considerable powers of persuasion. It was arranged for Brandeis to meet socially with two of the wavering senators on May 14; Brandeis face-to-face was a formidable advocate of his cause. Wilson not only publicly jawboned for his nominee, he also privately attended to pressing concerns of the doubtful group; direct help and hints of future patronage were powerful political levers. And with the committee vote finally set for May 24, such presidential "goodies" only accelerated the closer that day approached.

Notwithstanding these positive developments, the day before the vote a close political ally and friend of Brandeis was rejected by the full Senate for the position of Federal Trade Commissioner, with three Judiciary Committee Democrats voting against the administration's nominee (and with one committee member not voting, being back in Tennessee because of illness). That was surely not a good omen!

As the senators filed into the committee room on May 24, the chairman believed that the recent, intensive lobbying had resulted in nine sure votes for the nomination. The remaining question was Senator John K. Shields from Tennessee—he was on a train coming back to Washington, but (1) would he get there in time? and (2) would he vote for Brandeis? No one knew the answers to those questions.

Just as the roll call was getting under way, Shields (who one Washington wag said looked more like "a pirate than any man I ever saw") strode in and took his seat. When he was polled, Shields voted "aye!"

The Vote and Aftermath

Partisan politics and the imminent Republican convention no doubt helped to solidify the Democratic members of the committee. And with the majority vote approving the nomination, the Republican leadership knew the game was up as to Brandeis and wanted to switch the focus to national issues and the party's platform. As such, they agreed to a prompt vote by the entire Senate.

On June 1, in the space of a half hour with no debate, the Senate voted 47 to 22 in favor of the Brandeis nomination (the margin would have been smaller if a number of Republican senators had not already left for the convention). Brandeis heard the news when his wife greeted him: "Good evening, Mr. Justice Brandeis." Amid much public acclaim that the forces of bigotry and antireform had been overcome, Brandeis was sworn in as an Associate Justice on June 5 in the Supreme Court's chamber in the Capitol.

Postscripts

Senator Henry Cabot Lodge, who had been publicly mum on the nomination, ultimately went on to vote against Brandeis. In the general election that fall, he ran against and defeated "Honey Fitz" Fitzgerald. Lodge's grandson, Henry Cabot Lodge Jr., was defeated for reelection to the Senate in 1952 by John Fitzgerald Kennedy Jr. In 1962, Edward M. "Ted" Kennedy won his older brother's vacant seat in the Senate, defeating Lodge's great grandson, George Cabot Lodge II.

William Howard Taft was nominated by President Warren G. Harding to become Chief Justice. Once on the Court, he and Brandeis developed a good working relationship and a personal friendship. Brandeis at one point observed to Felix Frankfurter:

"It's very difficult for me to understand why a man who is so good as Chief Justice ... could have been so bad as President." Frankfurter replied: "[It] is very simple. He loathed being President and being Chief Justice was all happiness for him."

The New York Times, which had been a strong and vocal opponent of the Brandeis nomination, had this to say upon his retirement:

> The retirement of Justice Brandeis takes from the bench of the Supreme Court one of the great judges of our time. Nearly a quarter of a century has passed since Woodrow Wilson sent his nomination to the Senate. The storm against him at that time seems almost incredible now. From the first he vindicated the wisdom and the confidence of the farsighted President who appointed him to office. Year by year his stature as a judge has increased. His learning, his intellectual energy and his great integrity have long destined him to occupy a seat among the foremost judges of the court!